BAD GRASS NEVER DIES

MORE CONFESSIONS OF A DANGEROUS MIND

Also by Chuck Barris

Confessions of a Dangerous Mind

You and Me, Babe

CHUCK BARRIS

BAD GRASS NEVER DIES

MORE CONFESSIONS OF A DANGEROUS MIND

CARROLL & GRAF PUBLISHERS
NEW YORK

BAD GRASS NEVER DIES

Carroll & Graf Publishers
An Imprint of Avalon Publishing Group Inc.
245 West 17th Street
New York, NY 10011

First Carroll & Graf edition 2004

Some names have been changed to protect personal feelings
and privacy.

Library of Congress Cataloging-in-Publication Data is available.

ISBN: 0-7867-1379-8

Printed in the United States of America
Interior design by Paul Paddock
Distributed by Publishers Group West

for Mary,
the love of my life

"Forget about what you are escaping from.
Reserve your anxiety for what you're escaping to."
—MICHAEL CHABON

"Normal is a setting on your washing machine."
—RICK DEMARINIS

PROLOGUE

> *"I have come to believe that there can be no adequate preparation for the sadness that comes at the end, the sheer regret that one's life is finished, that one's failures remain indelible and one's success illusory."*
>
> —ANITA BROOKNER

t's September 2000 and I'm in New York-Presbyterian's Intensive Care Unit. I hate this fucking hospital. Especially the surgeons. They hacked up my back a few days ago like a bunch of goddamn sadists. Now every time they come to admire their work they probe the wound with thin silver picks and knives. It's pure torture. Sometimes I think that's why surgeons do it, probe around like that. They get their kicks by torturing patients, the vicious fucks. I can't see what's going on back there but I swear once in a while a surgeon used his fingers to open the wound, just for the fun of it. You know, ripped it apart so he could take a look inside. What the hell, it's only an incision. God forbid it should heal.

So here I am in my private room overlooking the Hudson

River with all these tubes and rubber hoses pushed into my body; one tube sucks out bad blood from inside my lung, one pushes antibiotics into my veins, one's for something else—I forget what. And I'm not feeling any better. If anything, I'm feeling lousier.

My sister and her husband Herman visit me almost every day. Today when they walked into the room Phoebe's jaw dropped and her face turned white. I had to pep her up. I said, "Hey, Pheeb, don't worry. I'm going to be fine." I gave her the thumbs-up sign. When she and my brother-in-law left I began to worry in earnest.

Was I *really* dying?

Later that same afternoon a specialist performed a procedure on me that almost put me away for good. While I waited to see if I was going to live or die I noticed a young intern standing beside my bed. I wondered why he was there. He could see I was frightened. I tried to hide it but I guess I couldn't. He said, "How are you feeling?"

"I think my days are numbered," I mumbled. "Maybe even my hours."

The young intern looked at me. His worried eyes showed both his concern for me and his inability to find something encouraging to say. And then it came to him. He smiled and said, "Don't worry Chuck, bad grass never dies."

He's right, I hadn't died yet.

I didn't die in Boston or Paris, I mused, or a bunch of other places. Not even in Mexico. Twice! No, *three* times! But Mexico was close. Especially the last two times.

PART I

"In all of life the odds are six to five against."
—WARD JUST

CHAPTER ONE

Let me tell you about Miguel Agular.

He was one despicable son of a bitch. Agular disliked everything in life with the possible exception of money, Spanish whores with big asses, and killing CIA agents working in Mexico and Central America. He had dirty fingernails, dirt in his ears, dirt between his toes, rotten teeth, and breath that smelled like a garbage dump. His nickname was The Ferret because he was a relentless, vicious little animal. The venomous cocksucker searched out our intelligence guys, dug deep until he scraped away their cover, then killed them.

Just like that!

The CIA didn't know who Agular worked for. Could have been almost anyone—the Sandies, the Contras, some Arab cell, or possibly a rogue terrorist group. What The Company *did* know were the names of some of his dead targets. Two of them were friends of mine. So you can see why I was thrilled the Central Intelligence Agency hired me to go to Mexico and kill the prick.

Oh, and one other thing. Agular was considered fearless, almost psychotically so. His rap sheet contained the simple sentence: "An experienced killer, always armed, confident, dangerous, unafraid." But let me tell you this. At that time I too was considered just as fearless, dangerous, and unafraid. The question was: Who would kill who first? Big shoot-out at the ol' OK Corral. The outcome of my mission was a hot bet around the corridors of the CIA and the Pentagon. Lots of money changed hands.

The timing for my departure was perfect. *The Gong Show*— an American television program I created, produced, and starred in—was on a two-week hiatus, one of those periodic breaks I gave the crew and staff so they could rest up, see what was going on with their lives. It was a great time to leave.

I arrived in Mexico on the morning of February 14, 1975. Mexico City was roasting. The sun was a white hot smear in the sky. There wasn't any relief from shade, not even standing in it. The smog and smell of diesel fuel was so thick you could cut it with a knife. The streets were jammed-packed with steaming people, the sidewalks with steaming dog shit. The humidity wilted my seersucker suit, made my blue sport shirt cling to my back. I looked like I just stepped out of a shower.

Along with the vile weather was the unfortunate discovery that the information the CIA had given me regarding Agular's whereabouts was worthless. So I fell back on tradecraft; checked out past tips, talked to known stoolies, followed ex-informants, examined old dead-drops, stuff like that. I hung around Agular's known haunts. I even went to Cuernavaca and Guadalajara. I found most of Agular's cronies, like Juan Carlos "The Lizard" Izquidero, Fernando "The Nose" Bernal, Patricio "Cool" Salinas, Juan "Little Fidel" Castro, Ligdano Guitierrez, even the desperado Juan Ulloa. But I never found Miguel Agular. So I went home. The highly touted Agular vs. Barris shoot-out ended up an anticlimactic nothing.

I returned to my office really bummed. Not only was my reputation tarnished, but I was also the center of a great deal of enmity from my fellow agents. The boys weren't angry that

4

I had failed in my mission. They were pissed over the loss of anticipated gambling profits. I quickly became The Company goat. Or black sheep. Whichever was worse. Still, the way I looked at it, I didn't kill the shitfuck Miguel, but he didn't kill me either. And I was on his home turf.

To tell you the truth, I was happy to get away with a draw.

CHAPTER TWO

t was 1978 and I was forty-nine years old, still single, still seeing Penny Pacino. We had been going out together for over three years now—off and on. Good old Penny. Actually good *young* Penny. The girl was in her twenties, statuesque and very pretty, her hair beautifully red with those freckles that I loved all over her face. She popped out a moronic malaprops or two on a daily basis and was a big pain, yet she protected me like a wolverine. One of my favorite pictures of the two of us was taken by a news photographer who caught us coming out of the NBC-TV studio artist's entrance. We had just been ambushed and surrounded by a horde of screaming lunatic fans. The picture shows me smiling and being all friendly-like, but Penny's not smiling at all. She's standing slightly behind me, her arm draped around my neck, her brows furrowed-up with concern and anger. She looks like a young female lioness. Her expression clearly says: Don't any of you dare harm a hair on this little man's head.

I love that photo.

Me? I had only two physical complaints. One was that my hearing seemed to be getting worse. The other was the size of my balls.

I had trouble hearing in the sixties, but now in the late

seventies the ears were definitely starting to fade. I wasn't hearing what people said. I was hearing different things. When someone mentioned behind my back that the deal fell through I thought he said, "I'm going to kill that Jew." I often thought about buying one of those big bronze horns to shove in my ear so I could understand what the actors were saying at movies and plays, but I worried that the person sitting directly behind me might complain.

I was also having trouble crossing my legs. My balls had grown. Their extraordinary length surprised me to no end, though I guess it shouldn't have. There's a baby picture of me on my bulletin board. It shows my father holding me up in the air above his head. I am six months old and naked. I have a pair of nuts on me that would make a grown man proud. It's no big deal about my balls. They're just annoying. They look like two large stones in condoms that have lost their elasticity. It's odd to have such humongous balls now at my age when everything else about me has shrunk.

On the social side, I was bored.

I was still working hard producing *The Dating Game, The Newlywed Game,* and *The Gong Show,* along with working as a hired assassin for the CIA and killing enemies for the United States. But the novelty of both endeavors had worn off. The TV game-show business had become old hat, and being CEO of a public company had become a major irritant. Most annoying of all were the dodos at the CIA. That collection of retarded Ivy Leaguers *really* disturbed me. No, more like exasperated me. Lately they had stepped up the heat down at Langley, bugging me on a quasi-regular basis for my failure to kill Miguel Agular. And, finally, the goddamn TV critics were starting to get to me. I remained their most hated entertainer; the Sultan of Schlock, the man who singlehandedly lowered the bar of civilization as they knew it, etc., etc., etc. The television writers seemed to wish I had never been born. I wondered if the public felt the same way. I found myself envying Oprah Winfrey, Alan Alda, Tom Hanks, people like that, darlings of their industries. But I figured when I started coveting the life of Alan Alda it was time to give it a rest.

I decided to chill in Beverly Hills.

Screw my various business and civic responsibilities. *The Gong Show* was on another two-week rest break. I could take off for a spell. I'd put a temporary lid on being Chairman of the Board of my public company, Chuck Barris Productions. I would think of a decent replacement for myself as host of *The Gong Show*. And I would most definitely put a hold on any future assassinations for the CIA. I would just drop out. At least for a little while.

I fled to my aluminum fold-up beach chair. The chair rested on the stoop of my Beverly Hills apartment on the corner of Charleville Street and South Rodeo Boulevard. The stoop was hidden from the street by overgrown green fronds so people walking past my apartment usually couldn't see me sitting in my chair.

But I could see them.

So there I was on a pleasant California morning in January 1978, meditating in my beach chair—thinking about my departure years ago from my last corporate job. It was when I was Director of Daytime Television, West Coast Division, American Broadcasting Company—a title I had suggested shortening to "Duke of Daytime," which for some strange reason upset everyone on the executive floor of ABC-TV. It never mattered to me that I upset the brass. Fuck the brass. I was leaving ABC-TV anyway. I was going to create my own television game show. I had an idea that fortuitously turned out to be *The Dating Game*.

On my last day at the American Broadcasting Company I discovered that my fellow employees put together a half-assed going-away party for me. I was given a Timex watch that three co-workers had chipped in to buy. I thanked the three from the bottom of my heart. Watery punch and some stale cookies were passed around, followed by a lot of staring at our shoes. One of my associates, a minor suit in the Sports Department, who I never liked and I'm sure was glad to see me gone, asked what I intended to do with myself. I was positive he was hoping I didn't have anything noteworthy in my future so he could stop worrying about my getting ahead in the business.

I told him for starters that that I was on my way to Las Vegas to get some sun and lose a few bucks gambling.

He asked if I was interested in rodeo.

I told him I was.

He said that ABC-TV Sports was covering the national rodeo finals held that weekend in Las Vegas. Would I like to go?

Sure, I said, I'd love to see the national rodeo championships.

No problem, he replied, here's what you do. When you get to Vegas go to the fair grounds. Find the ABC-TV mobile truck, walk in, and just tell them who you were.

Just Tell Them Who You Were.

Good title for a book.

I was chuckling to myself when I spotted a huge towheaded oaf wearing a three-piece seersucker suit standing below me on the pavement. The oaf was definitely looking for someone. I got the feeling it was me. I was right.

"I do believe I've found my man," he said as he began climbing up my front steps.

"Hold it!" I yelled. "Stop right there."

"Chuck Barris, right?" asked the oaf, coming no further. "Hey, I'm sure glad to see you."

The young man hadn't said much, but I could detect a southern accent. I love southern accents. Always have. Always wanted to date a southern girl just to listen to her talk. Hear her drop her "g"s when she spoke, say those funny little southern expressions like "mean as a snake" and "ugly as a bucket of rocks," shit like that. Maybe have her cook me some grits. (I love grits.) I've always thought southern girls with southern accents were sexy. But standing below me wasn't any sexy southern girl desiring to cook me grits. This was a large southern lummox. Big fucking difference.

"It *is* Chuck Barris, isn't it?"

"Yeah, I'm Chuck Barris."

"You're one of my hee-ros, man."

"Is that right? And who might you be?"

"Coulter Bean."

"So what do you want, Coulter Bean?"

"I'm from the Central Intelligence Agency," he said, all proud as a peacock, standing real tall.

"Well, pin a rose on your nose," I said, seeing my days on the aluminum beach chair fading away.

Coulter Bean laughed. The thought of pinning a rose on his nose was funny, I guess. He had a great laugh, too, and long arms. I mean his arms were *long*. Almost but not quite ape-like. During the next few years, I would find out the story about Mr. Bean's arms, but since time is fleeting I'll give you the highlights now.

Coulter Bean was born in 1946 at 135 Mt. Gilead Street, Orangeburg, South Carolina. He attended Orangeburg Preparatory High School and Harvard University, graduating from that venerable institution in 1968. After college Bean flirted with the idea of doing something for his country. One option was joining the Central Intelligence Agency. He spent a day in Washington, D.C., meeting with fellow intelligence personnel. He and the other prospects were given I.Q. tests and a written exam. Following lunch Bean was interviewed by a panel of seven men. Coulter wasn't sure if they were honest-to-goodness agents or just personnel department flunkies. It didn't matter. At the end of the day a CIA representative told Coulter the agency would be glad to have him. Bean thought about it for a couple of weeks then turned the CIA down.

Coulter's heart was with the New York Yankees. As a child Coulter dreamed of being a Yankee pitcher. He put himself to sleep every night counting opposing players striking out, one after another, after another, after another, after another. . . . He was his high school's star pitcher and All-Ivy League for three of his four collegiate years. His long arms were worth every inch of their unsightly length. Throughout his entire high school and college playing days Coulter daydreamed he was wearing the pinstripes of the Bronx Bombers and sitting in their bull pen. He fantasized—no, more like obsessed—about being the Yankees' ace relief pitcher, that someday the public address system at Yankee Stadium would boom: "Three up, three down. Coulter Bean has retired the side *again!*"

Unfortunately, things didn't quite work out the way Coulter Bean hoped they would. He did pitch for the Yankees but only on one of their minor league teams. He *was* good, shot up to triple-A like a rocket, then to the Big Leagues for a few games until he blew a rotator cuff and shot out of organized baseball like a rocket.

The CIA recruiters, never happy being bridesmaids, heard Coulter was gone from The Bigs and went looking for him. They found him working in his hometown of Orangeburg where he was teaching American History and Phys-Ed, and coaching the high school's baseball team.

This time Coulter signed up with The Company. Since then his duties have carried him all over the world and his smarts took him right up the corporate ladder. According to folks who worked with Bean, he never changed, never became a phoney sophisticate, a pompous worldly-wise clod or anything like that. He just remained the good-hearted oaf I got to know; always smiling and kidding around—and most importantly, always there when you needed him. What's the old saying? You can take the boy out of Orangeburg, but you can never take Orangeburg out of the boy. Coulter was that saying personified.

Okay, back to 1978 and my stoop in Beverly Hills, California. I gave Mr. Bean permission to come up the steps and sit down. I grabbed another beach chair, unfolded it, handed it to him, and said, "So Bean, corporately speaking, what are you to me?"

"Your boss."

"You *are*?"

"Think so."

"How old are you?"

Coulter placed his beach chair at an angle. That way when he sat he could stretch his legs halfway down the front steps.

"I'm thirty-two."

"So what's your title?" I asked.

"Don't know for sure."

"That clears things up."

"Thought it would."

"What exactly is it you want, Bean?"

"The Company wants you to go to Mexico."

"Why?"

"To try and find Miguel Agular again."

CHAPTER THREE

Coulter Bean and I were seated in a banquette at Nate & Al's Deli on North Beverly Drive. The place was packed. Big lunch crowd. Lots of noise. Lots of food being stuffed into lots of big mouths. Most of the mouths resembled pythons', able to unhinge so that a Westwood—two pounds of corn beef and cole slaw with a half a ton of Russian dressing on top, jammed between two thick slices of rye bread—could be ingested at once. A long line of obese, salivating people were waiting for seats.

I knew the hostess, Marion Klick. We were old friends.

Glick was the only hostess in America who couldn't read her own writing. She never knew who was next because she was unable to decipher what she wrote on her clipboard. Marion would always take care of me as soon as I walked into the restaurant. It didn't matter if I was alone or with ten other people, I got the next banquette. Or the next two banquettes. I had to hide behind the gefilte fish jars until the banquette was cleared and then stealthily slink to the table like a thief in the night so the long line of waiting carnivores didn't see me jump the line. If they did, they would have gladly hung me by the neck from a salami hook.

After we were seated, a waitress named Kay Coleman

walked up to me, poured coffee into my cup, and said, "Hi Chuck. How they hangin'?"

I was a little sensitive in those days about that particular greeting, what with my testicular problem and all that. I answered jovially, "Fine Kay. Everything's fine."

"You're lookin' good."

"Thanks, Kay. I'm trying to stay fit."

"Eat well, stay fit, die anyway," said Kay.

"Yeah, right."

"So whattaya goin' to have, Chuckie Baby? The sturgeon special, cream cheese, the works?"

"Too much, Kay. Gotta be able to keep getting into my jeans."

"It ain't the jeans that makes your butt look fat, Chuckie Baby."

"You should know, Kayzie."

"Does your friend want coffee?"

"Don't know. Why don't you ask him?"

"No thank you, ma'am," said Coulter Bean, drawling all over the place like a big show-off.

Kay loved the accent, especially the "ma'am" part, and smiled broadly at Coulter while she poured.

"Thank you, Kay, darlin'," said the show-off.

I thought Coleman was going to swoon.

One never forgot Kay's name. That's because Kay had a sign roughly a foot wide and a foot long pinned to her blouse that read:

KAY

Kay Coleman was fat and jolly most of the time. She was from Philly, like me. We spent many hours together talking about Spam, Tasty Cakes, Goldenberg's Peanut Chews, old

Horn & Hardart restaurants, and the Mummers Parade. Sometimes when the two of us were particularly homesick, we would telephone Philadelphia information just to hear the operator's accent. Made us feel better. Though Katherine Coleman and I were bonded ex-Philadelphians, that didn't make her my favorite Nate & Al's waitress. Arlene Malmberg was. Still is, for that matter. I love Arlene because her name pin is understated and she always knows the point spread on any game in any sport I care to discuss. Arlene was at another table that morning, so Kay was waiting on Coulter and me.

I ordered a *matzo brie.*

Coulter asked me to explain to him exactly what that was.

I didn't bother because I didn't have the time. I just told him to get something else. I suggested a baloney sandwich on white bread with mayonnaise. He thanked me and ordered exactly what I suggested. A baloney sandwich on white bread with mayonnaise! I was only kidding. Fucking mind-boggling.

Kay waddled off but Gloria Leon, another waitress, took her place by our table. Gloria's Mexican and very religious. She always wears a cross the size of the Eiffel Tower around her neck. She's short, with cute fuzzy red hair. Gloria gave me a big kiss on my cheek and asked God to bless me and my friend. "I light a candle for you two next time I go to church."

I thanked her.

Gloria said, "Your friend looks like a nice Christian man," nodding her head in Coulter's direction. Gloria was in her forties, married, and flirtatious.

"I can't vouch for his Christianity yet, Glo. I just met him."

"I *am* a nice man, Gloria," said Coulter, sucking around. "I go to church every Sunday."

"Going to church doesn't make you a Christian any more than standing in a garage makes you a car," suggested Gloria Leon, pouring both of us cups of coffee.

As soon as Gloria departed I turned to Coulter Bean and yelled, "Fuck Mexico City!"

"These waitress here sure are nice," said Coulter.

"Hey Bean, you hear what I just said?"

"Yeah, I heard. Calm down."

"I *can't* calm down."

"Try."

"Fuck 'try,' Coulter. I can't believe you guys actually want me to go down to Mexico City—*again*?"

"Shhhhhhhh." Coulter held a finger to his lips.

"Fuck 'shhhhhhhh,' Coulter."

A busboy with a pot of regular and a pot of decaf said, "Coffee?"

"No!" I yelled.

The stricken busboy quickly moved away.

And then to Coulter, "Again?! The Company *really* wants me to go back to Mexico City and find that prick again!?"

Bean lowered his eyes and said, "You didn't find him the first time did you?"

"Okay, so I didn't find him the first time." I was annoyed at the dig. One of those things I guessed I would never live down. "But *why* am I going back? You know I can't kill him. The CIA isn't in the killing business anymore. Not according to Executive Order #12333. The Prez says we can't be killing people no mo'. Not good for the Uncle's image. I'm sure you've heard about EO #12333, Coulter. They passed it just last year."

"I know about the order, Chuckie Baby, but . . ."

"Stop calling me Chuckie Baby."

". . . but you're not goin' down to Mexico City to kill Agular."

"I'm not?"

"No. You're going to offer him a job."

"To do *what*?!"

"Offer the prick a job."

"You've got to be kidding."

"I'm not," said Coulter.

The busboy with the pots of coffee returned. "Decaf or regular?" he asked. He had an accent and reminded me of the waiter in *Faulty Towers*. Without taking my eyes off Coulter, I placed my hand over my cup and said, "No thanks. My coffee's just right."

After the busboy left I said, "What kind of job, Coulter?"

"The Company wants you to give Agular a list of known terrorists living in Mexico and Central America and have Agular find them."

"And when he finds them, then what?"

"He kills them," answered Coulter Bean.

"What's Agular get out of it?"

"Money."

"How much money?"

Kay returned with the *matzo brie* for me and Coulter's Christian Delight. She asked if I wanted her to freshen up my coffee.

"Not now."

"What?" said Kay, a big note of hostility in her voice.

"Not now."

"How about some manners here as in, 'Not now, *thank you*, Katherine?' "

"I'm sorry. Not now, thank you, Katherine." I looked at my plate. It was overflowing with Jewish delights: lox, sturgeon, cream cheese, onions and tomatoes, a little gefilte fish, a slab of creamed herring, and so on. "Jesus, Kay, what did you do to me? I'm trying to stick to a balanced diet and your screwing it all up with your goddamn generosity."

"A balanced diet is a Dove Bar in each hand," said Kay, walking away.

I looked at Coulter. "The waitresses here are all comedians."

"I think they're funny," said Bean.

"Who gives a shit what you think? How much money, Coulter?"

"Fifty a pop."

"Fifty?!!"

"Yep."

"Thousand?" I asked.

"Yep."

"Dollars?"

"Yep. You can go as high as a hundred if you have to."

I gasped. *"A hundred thousand dollars!"*

"Yep."

" 'Yep, yep, yep.' Is that all you can say? Jesus fucking Christ." I felt deflated, defeated, I don't know what.

The busboy with the coffee pots was back. "Decaf or regular?"

"I thought I told you to go away and stay away." I shot the annoying busboy a blistering look. When I finished, I turned back to Coulter Bean. "Agular will never believe me. Even if I live long enough to get within talking range, he won't wait to hear what I have to say. He'll just kill me."

"No, he won't."

"You're sure?"

"Yeah, we're sure."

"What makes you so sure?"

"We paid a bunch of his close friends a lot of money to make Agular a believer."

"In what?"

"In you. We have reliable information that says he'll listen to you *and* he won't hurt you."

"And you believe him?"

"Yes, we do."

"Stop with this fucking *we* shit, Bean. Do *you* believe him?" Though I didn't know this Coulter guy very well, watching his eyes would tell me what he was thinking.

"I believe him," he said.

His eyes seemed okay.

"I've been informed personally," said Bean, "that he'll accept you *and* the deal if the money's right. I think fifty thousand . . ."

"And if the money's not right?"

"He'll let you go without touching a hair on your head."

"And you believe the lying fuck?"

"Yes, we . . . yes, I truly believe him."

"Hey Coulter, you're kidding about this assignment, aren't you. You're putting me on. They sent you here from The Farm to sort of play an April fool gag on me, right?"

"It's January, Chuckie Baby."

"Come on, fess up Coulter, you're pulling my leg." I reached across the table and punched Bean playfully on his shoulder. "Admit you're pulling my leg."

Before Coulter could admit anything, the busboy with the coffee pots was back. "Decaf or regular?" He sported an insolent smile on his face. He was enjoying tormenting me.

I grabbed my fork and, holding it like a dagger, placed it under the busboy's chin. "You come back here again you little prick," I hissed, "and I'll push these prongs right up between your fucking bicuspids." A foursome in the banquette across from us stared at me aghast. When I turned toward them they looked the other way.

The busboy fled.

I told Coulter that Agular would probably pay twice what we offered him to kill *me*.

"No he won't."

"Let me tell you something, Bean, the world's gone mad."

"Yeah, sometimes I do believe it has." Bean stretched his legs out in the aisle. "Only the boys at The Company say it's important you make this deal so that Agular dusts these other guys. Seems we can't get to them, but he can. And if nobody gets to these guys, they may cause big trouble in the good old U.S. of A. I mean like the Los Angeles airport gettin' blown to smithereens or somethin' in New York."

The pissed-off busboy holding his two pots of coffee scurried up to tell Coulter he couldn't leave his legs out in the aisle like that.

"Like what?" I growled.

"Like *that*." The busboy pointed a coffee pot at Coulter's legs.

"Why not?" I snarled.

"I trip."

"So fucking trip."

Coulter pulled his legs back.

"Let me tell you something, Bean. You don't know me from a hole in the head, but in my humble opinion if I get close enough to talk a deal with that bastard, you know what I'll do?"

"You'll kill him," guessed Coulter.

"Right."

"Wrong."

"Who says so?"

"I say so," said Coulter Bean. "You want to know why?"

"Why?"

CHAPTER *FOUR*

After lunch Coulter Bean and I walked down Rodeo Drive. There wasn't a cloud in the sky. Passersby strolled past the two of us, confidently munching their patty-melts-to-go. Drivers were happily taking right turns during red lights in their bright red Ferraris. We passed an outdoor newspaper and magazine shop. I noticed the *Los Angeles Times* had a front-page picture of a raging snow storm in New York. The City of Angels giving the finger to the Big Apple.

A gentle breeze blew up Beverly Boulevard. Though it was January, the breeze fluttered the short skirts of summer dresses worn by the sexy women walking by. Coulter didn't seem to notice. He was a happily married man. I didn't care either. My mind was elsewhere.

"So why won't I kill Agular?" I asked.

"Because," said Coulter, "if you try to get to Agular, one of his henchman will kill you first. Simple as that."

"How do you know that for sure?"

"Figure it out, Chuck. You won't be able to carry a gun. He'll pat you down before he sits with you. If you're thinkin' of plantin' a gun at the restaurant, forget about it. It'll be impossible. He'll change restaurants after you arrive and you won't know where he'll take you next. He won't stay if he sees you with someone else. And he'll have his bodyguards. My advice? Don't think about dustin' him, Chuckie Baby, the odds suck. I'm sure when you cool off and think about it, you'll agree with me. Besides, The Company wants him alive so he can get to those *other* assholes."

"I thought Agular was coming alone."

"What?"

"You mentioned Agular's bodyguards. I thought you said he was coming alone."

"He said he'd come alone but I don't believe him."

"So where's *my* protection in all this?"

"Hey, I agree it's a dangerous assignment, Chuckie Baby, but we've got it on good authority . . ."

"Here we go with that *we* shit again. What's with this *we* shit? *We* have it on good authority. What *we*? And on *who's* good authority? Good authority my ass. I ain't buying into this *we* crap or your goddamn *good authority* crap." I sucked some *matzo brie* out of one of the gulches between my teeth. Little holes and separations that my dentist, Bill Tanner, leaves behind in my mouth. He left this particular space between two back teeth during my last appointment. I call these little excavations Tanner Gulches. I once had a little piece of brisket in a Tanner Gulch for just short of two years. I got used to it. The piece of meat became a sort of pet. I missed the brisket when it was gone. "Listen Coulter. I'm really rusty these days, man. I mean *really* rusty. My reflexes are shot. Same with my motivation. Same with my . . ."

"I know how you feel."

"The *fuck* you do." The guy was really starting to annoy me. "How could you *possibly* know how I feel? You haven't a fucking clue how I feel, just like I haven't a fucking clue how *you* feel. Anyway it doesn't matter, Bean. I'm finished with the CIA. I've killed enough bad guys for my country to last me for life. I'm fed up and I want out. You know as well as I do that if you lose your nerve and don't quit, you're doomed. Where did I read . . . I read somewhere that you have to know when to get off the train. Nobody knows when to quit, when to get off the train. You know as well as I do, or maybe you don't, but knowing when to get off the train's the whole enchilada. Go out there feeling insecure, and the Grim-Fucking-Reaper will grab your ass for sure. Even a backward Southerner like you ought to know *that* by now. So go peddle this assignment somewhere else. Find another sucker to make a CIA killer rich. I'm not risking my ol' concave ass for something as dumb as that. I'll tell you this, Mr. Bean, I'm not going anywhere for you or the Director or the President of the United States *hisself*, as my driver Tyrell Massella would say, bless his little black heart. Know what I'm saying, Boss Man?"

Coulter Bean and I didn't speak again until we reached my stoop and were seated on the two aluminum beach chairs.

Coulter spoke first. "Listen Chuck, you know once you're in the CIA, you're in it for life. Unless of course you die or switch sides. Oh sure, employees retire, but they're mostly clerks and pencil pushers. Good killers like you are hard to find *and* hard to train. There aren't a lot of them out there and The Company usually likes to hang on to their investments. But you know that. I'm not tellin' you anythin' you don't already know."

"Yes you are. You're telling me I'm a dead man if I don't continue to carry out CIA assignments. Isn't that what you're trying to tell me with all that fucking Company gobbledygook shit? You've been given the authority to issue a death threat, haven't you? Not bad for a thirty-year-old punk who doesn't even know his goddamn title."

"A thirty-*two*-year-old punk," said Coulter Bean calmly. "Hey, Chuckie Baby, I'm like you, I work for The Company. Don't be mad at me. I'm just the messenger. Sometimes they make me do things I hate to do, too, like tellin' you about this Agular assignment. But I must admit most of the time I *like* what they tell me to do."

"Who gives a rusty fuck what you like."

"You back out of this, Chuckie Baby, and you'll *really* be between a rock and a hard place. You'll have the CIA lookin' for you *and* the bad guys, too."

"What bad guys?"

"Come on, Chuckie Baby, you've got to know they have you on their hit list."

"Goddamn it, stop calling me Chuckie Baby, Coulter, or I'll break your nose, and *who* has me on their hit list?"

"They do."

"Who's they?"

"Damned if I know. But whoever they are, it's not good to be on their list."

CHAPTER FIVE

Two months later I went back to Mexico City.

Once again I was looking for Miguel Agular. But this time I wasn't going to find the former murderer of CIA agents to kill him. No, this time I was going to meet the bastard to make him rich!

How's that for an ass backwards situation?

Mexico was hot as hell again. Not a breeze, not a cloud. Just sun, dust, stray rib-thin starving mongrels, and that same old lousy smell of smog and diesel fuel. I was in a parked taxicab, sweating through my sport shirt and seersucker sport jacket, de rigueur for clothing in Mexico City. I was watching the piece of shit Agular sitting outside at a restaurant table across the street. He was at a dive called El Sombrero. The Hat. Remember the poem?

> *A cat in a hat.*
> *In French,* chat chapeau.
> *In Spanish, it's a* gato *in a* sombrero.

I couldn't stop staring at Agular from my taxicab window. Weird how I failed to find him in '75 when I wanted to kill him, and now three years later there he was, fifty feet away. It was chilling, you might even say mesmerizing, to watch a feral killer, whose greatest joy would be ending my life and putting me in a pine box, sitting right across the street!

A cigarette hung from Agular's mouth. The smoke shut his left eye. A cigarette was always hanging from Agular's mouth, the smoke always keeping his left eye closed. I knew the dirtbag thought the cigarette thing with the closed eye looked cool and dangerous.

He was right.

It did.

Agular was at El Sombrero because he had been told by *some trusted friends* that I was coming to the restaurant to make him an offer he couldn't refuse. That big bucks were involved. Agular knew The Uncle had deep pockets and, as I said, nothing tempted the scumbag more than lots of U.S. dollars.

Even more than Mexican whores with big asses.

While I watched Agular, I seethed. The prick had executed two of my CIA buddies. First Hugh Jones, my classmate at Langley, then Danny "Ears" Endy, a father of six. And there he was, this killer reptile, sitting in the noonday sun, waiting for Chuckie Baby to make him rich.

"Go know," as my grandmother used to say.

Agular seemed nervous. More so than usual. He invariably played with his mustache when he was nervous. Since he was always a little agitated, he always played with his mustache. A little. That afternoon he was playing with his mustache *a lot*. And the silverware too. And his napkin. Then back to his mustache. Then the silverware again. Then out came the jackknife. Agular's trusty jackknife. I wondered if my two friends had their throats cut by that jackknife. Agular snapped open the blade and began cleaning his fingernails with its point. I snorted another laugh. I don't think Agular gave a shit about clean fingernails. I think he was convinced that cleaning his fingernails with a jackknife in restaurants frightened people sitting near him. He just wanted to scare people.

And he was right.

It did.

"The problem is," I said aloud to myself, "the more high-strung he gets, the more dangerous he becomes."

"Why you telling me, *amigo*?" the taxi driver said, annoyed.

"I wasn't telling you. I was telling myself. I was just thinking out loud."

Cab drivers with attitudes get on my nerves. Especially slovenly cab drivers like the one I had, with his crappy-looking straw hat on top of his head and those cheap sunglasses that had to be hiding a pair of bloodshot rheumy eyes.

"Do all Mexican taxicab drivers look and smell as bad as you?" I asked.

He didn't say anything.

Agular hadn't changed much. He must have been about twenty-five then, with a short wiry body, closely cropped hair, a narrow face, thin lips, and that lousy-looking pencil-thin leading-man mustache across his upper lip. He had slits for eyes and a mean expression on his face. (But then Agular always had slits for eyes and a mean expression on his face.) He was wearing a dirty camouflage army field jacket over a light tan colored sport shirt. The shirt was the color of his skin. Blue jeans and sandals rounded out his wardrobe. His sandals were under the table, his dirty bare feet were propped up on the chair I was going to use.

I watched Agular undress a young girl with his eyes two tables away. The girl didn't seem to mind, even though she was with another guy. She made goo-goo eyes back at Agular. He evidently had some kind of charisma women went for. Maybe Agular exuded death and destruction, traits certain females seemed to get all wet just thinking about. The pretty young girl was with a small guy, not small like Agular—not lean and sinewy and dangerous-looking—but small like a pussy, someone Agular could drop with one chop. So the dirtbag continued cleaning his nails with his jackknife and lifting his eyelids now and then to flirt with the pretty girl. Good way as any to pass the time until I showed up.

I decided to show up.

I got out of the taxi and said to the driver, "Wish me luck."

"For what, *amigo*?" he asked, licking a finger then turning a page of the girlie magazine propped up on the cab's steering wheel.

I slammed the taxi door and walked across the street. With my seersucker sport jacket in one hand and a black leather bag in the other, I approached Agular's table.

Dangerous Miguel.

Dirtbag Miguel.

The real thing when it came to perpetrating mindless violence. They say that Agular's the guy who put several bullets into the head of Jose Francisco Ruiz Massieu, the brother-in-law of former Mexican president Carlos Salinas de Gortari. There wasn't enough proof to put Agular away, so instead of being locked up in some crummy Mex maximum security prison for the rest of his life, the peckerhead was sitting at an outdoor café waiting to chat with the likes of respectable me.

When I mumbled hello, Agular just lifted his eyelids for a moment then dropped them. I was instantly infuriated. So I angrily pulled the chair out from under Agular's feet causing them to drop suddenly to the ground. Agular didn't like what I did with the chair, but kept his anger to himself and his head down. He rearranged his legs and went on picking dirt from his fingernails with the point of his jackknife. The chair thing was an act of egotistical stupidity on my part, a really dumb way to start the festivities, especially with a notoriously quick-tempered guy like Agular. I could have gotten myself killed before we even began. Shouldn't do that again, I told myself. Had to learn to keep my cool or I'd blow another mission.

While I was thinking those thoughts, I felt Agular's two Mexican thugs behind me. I didn't know when they arrived, only that they were there. I tried not to look back but I did. Sure enough there they were, two meatheads, standing shoulder to shoulder, arms hanging down and crossed at the wrists, doing the Mexican national soccer team protect-your-balls-during-a-penalty-kick pose. Typical thug position. Typical thug attire, too. Dressed like your everyday guns-for-hire. Loose flowered sport shirts hanging outside slacks, the shirts as big as tents that hid the weapons that were tucked in their waistbands. Both wore floppy sandals, had shaved heads and Zapata mustaches. The only difference was size. One was big. The other was bigger.

Agular nodded.

One thug stood me up, then pulled my arms above my head and held them there while the other one patted me down. The two fucks did that right there in the open-air patio of the restaurant, in front of everybody: diners, waiters and waitresses, people walking by on the pavement. Agular acting as though he and his henchmen were *policia*, behaving as though he owned the place, which—in some respects—I suppose he did. I mean who in their right mind was going to challenge Miguel "The Ferret" Agular? When the patter finished patting, he gave Miguel the "he's clean" sign.

Coulter Bean was right. If I had a gun, I wouldn't have had it anymore.

Agular smiled. He enjoyed making a fool of me in front of everybody. He was even now for the chair thing. He took a suck on the neck of his bottle of beer, lifted his droopy eyelids to make sure the sexy young girl didn't miss the performance, went back to cleaning his fingernails.

I sat down, placed the black leather bag on top of the table and ordered a Ginger Ale, no ice. "So," I asked rather stupidly, "how's the weather been?"

"That's what you come down here to talk about, the fuckin' weather?"

"Not really," I said trying to hide my jitters. "I'm just making small talk."

The lowlife looked up from his stiletto, locked his beady eyes on mine, and hissed, "Fuck small talk."

I looked at Agular hard, wondering what to do next. We were caught up suddenly playing bullshit mind games with each other. It was a stupid ritual and I wanted it to stop. I popped a piece of sugarless chewing gum into my mouth, offered the prick a stick by pushing the pack toward him. Agular examined his other hand's fingernails, started picking at them with his knife. His way of saying no thank you.

"What's in the case?" he asked.

"It's a bag, not a case."

"Okay, what's in the *bag*, fuckwad?"

"Hey, watch your language, Agular. Don't be bad-mouthing me, okay?"

"Then don't you be givin' me no fuckin' school lessons, okay?"

We stared at each other.

"Just watch your mouth," I growled.

"Fuck you," said Agular.

I was having a hard time turning this thing around, getting the two of us on some kind of good track. I took a deep breath. All I heard was background noise: recorded music, the hum of conversation, ice cubes tinkling in glasses.

"Okay, we straight?" I said, not knowing what else to say. "I won't give you any school lessons and you won't bad-mouth me."

Agular started laughing. When he stopped, there was a shit-eating grin on his face. "Yeah, we're straight," he said mimicking my voice, low and nervous, making me sound like the scaredy-cat I was, still being dangerously cutesy with me.

Agular returned to getting the dirt out from under his fingernails. "So what you got in the *bag*," he asked, never looking up from his lap, "some pussies for sale?"

"No, Agular, no pussies."

I realized I was at a definite disadvantage. For one thing, I hated the guy. For another, I was constantly trying to control myself and not do something stupid and blow this operation. For another thing, I didn't have a clue how to play him. Plus the fact that if he annoyed me beyond the pale, so what? What the hell could I do about it? Not a thing. Not if I wanted to succeed. I had to get him to do this thing or I failed. I didn't want to fail. Not again. And finally something about the set-up bothered me. Why were we still in the same restaurant? Coulter had said . . .

"I ask you, what you got in the *bag*?"

"I'm not going to tell you what's in the bag yet, Agular. Later, maybe, if you're a good little boy." Me, like a big schmuck, being dangerously cutesy with him again.

"I know it's for me, so fucking give it to me."

"I'll give it to you when I'm ready."

Agular folded his jackknife and slipped it into a pocket. A good sign. Then he stood up, threw some money on the table, grabbed the black leather bag and walked out of the restaurant.

A bad sign.

CHAPTER SIX

F irst I figured I blew it. Failed again. Then I panicked
What the hell was he doing and where was he going?
Before I could think of an answer, the two apes lifted
me out of my chair by my armpits and, using small jabs to my
back, pushed me out onto the street. The underaged girl
Agular had been flirting with watched in wonder, her mouth a
little "o."

And then brilliant me figured out what Agular was doing.
He was switching restaurants. Coulter Bean was right again.
The four of us crossed the street and walked a few blocks away
to another outdoor place. Agular and I sat down outside at a
table for two. The thugs plopped down into a banquette inside
the restaurant, but not far away. I watched them watching me,
even when they ordered their food from a blowsy waitress.

"Wha' the fuck you want?" snarled Miguel Agular, out of
patience, fingering his mustache. "Stop fuckin' aroun' and talk.
Tell me wha' the fuck you come here for or I'm outta here."

"I thought you knew what I came here for."

"My friends say you wanna make a deal. Gonna make me
rich. I figure wha' the fuck, I listen. Don't take too much work
to listen. But know this. I don't get convinced easy, no matter
what my friends say."

"No? How come? You don't trust your friends?"

"I trust my friends, but my friends are *stupido*. They don't use their heads like I do," Agular said, pointing to his own so I would know the difference between a head and, say, a leg. "Let me ask you a question. Why would the gringos send a big asshole like you to make a deal with me?"

"Watch your language."

"You, the rat turd who wants to kill me more than anybody in the whole world."

"I said watch . . ."

"Me, Miguel Agular, the guy who capped maybe one of your best friends. Maybe two. Maybe more. Jus' don't make sense. Am I right, *amigo*?"

I wanted to kill him right then and there. "First of all Agular, I'm not your fucking *amigo* . . . and . . . yeah, you're right, it doesn't make much sense."

"Seems to me nothin' but a big fuckin' trap. I mean you try to kill me once. Why not try to kill me again? But my friends, they say no trap. They make me promise to come and listen to wha' you have to say. They say I gonna be surprised an' I gonna be happy, too, but they don't tell me nothin' else. So like wha' the fuck is goin on?"

"You were supposed to come alone, Agular."

"Wha'?"

"I said you were supposed to come alone. Just you. How come you brought your cannons if you were supposed to come alone?"

"Yeah? So? My old lady suppose to shit strawberry ice cream. At least *she* think so." Miguel laughed hysterically at his joke, turned for approval from the thugs. They didn't know what the hell Agular was laughing about, but they ho-ho-hoed their fat asses off anyway. "Wha' the fuck you think I am, *stupido*, too?" Agular said to me. "I think it's pretty good I come at all. You know? At least I come."

"Yeah, at least you come."

"I come because my friends they tell me all that shit with the Sandies and Condies is finished. They tell me now everybody have different enemies. They tell me in these new times I can still make a lot of money. Maybe they tell me I have to change sides, shit like that. But dealin' with you . . . I don't know."

"I make you nervous, right?"

"*You* make *me* nervous? You fuckin' out of your mind?" Agular started pushing his silverware around, twirling the ashtray, playing with his mustache. "I say somethin' about bein' nervous? I don't say somethin' about bein' nervous, do I? Huh, do I? You think your pussy ass make me nervous? BULLSHIT. I come to hear wha' you have to say, that's why I come. So say somethin' quick or I'm outta here. You hear wha' I'm sayin'? Don't keep wastin' my time. Start talkin' already."

So now I was taking orders from the little prick. "We want to make a deal with you. We want you to go to work for us."

"We? Who's we?"

"My government. The Uncle."

"Yeah? The Uncle? So why they send you, limpdick? The Uncle knows we hate each other. So why they send you?"

I was stuck for an answer. Didn't think he'd ask that question. The boys at The Company didn't either. We all should have thought of an answer for that one. I mean, why *would* the CIA send me? I had to make something up. I decided to try honesty. Maybe toss in a little flattery to boot. "I'll tell you why. Because The Company knows I'm the best man for this job. The Uncle also knows I respect you. The Uncle knows I may be the only CIA agent who does."

"You ain't no CIA agent. You're a hired killer. Like me."

"Yeah, maybe, but The Uncle still knows I'm the best man for this job, that I respect you and that I'm the man you'll probably listen to. Even though you hate me as much as I hate you, you'll listen to me. Am I right or wrong?"

The scumbag thought about it, then bought it. Didn't want to lose the possibility of big bucks coming his way. Even threw in his own reason, said in a low voice, "The Uncle knows we ain't scared of each other."

"Yeah," I said, sucking up, "that's another good reason. Anyway, what I came to say is, The Uncle wants to work something out where you'll make a shit load of money."

"So maybe one of these days you gonna tell me wha' I have to do to make this shit load of money?"

"You have to find and kill targets we give you."

"Yeah. Good. What's targets?"

"People. Targets are people. You have to kill some people for us. Some of these people you might know. Some of the people you won't know. All you have to do is make the people disappear. Forever. No traces. The Uncle doesn't want to know what you did or how you did it, or *when* you did it. The Uncle doesn't want to know dick. Only that you *did it*. The Uncle wants results or he'll go find someone else. Understand so far, Agular?"

"Yeah. Sure." He laughed. Then he scowled. "So how much money we talkin' about?"

"Fifty thousand dollars a kill."

CHAPTER SEVEN

So there I was, sweating my ass off in the sweltering midday sun, watching a dangerous gunman watching me. Only dangerous me was weaponless. Thank God the dangerous gunman sitting in front of me was suddenly a happy gunman.

Miguel Agular appeared to be trying to find the right words to express his unmitigated joy at the possibility of earning fifty thousand dollars a kill if he was successful. His pea brain worked slowly like a crocodile's, but the words finally did come. They broke from his yellow toothed mouth like wild horses galloping in different directions.

"You shit me! You shit me! You shit me! You shit me! You shit me! You shit me!"

The two apes across the way looked up from their food wide-eyed with alarm, their guns drawn, not caring if the other patrons saw them with weapons or not. Meanwhile, Agular was sitting straight up in his chair for the first time that afternoon. Maybe for the first time ever. I had never seen Agular in any position but slouched. So when Agular sat up, his two *banditos* stood up, confused. Patrons started leaving the restaurant.

"That's right, Miguel, you get fifty thousand dollars every time you kill one of the people we tell you to kill."

"Fifty thousand dollars a cap!"

"Yeah, Miguel, fifty thousand dollars a cap." I hated calling him by his Christian name. I hated him, period.

"Fifty thousand U.S. dollars a cap!" he yelled again. Agular appeared to be verging on catatonia. Without looking at his trigger-happy bodyguards, Agular motioned for them to sit down by flapping his hand by his side as if he was dribbling an invisible basketball.

"Yeah . . . fifty . . . thousand . . . dollars," I said slowly, getting sicker and sicker every time I mentioned the figure.

Agular smiled from ear to ear. Another first. First time I ever saw the slimeball smile, let alone from ear to ear. Then, suddenly, his eyes became slits again. "How I know you tell the truth?"

"Because you're holding half the money in your lap."

"*Yeah!?*"

"Yeah. With each cap, you'll get half before the job and half after. The first half's there in the bag. Twenty-five thousand dollars. Here's the key. See for yourself."

I gave him the key.

He placed the leather bag on the restaurant table, unlocked its lock, pulled the bag wide open, and saw one hundred packages of crisp new twenty-dollar bills; two hundred and fifty dollars worth of twenties in every package.

Agular whispered, "Jesus, Mutha Mary, and Joseph." He closed the bag and called the two apes over to our table. When the thugs were standing behind him, Agular slowly opened the leather bag. The *banditos'* eyes bulged. Then they crossed themselves and kissed their thumbs.

Agular sent the thugs back to their table. When they were gone, he attempted a serious expression and tried hard to suppress the pleasure that had flooded his repulsive being. He wanted to be scary again but couldn't quite pull it off. He was too happy, a strange form of behavior for him to endure. Trying hard to sound suspicious, he asked, "Why you give this to me now?"

"That's good faith money."

Agular's facial muscles tightened. "Wha' the fuck's that?"

"Good faith money? It means we trust you." I thought I'd barf. "Like I said, Miguel, you get half before and the other half when you've done the job."

"Yeah? Good. I take the . . . what you call it?"

"Good faith money."

"Yeah, good faith money. I take the good faith money now." Agular closed the bag.

I couldn't remember ever feeling so lousy.

(Fucking CIA.)

"So when do I start?" he asked, a huge grin plastered all over his face, treating me to a grand view of his brown broken teeth and infected gums. "When do I get the first guy's name?"

"Within a week."

"How do I get it?"

"Someone will contact you."

"Contact?"

"Telephone you. Find you."

"Where?"

"The Uncle will let you know. We'll tell you how to find our man and how to know you got the right guy. The contact . . . our man . . . will give you an envelope. Inside the envelope will be the target . . . inside the envelope will be the person's name. After you read the name and know who you're after, burn the paper *and* the envelope. Understand? Burn the paper *and* the envelope. If you get careless and blow The Uncle's cover, you're a dead man. You hear? A dead man."

"Yeah, yeah, sure. I hear."

"I mean it."

"I fuckin' *hear*!"

"When you know who the guy is and where you can find him, kill him as fast as you can. We'll know if you've done the job or not."

Agular smirked. "Yeah? *How* will you know?"

"Believe me, Agular, we'll know." I didn't smirk.

"Yeah? Okay." Angular knew I was serious.

A waiter came to take our order. I figured it was about time. It took him long enough to come, and I was surprisingly hungry. Agular told the waiter to go away.

"So, after I kill the guy, wha happens?"

"After you kill the guy—and by the way, Miguel, sometimes it might be a woman . . ."

"Who the fuck cares."

". . . after you kill the person, we'll get in touch with you to let you know where to find the rest of your money. Twenty-five thousand dollars more. Okay? Understand?"

"Yeah, okay, I understand."

"When you cap one name, we'll give you another name. And then another and so on, until we're finished. Each time you cap someone, you'll put fifty thousand U.S. dollars in your pocket, right?"

"Yeah. Right. Simple." Agular thought for a moment, then said, "Why me?"

"You can get to these people. We can't."

"Yeah. Okay." Agular grinned, buying the answer. One of his gold teeth flared in the sun.

"One other thing, Miguel."

"What?"

"If you say you've killed someone and you haven't, we'll come and kill *you*. That's a promise." Those two sentences I didn't mind telling him at all.

"Yeah? You couldn't do it before. How you gonna do it now?"

I flared. Agular noticed it. "We'll do it this time," I said. "Count on it."

"Okay. Okay." He felt too good to bait me.

I couldn't quit. "They'll send a better killer this time, Agular. They'll send someone better than me."

"*Okay!*"

Neither one of us spoke for a moment, then Agular said, "So how do I know The Uncle won't kill *me*?"

"Kill you?"

"Yeah, kill me. After I finish with your fucking list."

"We might need you again."

Once again Agular considered what I said. "Yeah, that's right, you might."

Agular lifted his eyelids and stared at me.

I wondered what was up.

"I'm finished talking," he said. "You finished talking?"

"Yeah, I'm done."

"Okay," said Agular, "let's have a drink." He slapped the top of the black bag on his lap. "I even pay."

"Can't, Miguel," I lied, suddenly stressed. (Thirty seconds more with this bohunk and I'd kill him with my bare hands.) "I can't, Miguel. I've got to go. Got to get back to Washington. Tell my boss we have a new, uh, partner."

"I get a cab for you. Least I can do for my new *partner*."

Agular and I got up from the table. He draped his skinny arm around my neck. I shook it off. He didn't seem to mind. His newfound riches must have softened the insult. The four of us walked out to the curb, the two bodyguards staying close behind me. They still didn't trust the CIA guy worth a damn.

Agular whistled. A taxi pulled up.

"Same goddamn driver I had before," I said.

"How can you tell?" he asked.

"Same straw hat. He's dumb as shit."

"They all are," said Agular. "Give me a ride?"

"Where to?"

"Back to El Sombrero. I wanna see if that little chickie's still there."

I couldn't stand the thought of being with the prick another second. "The El Sombrero's only three blocks away."

"So what?" snapped Agular, his eyes quickly turning to slits, instantly angry. "Wanna give your new partner a ride or not?"

I told Agular to get in.

The two of us climbed into the back seat, me first then Agular and his bag. He wanted his bodyguards to get into the taxi but there wasn't enough room. One of the fat *banditos* could have fit in the front seat, but the other bag of shit was much to obese to sit in the back with Agular and me.

"You two walk," Agular told the bodyguards in Spanish. "Keep each other company. Meet me at El Sombrero."

The one in the front reluctantly got out. The two stood in the street side by side, frowning.

"El Sombrero, *por favor*," I said to the taxi driver.

The driver mumbled something in Spanish through his rearview mirror.

I asked Agular to translate.

Agular told me the driver said it was only three blocks, we should walk. I started to get out of the taxi. Agular stopped me by putting his hand on my arm. The apes on the street were paying attention again. Agular leaned forward and yelled something in Spanish directly into the driver's ear.

The driver pulled away from the curb immediately.

"What did you tell him, Miguel?"

"I say if you don't start drivin' I break your neck then fuck your mother." Agular opened his mouth wide and howled. Then he seemed to suddenly chill out. He leaned back against the seat with the black bag on his knees, and closed his eyes.

Maybe he was praying?

To what God, I wondered.

I looked out my window. I couldn't look at Agular. Not another minute. I was furious at everyone: Agular, the CIA, Coulter Bean, everyone. I just gave the killer of two of my friends twenty-five thousand American dollars. How awful was that? I sat there in the taxi pissed. How could The Company be so fucking dumb?

The cab driver stopped at the first corner for a red light. The light turned green but the cabbie didn't go anywhere.

"Drive!" yelled Miguel, his eyes still closed.

The taxi driver, Coulter Bean, twisted his body around to face us, said, "Bye-bye, shithead," and shot Miguel Agular right between the eyes.

CHAPTER EIGHT

The force of the shot threw Miguel Agular's body back against the taxi's rear seat, where it stayed. There was a neat little hole just above Miquel's nose.

The taxi smelled of cordite.

I smelled of shock.

Coulter Bean slid his automatic and silencer back into the inside pocket of his jacket and turned to face the red light. His two passengers—one alive and dumbfounded and one dead and dead—sat quietly in the back of his cab.

When the traffic light changed to green, Coulter made a sharp right and took off. Agular fell across my lap. I pushed him back to a sitting position. Ten minutes later, Coulter pulled into the short driveway of a row house at an address known only to him. I was still mute from what I had seen, my heart still thumping up a storm.

We were in front of a two-car garage door. Coulter pushed the button of a remote control and, once the garage door had slid up, parked. He left the body in the back seat, grabbed the black bag from the corpse's lap and stepped out of the cab. Coulter pointed to the 1976 Volvo parked in the adjoining space. He opened the door on the driver's side and climbed in behind the steering wheel as I walked around the rear of the car and slid onto the passenger seat beside him. He backed onto the street, shut the garage door with the remote control, and we sped away.

After a few minutes Coulter turned to me and said, "Airport, *amigo?*"

I nodded, barely able to say, "Sounds good to me."

Nine minutes later, we were free and clear of the city.

Roughly twenty-five minutes after seeing Miguel Agular shot dead as yesterday's newspaper, my voice returned in full.

"Jesus Christ Almighty!"

"You called, *amigo?*"

"Want to tell me about it?"

"What's to tell?"

"What's to tell?! I thought you were along as backup, you know, protection in case something went wrong, shit like that. Why the Christ didn't you tell me you were going to shoot the prick?"

"We figured . . ."

"There goes that *we* shit."

". . . *they* figured it was better to do it this way. Then you couldn't accidentally give anythin' away or play it any way but the right way, simply because you didn't know any other way to play it. Does that make any sense?"

"I'm not sure."

"Otherwise you might have been doing more *actin'* than normal and fuck it up by *pretendin'* to be a courier, if you knew all along that at the end of the day I was going to shoot the skunk. By *not* tellin' you, you were pissed all the time you were with him, which would have been normal for you in that situation. And Agular could tell you were pissed. That way, he was never suspicious. You *were* pissed all the time you were with Agular, weren't you?"

"Yes I was."

"Which was normal. And consequently, Agular didn't sense anythin' amiss. I'm sure he figured what you said was true, mainly because he could tell you hated havin' to say what you were sayin', what you were *ordered* to say. Agular's usually sharp instincts had to be tellin' him you were bein' truthful, because as far as you were concerned, *you were* bein' truthful. Am I right?"

"Yeah, you're right. I guess even a dimwit like Agular had to see I hated every minute of being in his company."

"Right, that's why he believed you. See? Sometimes those boys down there on The Farm ain't always as dumb as we think they are."

"*Up* there on The Farm, dimwit. The Farm's in Virginia. We're in Mexico."

"You sure the United States isn't south of Mexico?"

We didn't speak for a moment or two.

"Still, Coulter, you were really cool. It would have been a bitch if you got fucked up and weren't right there when we came out of the restaurant . . ."

"That wasn't hard."

". . . and killed the motherfucker before he knew what was going on."

"Yeah," said Coulter Bean smiling, "that *was* pretty good."

"It was better than pretty good. Come to think of it, it sure was a dumb move on Agular's part, getting into our cab like he did without his bodyguards. He wasn't thinking, was he? I guess the money made him loco. That's not like Agular, to let his guard down."

"Past tense," said Coulter. "That *wasn't* like Agular to let his guard down."

"Yeah, past tense, right."

Saying "past tense" sure made me feel good. I was never so happy to see someone dead as that shit Miguel Agular. I stared

45

out my window at shantytowns, battered cars on cement blocks, and those ubiquitous rib-thin stray dogs looking for garbage on muddy, potholed roads. Welcome to Mexico!

"Jesus, Coulter, what if Agular ended up not wanting a ride back to El Sombrero?"

"I wasn't plannin' on him wantin' a ride."

"You would have had to shoot him in the street."

"That's what I thought I'd have to do in the first place."

"And his two bodyguards. You would have had to shoot them too."

"I know."

"We were lucky, Coulter."

"What's this *we* shit?"

"I can't believe we finally got Agular."

"My granddaddy used to say, 'Sometimes you eat the bear. Sometimes the bear eats you.' "

"So many things could have gone wrong."

"True, but ain't that always the case?"

"My only real complaint's that lousy attitude of yours, Coulter."

"What lousy attitude?"

"You know, when we were parked across from El Sombrero and I was watching Agular, you weren't much fun. You were, I don't know, sullen."

"I was nervous."

"You get sullen when you get nervous, do you?"

"I do."

Silence.

"Tell you the truth, Chuckie Baby, I'm glad we dusted that skunk."

"You can say that again."

"Tell you the truth, Chuckie Baby, I'm glad we dusted that skunk."

"Give me a break, Coulter, and stop calling me Chuckie Baby. It annoys me."

"My granddaddy had a saying about guys like Miguel Agular."

"Yeah? What did he say?"

"Never trust a man, not even your brother, if his hair is one color and his mustache another."

"You sure had one smart granddaddy, Coulter."

"Yeah. He also said beware of grown men who wear their college class rings."

"Really?"

"Yeah. Granddaddy seemed to think guys who wore their class rings were gayish."

"Gayish?"

"You know, maybe had a few homosexual tendencies."

"Your granddaddy was a homophobe?"

"No way," said Coulter. "Granddaddy always wears his Emory class ring."

I sat quietly wondering about Coulter Bean and his god-damn Granddaddy.

"CB and CB," I said eventually.

"What?"

"That's us, Coulter. CB and CB. Chuck Barris and Coulter Bean. Two CBs. We CBs are the best."

"With a little help from Count Basie," added Coulter.

"And Carol Burnett."

"And Charles Barkley."

"Good one, Coulter. And how about Charlie Barnett."

"Who?"

"Charlie Barnett. He was a famous dance band leader. Before your time."

"Charles Barkley," said Coulter.

"You already mentioned him. Cousin Brucie," I said. He's a disc jockey in New York."

47

"His first name's *Cousin?*"

"Yeah," I lied.

We started laughing. It came suddenly then grew and grew and grew. After a few minutes the laughter turned into hysteria. Soon tears were pouring down our faces and our sides were killing us. I guess all those hours of pent-up nervousness were pouring out of Coulter and me in the form of uncontrollable, spastic laughter. Coulter had to pull off the road and stop driving. We sat there in that steamy Volvo, laughing and wheezing and choking and coughing for almost ten minutes. I thought I might die.

(Has laughing ever killed anyone?)

My ribs hurt so badly I had to get out of the car and move around in the dusty gravel by the side of the road. I walked bent over, holding my sides. Eventually we both simmered down. I got back into the car and we drove off. Two really happy killers on their way home.

"Hey, Coulter."

"What?"

"That list of terrorists that Agular was supposed to get to, do those terrorists really exist?"

"Yeah, I think they do. I'm not sure. Why?"

"I was thinking. Maybe you and I should go after those guys. You know, fifty big ones a pop."

"My granddaddy used to quote an old Latin sayin' about situations like that."

"Yeah," I said feeling like Bud Abbott, "what Latin saying?"

"*Quieta non movere.*"

"Which means?"

"Let sleepin' dogs lie."

"Your granddaddy knew Latin?"

"Yeah, he did. You know, Chuckie Baby, I kind of like this straw hat and these crummy sunglasses."

"Wear them in good health," I said. "And Coulter, do me a favor. Stop calling me Chuckie Baby."

And then guess what? We started laughing again.

CHAPTER NINE

I stopped laughing in 1980.

I was living in Malibu, California. It was June. I had just turned fifty-one. A girl I loved, Lucy Sue Glop, who I had been seeing before Penny Pacino, died in a plane crash and a film I produced and directed called *The Gong Show Movie* tanked big time. I had just returned from Lisbon, where I had traveled to see a girl who I suspected, unbeknownst to Penny, might become the new love of my life, only to discover in Portugal that she had a black front tooth. I had met the lady briefly in an airport lounge in St. Louis. When I asked her where she was going, she said Lisbon, and challenged me to meet her there. Like a horny fool, I went, only to discover the first night that she had a jet black dead tooth front top right. I didn't remember her having a black tooth in St. Louis, so seeing it when she smiled was rather traumatizing. In fact, I thought the black tooth, along with a cholera epidemic and a political uprising taking place in Portugal's streets, were good enough reasons to cause me to suffer my first nervous breakdown. I remember panicking and calling Penny in Los Angeles. Whenever I was in the throws of a major anxiety attack, I would immediately telephone Penny.

"Come to Lisbon, Pen," I remember whining. "Please. You gotta come. You gotta get me out of here."

"What's the matter?" I recollect her asking.

"I'm having a small nervous breakdown "

"How small?" she asked.

"Small."

"Well, if it's a small one, come home yourself. I'm busy right now trying to find a life of my own. You have the fortissimo. Bug off."

"Fortitude," I said.

"What?" She sounded angry.

"Fortitude, not fortissimo. I have the fortitude. And I changed my mind. It's not so small."

"What's not so small?" asked Penny.

"My nervous breakdown."

"You just want to hump a little."

"Hump? What are you talking about, Pen?"

"You know, you just want to scootch around."

"Jesus Penny, we can scootch around when I get home. Right now I'm laying here inert, in the throws of a major breakdown. Humping is the last thing I want to do. I just want you to come and save me. I want you to bring me home."

"I can't believe you're asking me to do this. What happened with the girl you went to see?"

"How did you find out about that?"

"Never mind. What happened?"

"She had a black tooth."

Penny laughed. That was one of Penny Pacino's great traits. If something struck her funny, she laughed, no matter what.

"Aw, come on, Pen. I miss you. I really do. I love you so much. Maybe when you get here we'll go to Paris."

"See! You just want to hump."

Penny came and got me. She was angry about the girl with

the black tooth, but she still came and got me. She arrived in Portugal pissed. The problem with Penny was that when she was mad she looked adorable.

"You look cute, Penny," I said when I picked her up at the Lisbon airport.

"You always used to tell me I looked cute, but you don't anymore."

"I still do."

"No you don't."

"I just did, for Christ's sake."

Penny never stayed mad very long. She didn't in Portugal, either.

We did go to Paris and we did scooch around, just like Penny said we would. We ate at great little bistros, walked the streets at night, reviewed our lives on the various bridges that crossed the Seine.

"Remember the time you tried to kill yourself?" I asked.

"Because I caught you with that tropplop."

"Trollop. You tried to do it by drinking champagne. When I came to your place, you were passed out on your bed with seven or eight empty splits all over your bedroom floor."

"They didn't have any large bottles at the market."

"At first you scared me to death."

"You were such a shit in those days."

"Remember the time I stood you up at the Metropolitan Museum and you waited in front of the place for hours?"

"See what I mean."

"You're right, I was a jerk."

"You used to make me cry a lot."

"You still cry a lot."

"You're always sweet to me when I cry."

"But I've changed, Pen, haven't I?"

"Not a whole hell of a lot. But I love you and I always will."

"I love you too," I said on that bridge and hugged her hard.

Penny said, "I told you once before when I'll figure you out, but I'm sure you forgot."

"I remember when."

"You do not. When?"

"You said you'll figure me out when we're old and gray and we're sitting in our rocking chairs."

"Right!" she said all surprised that I remembered.

That was a great night in Paris.

Anyway, the trip back to Malibu from Europe was exhausting. I was getting too old for that kind of shit, chasing girls from continent to continent. My programs, like me, were getting old too. Their ratings were slipping. That's what the Vice President of Television Network Programming called to say.

CHAPTER TEN

"There's slippage, Chuck."

"Slippage?"

"Yes, slippage." The speaker on the other end of the telephone was one of the corporation's many Vice Presidents, Edward T. Vane. Mr. Vane spoke in the funeral manner of a brain surgeon announcing the presence of a terminally malignant tumor in my head. "I'm afraid to say there's slippage."

He was right. There *was* slippage. That's because instead of paying attention to either of my old shows—*The Dating Game* or *The Newlywed Game*—I was concentrating on *The Gong Show*. In fact, I was more than concentrating, I was obsessing. I insisted on auditioning every act, then choosing and rehearsing the ones I wanted. I wrote the script, rehearsed the band, selected the celebrity judges. I had to be sure the show I fronted was as close to perfect as possible. Still, with all my effort and attention, *The Gong Show* was headed south, too.

For the vast majority of the world not familiar with my television programs, *The Dating Game* offered a pretty girl the opportunity to question and then choose one of three eligible bachelors she couldn't see on the other side of a partition. In the daytime version, the lucky pair spent a "night on the town," consisting of dinner for two and a couple of glasses of cheap wine from a screw-top bottle at a cheesy bistro in down-town Los Angeles. The prime-time or evening version of *The Dating Game* sent the couple and a chaperone to romantic cities all over the world. Sometimes I went along as the chaperone to kill some enemy of the United States for The Uncle.

The Newlywed Game was a television program whereby married couples, wedded to each other less than a year, competed for prizes by answering the greatest number of correct answers to personal questions about each other. *The Newlywed Game* was the simplest format of any game show ever. All a daily show needed was four couples, eight questions, and a washer-dryer.

The Gong Show was a variety program that showcased mostly awful talent competing against each other for the paltry amount of $107.28 and a small disgusting trophy no one would want in their house. As I said, for reasons too complicated and boring to explain, I was the host of *The Gong Show*. It was the first and only television show I ever created where I also acted as master of ceremonies. Though hosting the show was enormous fun, my deciding to do it might have been a grave mistake. *The Gong Show* would change my life. Some said for the worst. Others disagreed. I'm still trying to figure that one out. No matter what anybody thinks, no matter what I accomplish before I die, *The Gong Show* will always be my legacy. My grave stone's epitaph will probably read:

CHUCK BARRIS 1929/?

GONGED AT LAST

R.I.P.

In an effort to save *The Gong Show,* I did the equivalent of pouring gasoline on a roaring fire. I ratcheted up the show's energy past the point of no return. Energy was the last thing the *The Gong Show* needed. Sanity would have been preferable.

At least that's what I think now. Perhaps I was ahead of my time back then, which to me is as bad as being behind the times. No accolades should be given to either. In my opinion, being ahead or behind the times are both failures in the world of creativity.

In any case, my new and misguided ratcheted-up perform-ance in front of the cameras appeared to a goodly number of viewers as the actions of a crazed buffoon on a strong dose of drugs. Fortunately, I've never taken drugs. Ever. I'm an extremist by nature. When I chewed gum I chewed twenty packs a day. When I smoked cigarettes I was a walking chimney. When I started on cigars I went through at least fifteen a day and sucked their smoke into my lungs as if I were a human vacuum cleaner. I knew that if I so much as sniffed a drug I would have become an instant junkie, and a junkie is the last thing you want to be when you're running a public company.

Anyway, accelerating the wildness factor on *The Gong Show*, pushing the envelope of good taste to the extreme, was defi-nitely *not* the thing to do. In those days, new TV audiences, the growing Reagan Republicans, of which there were tons, and the freshly vociferous Christian Majority relished blandness and repetition, such as *Wheel of Fortune* and *Jeopardy*, Perry Como and Andy Williams. Not lunacy and change, i.e. *The Gong Show*. The pendulum had swung. Soon I would no longer be in fashion.

I should have known better, but I didn't. I figured if the studio audience loved my craziness, and I thought they did, then so must the rest of the world.

"Studio audiences always love everything that's happening in the studio," my beloved announcer and showbiz veteran Johnny Jacobs told me one night. "But," he added gravely, "it's the audience at home you have to worry about." I should have listened to Johnny.

The funny thing is, I always thought my stupid antics on *The Gong Show* were the cause of my company's downfall. But I was wrong. They weren't. A new show was.

It was called *Three's a Crowd*.

CHAPTER *ELEVEN*

The premise of *Three's a Crowd* was: Who knows the husband better, his wife or his secretary? The original Eternal Triangle. The Garden of Eden. The husband was Adam. The wife, Eve. The secretary, the snake. The Bible's premiere story extrapolated and formatted for syndicated television. A guaranteed surefire hit. At least I thought so.

But I was terribly wrong.

What I didn't realize was how venal and heinous my creation was.

Three husbands came on stage. The "evil" host asked the husbands four questions. A sample question: How many presents has your secretary bought your wife, for you, this year?

This following transcript is a portion of *Three's a Crowd* show taped in 1979:

> *Husband Number One: "My secretary never bought my wife a present for me. Zero."*
> *Husband Number Two: "Zero."*
> *Husband Number Three: "Me, too. Zero."*
> *The secretaries join their bosses on stage and are asked the same question.*

Secretary Number One: "Two. I bought his wife two presents."

Husband Number One holds up his card with "O" on it and mutters: "Bullshit." (Which we bleep.)

Secretary Number One: "What do you mean (bleep)? You forget about the little see-through nightie I bought her for Valentine's Day?"

Husband Number One: "Oh, Jesus!"

Secretary Number One: "Or the pearls I bought her when she had the baby?"

Husband Number One (his face in his hands): "Oh, God! Oh, God!"

Evil Host (giggling): "Okay, no points for Secretary Number One. Secretary Number Two?"

Secretary Number Two: "This year? Try this month. Three presents this month!"

The studio audience gasps.

Husband Number Two holds up his card with "O" on it and (trying to be cute) says: "I forgot how thoughtful and generous I am. Heh, heh, heh."

The studio audience is deathly quiet.

Evil Hosts: "Too bad, Secretary Number Two, no points for you either. How about you, Secretary Number Three?"

Secretary Number Three: "I've lost count."

Evil Host (chuckling): "Now, now, now. I need a number."

Secretary Number Three: "Okay, okay. Four. No five. Five!"

Husband Number Three holds up his card with "O" on it: "I think I'm in trouble."

Evil Host: "I think you are too."

And then the wives make their entrance. The unit is complete. The husband is in the center, his wife and secretary at his sides.

Evil Host: "Okay, Wife Number One, how many presents did your husband say his secretary bought you on his behalf last year?"

Wife Number One: "How many presents did she buy me?"

Evil Host: "That's right, your husband's secretary bought for him that your husband claimed he bought for you."

Wife Number One (smiling): "Well, he better had said none if he knows what's good for him."

Husband Number One (still numb from his secretary's answer) holds up his card with a large black "O" on it and smiles weakly.

Evil Host (happy as a clam): "Correct! One point for Wife Number One!"

Wife Number One: "Thank God."

Evil Host: "But unfortunately that's not what your husband's secretary said. Please hold up your card, Secretary Number One, and show the missus."

Secretary Number One holds up her card with a large black "2" written on it.

Wife Number One: "What's that sign say? Two? TWO! Two what? What's that mean? She bought two presents for me? She's got to be kidding. What presents?"

Secretary Number One (leaning around her boss so she can face his wife): "Your little nightie last Valentine's Day, and . . ."

Wife Number One (completely befuddled): "My nightie . . ."

Husband Number One: "Well she . . ."

Secretary Number One (continuing): ". . . and the string of pearls when you had your baby."

Wife Number One is visibly mortified . . . and crushed.

She quietly begins to sob.
Her husband stares at her, shattered.
His secretary looks straight ahead, grinning.

Three's a Crowd was much too powerful, too malevolent. I couldn't watch it. It wasn't my type of program. Maybe I was ahead of my time yet again. Maybe happy television shows were on their way out and mean-spirited programs that loved to humiliate contestants were on their way in. Maybe I was in the vanguard and didn't know it. It didn't matter. I hated the show. It wasn't fun to produce. I retreated to my old vow: If it ain't fun, don't do it. So I didn't do it. I pulled the program off the air.

I didn't know it, but it was the beginning of the end of my television career. The times they were a-changing. Like I said, the pendulum had swung the other way. This sweet little guy from Bala-Cynwyd, Pennsylvania, had become television's Public Enemy Number One. By the end of 1980, all of my other programs would be canceled. *Daily Variety*, the show business trade publication, ran a headline that read: *BARRIS GOING, GOING . . . GONG!*

At some point during that depressing period of my life, my girlfriend Penny Pacino and I traveled to Philadelphia to see a New York Rangers–Philadelphia Flyers hockey game. We were guests of Ed and Myrna Snider, the team's owners. We sat in the owner's box. I was in a pathetic funk. We hoped the hockey game would cheer me up. For a while it seemed to be doing just that. And then during the second period, Snider—anticipating a pleasant surprise for me—placed the following message in lights on the huge four-sided electronic scoreboard that hung over the arena's center ice:

LET'S GIVE A BIG SPECTRUM WELCOME
TO THE HOST OF THE GONG SHOW, CHUCK BARRIS

The sell-out crowd of 16,005 *booed*!
They fucking *booed*!

CHAPTER TWELVE

Instead of going back to Los Angles after that disastrous hockey game, Penny and I moved into the Wyndham Hotel on West Fifty-Eighth Street in Manhattan. There wasn't any point in flying back to Hollywood to run my company. I was too much of a basket case to be an effective Chief Operating Officer. Somehow or other I had to get rid of all the anger, bitterness, and hurt that was roiling around in my system. I needed some kind of cathartic cleansing or I'd go out of my goddamn mind. I thought if I committed my misery to paper, I might be able to exorcize some of the pain and unhappiness from my body. Who knows, perhaps I would use the material down the road in a book or a magazine article or something.

"At least you won't be walking around like a clinically depressed psycholic," said Penny helpfully.

"Psychotic," I said, staring at nothing.

The Wyndham Hotel had monthly rates.

That's the reason I picked the place.

"How long do you think this catharsic thing will take?" asked Penny, unpacking some new boxes of clothes that had been Federal Expressed from Los Angeles to the Wyndham.

"A month, tops."

Two and a half years later—in August 1983—I finished a manuscript of a book I called *Confessions of a Dangerous Mind*. I thought the book was surprisingly good. And funny too, which was peculiar. I certainly didn't feel very funny when Penny and I checked into the hotel back in '81.

"Get it to a good agent," advised Penny, who over the years had grown excited about *Confessions*.

The best and most powerful agent in New York at the time was a guy named Mort Janklow. For all I know, he still is. I only knew him by name but took it upon myself to telephone Mr. Janklow and ask if I might send him a copy of my manuscript. He was gracious and polite, said it would be a pleasure to read *Confessions of a Dangerous Mind* and promised to give me an answer in no more than two weeks. I found all of this both exciting and flattering, maybe even mind-boggling. *The* Mort Janklow was actually going to read *my* manuscript!

Two weeks became three weeks, then four weeks, then five, then six.

I wondered if it was possible that Mr. Janklow had lost my manuscript and was ashamed to tell me. So I called him.

"Trash!" he proclaimed. "Your book is pure and simple trash." (I wrote on a little yellow pad of paper, "pure and simple trash.") "How could you expect anyone to read such drivel?" (I wrote on the little yellow pad, "drivel.") "The most ludicrously bizarre story, totally unbelievable, yet you have the unmitigated gall to call this . . . this . . . *thing* your autobiography!" (I wrote down "ludicrous" and "unmitigated gall" and "thing.")

I said, "I call it an *unauthorized* autobiography."

"Yes, yes . . . unauthorized. What the hell's that supposed to mean?"

"It was just a play on . . ."

"I would be *embarrassed* to be your agent," continued Janklow, his voice rising and rising. "I would be mortified to represent something as reprehensible as this book." (I wrote on the little yellow pad "Mortified Mort" and "reprehensible" and put the pencil down. I was tired of writing down Janklow shit.) "This piece of crap deserves nothing but reproach," he said. "If you are the least bit talented, then your manuscript doesn't show it. It's a severe waste of everyone's time. You show a shameful lack of concern for a reader's intelligence."

Eventually he hung up.

I looked up at Penny. She had been standing beside me during the telephone call. I showed her the little yellow pad of scribbled comments. She cried. I would have joined her if it wasn't such an unmanly thing to do.

To describe me in the minutes that followed Janklow's telephone call as being catatonic would have been putting it mildly.

I was beyond catatonic.

When Penny stopped crying, she ran to the refrigerator and returned with a carton of Ben & Jerry's Vanilla Bean Ice Cream. That's what Penny always did in a crisis involving me, shoved ice cream in my mouth. And it usually worked. I'd chill out almost immediately. Once, after dinner, we walked out of a restaurant on Beverly Boulevard in Los Angeles to find our brand new Ford Mustang's side window gone. Inside, the radio and CD player were gone too. The thief must have used a Great White Shark to bite out the equipment. In my entire life, I never saw such a gaping, tearing, jagged hole in a dashboard. So what did Pen do? She brushed away some shards of glass, pushed me into the car and drove like an ambulance driver, her hand constantly on the horn, to the nearest Baskin & Robbins for some coffee ice cream. B&R's coffee ice cream is one of my favorite flavors. It worked like a charm.

But no amount of ice cream seemed to help me crack the

funk I was in after I hung up from Janklow. So, holding me under my arm, Penny walked me out of our hotel room and into an elevator. The elevator traveled up several flights. When its doors opened again, Penny guided me to John Cassavetes's and Gena Rowland's apartment. John was editing his latest film in the Wyndham's basement. Penny described to John and Gena why her boyfriend was sitting on their sofa mute and wide-eyed. She showed them my scribbled notes. John telephoned Ben Gazzara and Peter Falk, who were also staying at the Wyndham. The three guys took me to dinner that night. We all got plastered.

The next morning, I started down a list of publishers that I found in a *Book World* magazine. I sent my manuscript to the editor-in-chief of every company, one at a time. They each rejected my manuscript, one at a time, except the tenth publisher, St. Martin's Press. Tom McDermott, CEO of St. Martin's, loved the book and approved a huge first printing of 100,000 copies. When *Confessions of a Dangerous Mind* finally arrived in bookstores in 1984, I was so proud I thought I'd burst. So was Mr. McDermott.

And then the literary critics got their hands on *Confessions* and started writing their reviews. After reading a few of them, I was convinced that they'd never read the book. The literary critics picked up where the TV critics left off. "What sort of an *unauthorized autobiography*," they groused, "would you expect from the guy who gave us *The Dating Game* and *The Gong Show*? His premise is absolutely ridiculous. He says that while producing schlock television programs on national TV, he was also an assassin for the CIA, killing enemies of our country! Puh-lease."

Being crucified by the nation's television critics never bothered me. Not in the beginning. I mean what *do* envious TV critics criticize? Programs we get for free! So who cares? They can rant and rave all they want, but television viewers will watch whatever they feel like watching. TV critics' bad reviews never stopped a hit from occurring. But critics of books, plays, musicals, movies, records, and CDs, stuff like that, now *that's* a different story. Those critics have an impact because books and plays and all the rest cost money. A bad review gives the public a reason to stay away from the box office or the bookstore. Bad reviews will usually guarantee the failure of all those endeavors. The literary critics certainly affected the sales of *Confessions of a Dangerous Mind*.

The book disappeared from the bookstores.

For the next two years, I dragged Penny from Los Angeles to New York and back to Los Angeles, trying to figure out what to do with our lives. Then one day—just like that!—it dawned on me. I would marry Penny Pacino before I lost her for good. I accomplished that goal in an impressive ballroom of the Beverly Hills Hotel in California. It was a big wedding, with all our friends and whatever family we had left. The second and final part of my plan took place two years later. That's when I woke up one morning and said to Penny, "We're outta here!"

"Where are we going?"

"To the south of France."

"Why?"

"I'm going to write the Great American Novel, like Hemingway and Fitzgerald. *Confessions* was practice. I'm going to write a novel, a wonderful love story."

"That's nice," said Penny smiling. "What are we going to use for money?"

"I sold my company!"

PART II

"Antonia knew when enough was enough."
—FROM THE MOTION PICTURE *ANTONIA'S LINE*

"A tremendous amount of your life is spent accumulating and fussing over assets (cash, stocks & bonds, cars, antiques, vacation homes), time that could have been spent with family and friends or fishing or traveling or quite simply fucking."
—JONATHAN HULL

CHAPTER THIRTEEN

It's July 1994, and I'm trying to park my car. I'm near the town square that's called the Place des Lices. A stupid French driver with an attitude just cut me off.

"*Manges merde et morte,*" I yell at him. (Eat shit and die!)

He says something in French.

I reply, "*Donnez-moi un casser, anetrou!*" (Give me a break, asshole!)

I love speaking my version of the French language. Penny and I have been in France almost nine years and neither of us has yet become fluent. But I come close with my pig-French. At least I think I do.

Most of the time we lived in the south of France just outside the little fishing village of Saint Tropez. Our beautiful home was situated in the hills, ten minutes from the port. The views from our house were mind-boggling: the Mediterranean Sea in front of us, the fortress town of Ramatuelle above us. There were vineyards surrounding our property, with large full fruit trees lining our driveway. The smell of the sea mingled with the lemon and orange trees was not to be believed. To this day I remember it—and miss it. The smell, that is.

In Saint Tropez we had a brilliant Labrador Retriever named Buddy, a fire-engine red Porsche convertible named Speedy,

71

and a forest green Range Rover named Boring. And then one day Penny bought me (with my money) a surprise birthday present. It was a sleek all-wood Italian speedboat. It had nine coats of varnish and two shiny 750-horse power Rolls-Royce inboard engines. It was thirty-two feet long and weighed three tons. The off shore racer was a classic all-wood beauty, the most magnificent boat I'd ever seen. It was a Riva. To anyone familiar with classic all-wood boats, the Italian-made Riva was the best. Unfortunately, the first time I soloed as captain of the racer I crashed. Twice. They weren't serious crashes, more like hard bumps; one into a dock and one into another boat.

I christened my ship Bam Bam.

When I wasn't speeding around the Mediterranean in Bam Bam, I was attempting to write the Great American Novel. I pretended I was either F. Scott Fitzbarris or Chuck Hemingway, depending on how I felt that day. I wrote in the morning and played *boule* in the afternoon. *Boule* is a game where two teams of two or three players compete against each other. The first team to score thirteen points wins. A player throws one of two solid iron balls roughly the size of a baseball ten to twenty feet away, rolling it as close as he can to a small wooden ball called a *petanque*. The closest balls to the *petanque* at the end of the round received a point each.

Playing *boule* was a way of inserting myself into the life of the village. It all was part of becoming one of them. It was hard for an outsider to become one of them. Cracking French hatred, envy, and bias toward Americans wasn't easy. Me trying to become an accepted *boule* player on the Place des Lices was sort of like Jackie Robinson breaking into major league baseball.

The locals called me, among other things, *le americain* (the American). At first when the frogs said *le americain*, they spit the words out as though the phrase tasted like chewed aspirin. I turned the other cheek. I turned the other cheek a lot during my life in France. I guess it's what you have to do when you play out your Walter Mitty expatriate dream thing, especially in small fishing villages along the southern coast of France.

Anyway, I became the pushy little guy who always hung around the *boule* games, always wanting to play with The Big Boys. Playing with The Big Boys was Saint Tropez's equivalent of making the major leagues. When I finally did get my chance to play with them—*voilà!*—I was good! I mean *really* good! After what seemed like years and years of trying, I finally found a sport I could excel in. I invariably rolled the *boule* ball right up next to the *petanque*. I mean, right up against it! This exasperated The Big Boys. They absolutely hated the idea that an American could play their national game as well or better than they could. Sort of like Johnny Halliday coming to the U.S.A., pitching for the Yankees, and winning the Cy Young Award.

Anyway, who would ever have believed that eventually The Big Boys would accept me on a regular basis and that toward the end of my stay in Saint Tropez, I would be recognized as one of the best *pointers* on the *Place des Lices*. Or that every July 4th, the Tropezzians would have a *Chuck Barris Championnat de Boule*—a *boule* championship in my honor!

Well, they did.

What a life Penny and I had in France. I would get up every morning to the refreshing smell of the Mediterranean. I'd drive to the port, park near *Le Gorille Bar*, stretch for a minute or so by my car and examine the sea. Was it flat or rough? Was it good for taking Bam Bam out or not? I would stand there with my hands in my pockets mesmerized by the sleeping yachts pulling at their ropes. They reminded me of beautiful mansions lassoed to iron cleats. Often I would think that if I hadn't sold my company and had worked another five years or so, I could have afforded one of those mansions. But then if the rabbit hadn't stopped to take a dump, the fox, etc. After a few minutes of

CHUCK BARRIS

absurd fantasizing about sailing off in one of those incredible yachts, I would walk up the steep alley between the bar and the bakery to the stationery store that sold newspapers and magazines. I bought the *International Herald Tribune* and read the headlines while walking back down the alley to Le Gorille Bar. Inside the bar, I would order my first bitterly strong espresso of the day—the "American coffee" was ridiculously weak, I was caught between a rock and a hard place—drop in the requisite two lumps of sugar and stir. The French love to stir. They stir everything for hours. It's one of their many retarded traits. Since I had turned into a big suck, always wanting to be one of them, I stirred my two little lumps of sugar in the tiny demitasse cup with my tiny spoon for the mandatory twenty-five minutes, just like all the other misfits. I'd take a swig, wince, turn to the sports page, and read sports scores that were at least two days old. When I finished my coffee I would go back to my house to spend the rest of the morning writing.

At one o'clock Penny would call me down from my office for lunch. The meal was served on the portion of our terrace that overlooked the sea. The weather was generally beautiful. When she wasn't plastered, lunch was prepared by our cook Mrs. Selig, a robust, red-cheeked drunk who created magnificent meals. At least two days a week we would go running to a ditch by a road that led to our house to rescue Mrs. Selig. She would be sitting potted and patient, smiling at us from her upside-down Peugeot.

Lunch usually consisted of grilled fish purchased that morning at the port, delicious cooked vegetables, a salad of fresh tomatoes and crisp lettuce with a magnificent dressing, warm baguets, some fluffy dessert, and iced tea. Penny and I ate listening to music from speakers attached to the veranda's ceiling. Sometimes we got up and danced to "Hotel California" or "You Were on My Mind" or "String of Pearls," filling the vineyards and forests surrounding our house with our music. After lunch, Penny and I would make love or I'd nap in a hammock tethered to two trees, lulled to sleep by breezes blowing up from the sea.

In the afternoon I'd drive back to town to the Place des Lices for *boule* with The Big Boys. We would have drinks afterward in the Bar des Lices, a restaurant on the square that catered mainly to the town's *boule* players. After a *Perrier menthe* or two, I'd say good-bye to my fellow players and race across the village to the port, running all the way. I wanted to get there before the sun set. Penny was usually waiting onboard Bam Bam, sometimes with a few of our friends. I'd get in the boat, start her up, and off we'd go.

Bam Bam would always growl at the ridiculously slow speed we were forced to maintain inside the marina. But once we passed the port's entrance, she howled with delight like the beast she was. I would make a wide arc and maybe do a couple of figure eights. My cowboying forced my passengers to hold on to their hats with one hand and the skyward half of the boat with the other. Everyone straightened up when I pointed the boat's bow toward the horizon, and away we went.

Soon we would arrive at that place where we were the only boat on the sea. I would cut the engines and Bam Bam would drift. The women would move to the front of the boat, their backs to the men in the rear. We men would strip down to the buff and dive into the blue-green delicious Mediterranean water. Next, came the women, if they wanted to. At this point, while treading water, I'd usually howl, "Ain't this the life?"

Later, some of us had that great after-swim cigarette. Then wine, beer, chips, pretzels, sometimes champagne. Bam Bam gently rocked back and forth while we ate and drank. Some of us would doze, anesthetized by the exercise, the warm winds, and the sound of lapping water against Bam Bam's hull. After the sun set behind the distant hills, we would head back to port and then home for dinner. During the colder months, Penny and I usually ate our meals sitting on pillows by our huge living room fireplace, eating more of Mrs. Selig's delicacies: a juicy pot roast, crispy small brown potatoes, buttery string beans, a lemon meringue tart for desert. I loved those days and nights.

The only bad moments I can remember was the day our dog Buddy died, the night the wild boars attacked our house, and the night they painted our front door.

Buddy, we called him Buddy The Wonder Dog, was eighteen months old when he died. He died pissed at me. He wanted to go with me to the Place des Lices to watch me play *boule*. I almost took him. Almost. But I didn't take him. At the last minute I changed my mind. I didn't want the responsibility of chasing after him when he went off to pick a fight with another dog. So I drove away and left him staring angrily at me by the front door.

Now, I must digress.

Buddy The Wonder Dog. He was the joy of the neighborhood's kids. They would come to our house to watch Buddy dive for rocks.

I'd say, "Okay ladies and gentlemen, here comes Buddy The Wonder Dog, doing his amazing trick of bringing back the rock from miles and miles down in the murky bottom of this deep pool."

One of the children would throw a large stone into our swimming pool. Buddy would jump right in and go to the bottom to bring it back. When Buddy dove down, he used his tail as a propeller. It became straight as a stick and wagged a hundred miles an hour it seemed, propelling Buddy down to the bottom of the pool. The dog often failed to bring the rock back the first time. Every time he failed the kids sighed, terribly disappointed. But they all kept rooting Buddy on. Down he'd go a second time and often a third, fourth, and fifth time. When he failed, Buddy would come up for air, hang by the side of the pool with his two front paws and gulp the sea breezes for all he was worth.

"But Buddy never gives up," I would tell the kids, "and Buddy never fails. A lesson for all of us to learn. So keep rooting him on, kids."

And down Buddy would go again. And again, until he came back with that rock. And when he did, the children would jump up and down, hooting and hollering, clapping their little hands, smiling from ear to ear. Buddy The Wonder Dog.

All that diving had hurt Buddy's ears and made him deaf. The day I went to the park without him, he went off disgusted to find a chicken or two, didn't hear the motorcycle coming, turned to cross the road and walked right into it. Buddy died instantly.

Penny was devastated. We all were, but none of us like Penny. She cried morning, noon, and night. For days and days. No matter what I said, nothing changed Penny's distress, nothing helped her grief.

And then the wild boars came. Buddy's death and the boars took place in September, the dry season. The wild boars were dying of thirst. They came down from the hills searching for water.

I woke up three mornings after Buddy died and walked out of the bedroom onto the terrace. I looked at our grounds. I wondered why the gardeners had decided to dig up all our beautiful lawns. Was this something they did yearly? To fertilize or replant or something? Then I realized it wasn't gardeners who had done that. Gardeners wouldn't destroy plants, kill trees by digging deep down into their roots, crack, and overturn flagstone walkways. It was a herd of wild boars.

"They're avenging Buddy's death," said my grief-stricken wife, standing beside me, holding a thin robe together at the neck.

And the time they painted our front door. But that's another story.

But other than those three terrible times, Saint Tropez was a dream come true. I loved Penny, Penny loved me, and most of the time all was right with the world. Days and nights like those in Saint Tropez were absolutely magical. I was sure they would go on forever.

But they didn't.

Life's strange that way. Up one day, down the next. And never any warnings. Little did I know that just a few years later I would lose everything I just described to you. The Lord giveth and the Lord taketh away. Sometimes He giveth back. Sometimes He doesn't.

But, as usual, I am getting ahead of myself.

So there I was, living the good life in the south of France, the expatriate writer penning the Great American Novel on the French Riviera. I was fulfilling a boyhood dream. Who would have thunk it? Me, little Chuckie Barris from Bala-Cynwyd, Pennsylvania, never knowing what I wanted to be or do—and no one to help me figure it out—living like a bunny rabbit in the south of France with his beautiful wife, his fastidious housekeeper, his drunken cook, his polished Riva speed boat, his red Porsche, and his new wonder dog, a Lab pup named Willie.

And then—just like that—things suddenly changed.

CHAPTER FOURTEEN

I t all started on a warm sunny afternoon in July 1994. I was sitting on a bench holding an ice cream cone, licking away, watching the passing parade go by on the Place des Lices, a small park maybe two city blocks long and one city block wide. The park is surrounded by outdoor cafés and shaded by large leafy trees. It's the place where the *marché*—the open air market—appears every Tuesday and Saturday. It's where the broken-down traveling circus performs on holidays and the local political and religious ceremonies take place. All other times, the Place des Lices is where the town relaxes, gossips, and plays *boule*.

It was the height of the tourist season. The streets were jammed with traffic, the park with tons of Americans, English, Germans, Italians, Poles, local Tropezzians, dogs, cats, and young mothers with their babies. Everyone was wearing different kinds of sunglasses, the young showing off sunburned body parts, the affluent carrying shopping bags crammed with expensive goodies from the village's trendy stores. Most of the heavy bags were being lugged around by American husbands, once powerful Titans of Industry, now sad and broken old farts yearning for their lost power. Those men reminded me of something Russell Banks wrote: "It's a terrible thing for a man to endure, to be nothing after having been something." Sallow-faced and stooped-shouldered, retired and forgotten, these one-time leaders of men had disintegrated into shrunken, pitiful has-beens working Europe and Asia, carrying their wives' booty from store to store like high-class Sherpas, thinking: Is this all there is? Is this the way it's supposed to end? Is this why I worked my fucking balls off my entire life? To do this Sherpa shit?

The wives knew exactly what their husbands were thinking, these women with mental problems of their own. The women would berate their husbands constantly, using variations on the following theme: Carrying my shopping bags is a hell of a lot better than sitting in a fucking wheelchair on Seventy-Fourth Street in front of our apartment building while the *shvartza* wipes snot from your fucking nose and drool from your fucking mouth, isn't it? If you had the choice, which would you take, you *putzola*?

They were scary, those wives of ex-Titans. Tough, marriage-hardened women. Wrinkle-free broads in their fifties and sixties, trying to buy back their youth with their grotesquely fat collagen lips, their Dr. Schlosser number six–type noses, and their mean expressions that no surgeon living or dead could alter. As Charles Baxter wrote: "Men leave behind their objects. Women leave behind memories of their good looks." Nasty women, those wives of ex-Titans crisscrossing the village square that afternoon in July, thinking to themselves as they walked by my bench: Fuck that *fercockta* husband of mine. I worked hard for my money, didn't I? Haven't I suffered sufficiently, God? A female Job down to the soles of my feet, no? Isn't forty years of marriage to that boring, selfish, moody, lying, cheating, self-centered control freak enough? Four decades of waking in the middle of the night to the lilting sounds of Mr. Wonderful farting or belching or regurging his

goddamn dinner out his nose. Endless years of jamming suppositories up his stinking, wrinkled ass. Cutting his jagged
smelly toenails. Sitting through a dozen trips to the hospital.
Forever picking glop out of his filthy, hairy ears. The arrogant
prick deserves everything he gets. His hernias, his piles, his
colon bag, his humongous prostate, his high blood pressure,
his palsy, his incontinency, his diapers, depressions, strokes,
hearing aids, trifocals, heart attacks, cataract operations, dental
implants, and gout. If my Sherpa-husband is getting annoyed
following me around with my shopping bags, let the pathetic
sack of shit fly home. Go already! Go back to your heating pad
and your hemorrhoid cushion. Go back to your Mylanta, your
Sudafed, Hyzaar, Celebrex, Ambien, Lipitor, Halcion,
Prochlorperazine, Flumadine, Vioxx, Chlor-Trimeton, and
Prilosec. Go back to thinking about dying twenty-four hours a
day. Go back to revising your last will and fucking testament
for the umpteenth time. Go dream your nightly nightmare of
being lowered into the abyss while *my* brothers and *my* sisters
pass around *your* gold wristwatches and *my* nieces and *my*
nephews divvy up *your* alligator and lizard wallets you bought
at Hermès in Paris before the ban on billfolds made from skins
of endangered species. Go, Mr. Wonderful, go home already.

So there I am sitting on my bench, licking a dip of *la fraise*
(strawberry) and a dip of *la vanille* (vanilla), minding my own
business, when I notice a man and woman looking my way.
He's sucking on an ice cream cone too. So's she. Typical Ice
Cream & Crêpe tourists. They come by ferry from St. Maxime
for the day, to clog up the town's restaurants, parking lots, and
port. They wear uniforms of pink tootie hats embellished with
green palm trees, Bermuda shorts hiked up their fat ass cracks,
black ankle socks, and brown Florsheim shoes. The pair of Ice
Cream & Crêpers that stopped a few feet away tilt their heads
in unison and stare at me. After a few minutes they walk over

and sit down on the other half of my bench. I knew they would.

"You're an American, aren't you?" asked the husband. He talked while he licked, his tongue wrapped around his cone like an anaconda, making his words barely understandable.

I grunted an answer and continued staring straight ahead.

Ignoring my hostile attitude, the wife pointed her finger at my ear and shouted, "Hey, aren't you the guy . . ." She squinted and looked closer, as if I was small print. That made her unattractive face downright revolting. And then she screeched, "You're . . . You're . . ."

"Of *course!*" boomed her husband, leaning around his wife to get a better look at me, "You're the guy from that TV show!"

"*The Gong Show!!*" hollered his wife, her mouth agape, ice cream dripping down her chin.

"Yeah, yeah," said the husband, "*The Gong Show*! Say, whatever happened to you? We thought you were dead. We're from Detroit. How ya doin'?" He pushed a sticky hand behind his wife to shake one of mine.

"Life," I said, ignoring his hand, pretending to have a problem with my right sneaker.

I hate when I do that, ignore someone's body part, but I usually can't help myself. I figure it's some sort of aberration inflicted on my psyche from Instant World-Wide Television Recognition. Some human beings revel in it. Some abhor it. I'm one of the abhorrers. On the other hand, my buddies Dick Clark and Al Pacino live for that recognition. When their personal acknowledgment by the rest of the world is over, they'll both lay down and die. If they haven't died already, that is.

"What?" said the husband, his hand hanging in midair like a hunk of dead meat.

"You asked what happened to me. *Life* happened to me," I said, continuing to examine my sneakers.

"He's not very sociable, is he?" snorted the wife, as if I were a deaf dalmatian sitting on the end of their bench.

"Fuck him. Let's go," harrumphed the husband, wiping his hands on his jeans.

The two stood up and walked away.

Another man sat down as soon as they left. He said, "You're Chuck Barris, aren't you?"

(One of those days.) "Yes, I am," I growled.

"Thank God," said the stranger, visibly relieved. "I need you to do something for me."

"Only if you have a pencil and a piece of paper with you," I snapped, thoroughly annoyed.

"A pencil and pa . . . I don't want your autograph," said the stranger nicely.

"Oh?" I said, feeling vaguely disappointed. "Then what *do* you want?"

"I want you to kill someone."

CHAPTER FIFTEEN

My *boule* game was forming on the Place des Lices. I saw my teammates looking around for me. I wanted to wave and tell them I'd be right there but the man sitting next to me on the bench caused me some concern. All my instincts said a WASPY bad news omen had just arrived.

I told the stranger I didn't kill people.

"Your code name is Sunny Sixkiller, is it not?" he asked.

I didn't answer him.

"I know it is," he said.

"Whomever you got your information from doesn't know his ass from first base."

"It's whoever and I got my information from Coulter Bean. Do you know Coulter Bean?"

"Yes. He's the one who told me it's *whomever*. You're from the CIA, right?"

"Yes."

"Why didn't you say so in the first place?"

"I was going to."

"Show me some ID."

"I never carry identification, Chuck. I'm afraid I'll leave it somewhere."

"Okay, then what's *your* code name?"

"It's Harry Covaire."

"What's your real name?" I asked. "You're calling me by my real name, so what's yours?"

"Harry Rollins."

"Like I said, I don't kill people, Rollins. You've heard of Executive Order # 12333, haven't you? That's the one ordained by President Reagan abolishing government-sponsored assassinations?"

"There have already been a number of exceptions to that order, Chuck. May I sit down?"

"You're already sitting down."

"Oh, so I am," he said, somewhat surprised.

Harry Rollins was a tall, well-built man who could have played football in college. (Who knows, maybe he did.) Rollins appeared to be my age, though possibly a smidgen older. Late sixties, I'd say. He had a shock of gray hair parted on the side, with a wave that had been sprayed in place. The wave tried to hide a faint *Y*-shaped scar in the center of his forehead. Rollins wore large tortoiseshell-framed glasses. He smoked a pipe, was dressed in a suit and tie and, even though it was a hot July afternoon, had on a belted Army-green raincoat with the collar hiked up around his ears. If I were producing an espionage movie, called central casting, and asked for a spy, they would have sent me Harry Rollins.

"By the way," I said, "I'm retired."

"I wasn't told that. In fact, I was told the opposite."

"What were you told?"

"I was told you were still active. In any case, we must go."

"Go? Where?"

Rollins didn't say. He just stood up, pulled me up beside him by my arm, hooked his in mine, and off we went. We walked out of the Place des Lices and onto Avenue Henri

Bruni, the street that led to the port. I couldn't help but notice that Harry Rollins limped. The hobble certainly didn't slow him down. We cantered along at a brisk pace for five or ten minutes, looking like two fags taking their afternoon constitutional. It was his arm through mine that gave us that swishy look. I noticed Rollins was smiling. His smile seemed to be a permanent fixture on his face. It was a nice smile, constant, and tolerant without being condescending—the smile of a basically happy man.

Rollins stopped suddenly.

We had arrived at his automobile. It was a well-used antique Rolls-Royce, a model from another era. Sort of a Roaring Twenties-ish thing, the English version with the steering wheel on the right. Rollins limped around to the street side and opened the passenger's door for me. I got in. Rollins shut the door, limped back to his side, positioned himself behind the steering wheel, and off we went. One thing about Harry Rollins. He was a gentleman.

"Graduated college I suppose?" asked Harry.

"Yes, I did."

"Where'd you go?"

"Penn."

"Oh, an Ivy Leaguer."

"Right."

Harry Rollins began singing; "Drink a highball at nightfall, be good fellows while you may."

"Yep," I said, "that's my alma mater."

"Join me," he suggested. Without waiting for me to agree, Rollins continued singing. "For tomorrow may bring sorrow, so tonight let's all be gay. Tell the story of glory of Penn-syl-vay-nigh-ya. . . . Drink a highball at nightfall. Here's a toast to dear old Penn. School after my own heart," said Rollins.

"Oh? How come?"

"Drinkers."

"I wouldn't say that."

"Oh, it's all you Penn people talk about. You guys even *sing* about drinking. It's in your alma mater, for God's sake. Highballs, highballs, and more highballs."

I nodded. The man had a point.

Harry Rollins didn't seem to be such a bad guy after all. Nowhere near as bad as I thought he might be. I'm always doing that, thinking the worst about people. Problem is, I'm usually right. We drove in silence for a while. And then Rollins suddenly took a sharp right, throwing me against his left shoulder, hard.

"Sorry," he said, smiling.

The Rolls-Royce had entered a rain-rutted, rock-strewn trail that wound its way up into the Rematuelle hills. On the right side of the road was heavy brush. On the left side were acres and acres of fenced-in land.

"Dupee's property," said Rollins, noticing me looking. "Weird duck, that Mrs. Dupee. Weird duckette, I guess I should say." Rollins laughed at his little play on words. Because of his pipe, when Rollins laughed or talked, he did so out of the corner of his mouth, like Popeye.

"Why is she weird?"

"Well, for one thing, she has her version of Noah's Ark in there. Two of everything."

I looked at the property. I saw two ponies, two horses, two peacocks, two lambs, and two goats.

"There are more pairs of animals. Lots more," said Rollins. "They're all over the place."

I noticed signs were posted here and there along that sorry excuse of a road, warning trespassers to beware of wild boars, poisonous snakes, rabid dogs, and other terrors of the forest.

"Are those her signs?" I asked.

"No, mine."

"Really? Are there snakes and rabid dogs around here?"

"No."

"Then why the signs?"

"To keep the tourists away."

"I don't see any tourists."

"There never are any."

I was riding with the Mad Hatter.

At the end of the tortuous road was Rollins's home. It was hard to judge the size of the place, tucked away as it was among the trees. Rollins parked his car under the thick leafy branches of a grand-looking something or other. I don't know tree names. I only remembered this one as being large and leafy. The two of us walked about a hundred yards to his house. On the way I noticed a swimming pool half-filled with brown water and leaves, and a tennis court gone to seed. Rollins led me to a long, wide terrace, where iced tea and snacks were already in place.

"I would be happy to offer you something stronger," he said. "Wine, scotch, Jack Daniels, cognac, you name it."

"I'm happy with the iced tea," I said.

Rollins took his leave to do something, perhaps shed his raincoat and change into more comfortable clothes. While he was gone I looked around his living room for signs of life. Hopefully, a framed photograph of a wife, a child, some other family members or friends on the fireplace mantle, or on an end table, or the piano. Somewhere. I saw nothing. Not even a photograph of Rollins. Just paintings.

Weird.

Harry rejoined me on the terrace. He had changed into a sport shirt and a pair of long, baggy shorts, no socks and sandals. He cleared his throat for several minutes before saying, "First things first. Please call me Boo Boo. It's short for Boola

Boola. It's what my classmates called me at Yale. Apparently I was a gung-ho undergrad." Rollins smiled shyly. "Cheerleader, head of this club and that club, a Whiffenpoof, the works. Hence the nickname. Boola Boola. Boo Boo for short."

"What is it you want, Harry?"

"Boo Boo," he said, embarrassed.

"Boo Boo."

Rollins coughed into a closed fist, wiggled his ass into a more comfortable position in his chair, fiddled with his pipe, pushed it into the corner of his mouth, cleared his throat, and smiled. Then frowned. Then said, "There's an Egyptian scientist trained in biological warfare. The scientist is also a known leader of an Egyptian-Iraqi terrorist group. We've picked up chatter that her cell is planning to attack big cities in the United States. Why? Anger at the U.S. for our backing Israel, for keeping troops in Saudi Arabia, who knows why? Most likely they'll come with biological weapons. That's this terrorist's forte. I haven't been told what form these attacks might take. Anthrax perhaps. Smallpox. Poison our reservoirs. Or what duration of time we're talking about. Months from now? Maybe years from now? God only knows. One thing for sure. The possibility of Omar's faction causing something devastating to happen to American interests around the world is very real. As I said, this particular Egyptian scientist is the group's leader, their guru, and the genius behind their hideous plans. This terrorist must be stopped at all costs."

"You mean eliminated," I said.

"Yes . . . well . . . eliminated." Boo Boo Rollins took a sip of iced tea and continued. "You've been assigned to do the job."

"What job?"

"The elimination business. Please understand, it is not me but The Company that is insisting on your participation. I am simply the messenger boy."

(I was tired of messenger boys.) "Why me?" I asked.

"Why you? For the job? Simple. You are a trained assassin."

"Shit, Boo Boo."

Now I was really annoyed. I didn't know which was worse, Trained Assassin or Host of the Gong Show. Both titles were going to follow me into my grave.

CHUCK BARRIS 1929/?

TRAINED ASSASSIN, ASSASSINATED

R.I.P.

You are what you are, I told myself, so shut up and accept it.

"I'm sorry, Boo Boo, my mind just wandered. What were you saying?"

"Yes . . . well . . . I was saying . . ." Harry "Boo Boo" Rollins played with his pipe. Tamped it with his forefinger a little and put the pipe back in his mouth. Checked the end of his forefinger. Flicked some tobacco off it with his thumb. ". . . you're here and the target's here."

"Here?! The target's in Saint Tropez?"

Boo Boo smiled and nodded.

"So why don't *you* do it?"

"I just *told* you," he said, the smile gone, in a bit of a snit, "*you're* the killer. I wouldn't know *what* to do. Heavens, the thought of me having to . . . having to . . ."

". . . eliminate someone . . ."

". . . Yes . . . the thought makes me sick in my stomach. I guess that's why I do what I do and you do what you do."

"What if I told you, Boo Boo, that nowadays *eliminating* someone makes *me* sick in my stomach too."

"Yes . . . well . . ."

"Besides, Boo Boo, there's an old saying that makes a hell of a lot of sense."

"And that is—"

"You don't shit in your nest."

"Excuse me," said Rollins, "but I . . . uh . . . I don't *get* it."

"I *live* here, Harry, for Christ's-fucking-sake! I *live* in Saint Tropez!"

"Yes, well . . . no matter."

"No matter? No matter? I'll tell you what the matter is. The matter is not only will I have to kill this terrorist, but I'll also have to make sure the body disappears, that's what the goddamn matter is!"

Silence for a moment or two.

Then I asked, fuming, "How many on the rest of the goddamn team and what's the gender breakdown?"

"There isn't any team."

"*No team*! I'm supposed to do this job solo?"

"Yes . . . well . . . it's too small a town to have a team. The Egyptian would spot a team quickly. Going solo makes your being spotted more difficult."

"What if the target *does* spot me?"

"Don't let that happen," said Boo Boo rather sternly.

I sighed. "So what's his name?"

"The target's not a him. It's a her."

"A *woman*!" I wasn't thrilled. I told Boo Boo I never liked to be part of a plot to kill a woman. "It's . . . it's unlucky."

"Yes, well . . . I'm sure you've killed several women during your many years with The Company."

Patricia Watson's face came immediately to mind.

Patricia Watson was a beautiful, bright young woman. A graduate of one of the Seven Sisters. I forget which one. She entered my life like a thunderbolt or a tornado or something, blowing away any female competition—including Penny Pacino. As it turned out, Patricia Watson was a mole, a double agent, and a murderess. She killed my best friend Jim Byrd, among others. When Watson's identity was secured I was given the assignment to eliminate her. In the movie *Confessions of a Dangerous Mind* I was shown poisoning Patricia Watson in her apartment in Boston. The killing took place in her apartment. That part was true. But I didn't poison her. I shot her through the chest while she sat in her favorite chair.

"I've eliminated one woman," I told Rollins, "and didn't like it. I didn't like it at all. Not one fucking bit. There's something wrong about killing a woman. At least to me."

"An enemy of the United States is an enemy of the United States, no matter what the gender," said Harry Rollins sitting up straight in his chair all high and mighty.

"Still . . . something about killing a woman . . ."

"I'm sure you'll pull it off without a hitch, Chuck."

"Easy for you to say, Boo Boo. What's her name?"

"Her name, or at least the one she goes by, is Naila Omar."

"Naila Omar," I repeated.

"She's a doctor, a scientist." added Boo Boo. "Dr. Naila Omar."

Harry Rollins handed me a heavy manila envelope. "Familiarize yourself with the contents of this package. It will be helpful to you. Keep in mind that Omar leaves Saint Tropez periodically but always returns. Or at least has been returning. I mean, usually. She's not here now. I seriously hope for all our sakes she hasn't left for good."

Harry "Boo Boo" Rollins stood up. The meeting was over. It was time for me to leave. He showed me out of the house. His Rolls-Royce was purring at the foot of the steps. A driver dressed in gray livery sat behind the steering wheel, looking straight ahead.

CHAPTER SIXTEEN

Woman target or no woman target, the adrenaline started flowing again. Writing the Great American Novel was more boring than I had realized. Now all of a sudden I had a reason to rise and shine. The old get-go was back and pumping. I guess there was something in my DNA that got a charge out of this assassination shit.

During the entire week after my meeting with Harry "Boo Boo" Rollins, I plotted and planned, planned and plotted. I read and reread all the material in the manila envelope Harry had given me. I committed most of it to memory. I took up some serious surveillance around the Egyptian terrorist's hotel, which was in the port at the beginning of town. When I wasn't watching the comings and goings of the hotel's clientele, I was studying and restudying the photographs of Dr. Naila Omar. I carried one particular picture in my pocket. It was a head shot. She looked ugly as mud.

One morning I sat down in my office and considered the best plan of attack. At first I thought it was best to shoot the terrorist and toss her into the sea. If that was the case, here's what I would have to do. I would need to break into the terrorist's hotel room, shoot her with my Stechkin revolver and silencer (I find the Stechkin the best gun in the world for close work), wrap her in one of the room's rugs or blankets, and get her down to my car. Then drive to the marina, put the terrorist in Bam Bam, and head out to sea. When I was unable to see shore anymore, I would slide the woman and rug into the empty canvas sail bag, wrap the bag in heavy chains and anchors, and toss her into the Med. If that was my plan, here's what I would need from the town's ship's store: I would need rope, an empty canvas sail bag, two medium-sized anchors, and some heavy anchor chains.

I took my shopping list to Saint Tropez's ship's store.

I asked the clerk, an ugly girl with large steel-rimmed glasses, for two anchors, some chains, strong rope, and a large sail bag. I explained all this to her in my pig-French.

The clerk replied in English, "We don't carry almonds, twine, suitcases, or suppositories in this store. You will have to go elsewhere to buy those things. This store sells only items for boats. Boats of any size, but boats."

Embarrassed, I tried again. This time I spoke English. I ordered the anchors, chains, rope, and a sail bag.

The ugly girl asked me if I intended to kill someone.

"Of course not!"

"Then why do you need a large canvas sail bag and anchors?"

"I need a large *empty* canvas sail bag to put a large sail into, *merde-pour-cervelle.*" ("Shit for brains.")

"What did you just call me?"

"I called you *merde-pour-cervelle.*"

"What's that mean? Are you speaking French?"

"Yes, I'm speaking French."

"You are?"

"Yes, I am. Pig-French."

"So what's it supposed to mean, this pig-French?"

"Forget it. Actually I confess. You're right. I *do* intend to kill someone. My girlfriend. After I kill this . . . this . . . *putain* I'm going to slide her corpse into the empty sail bag I've been trying my best to get you to sell me, wrap the bag in chains with the anchors attached, the same ones I'm trying to get you to sell me, then dump her body from my boat into the deepest part of the sea."

"What did this girlfriend of yours do?"

"She was unfaithful. She cheated on me."

"Oh my God. Who with?"

"Your boyfriend."

The clerk gave me the chains, anchors, sail bag, and rope. I think she wanted to shut me up and get me out of her store. She also awarded me one of those contemptuous frog looks, a revolting down-the-nose job it has taken the French centuries to perfect.

I put all the objects of death into the trunk of my Citroën *Deux Cheval*, drove down to the port, parked, and stored them in Bam Bam. When everything was shipshape, I returned to the port and continued watching the Egyptian terrorist's hotel.

I spent most of my surveillance time in a dingy café around the corner from the hotel's main entrance, where I had a clear view of anyone entering or leaving the building. I sat on a wooden chair that wobbled by a small table that wobbled. No amount of matchbooks could fix either one. Most of the time I watched the hotel. Occasionally I would pee. Other times I tried teaching myself French by reading the *Nice Matin* newspaper while consulting a paperback French/English dictionary. I also directed my attention to the café's bartendress now and then.

She fascinated me.

The bartendress was a young girl barely out of her teens from Manchester, England. She was small and skinny—almost anorexic looking—with dirty hair. Two of her teeth were missing on the upper left side of her mouth. She favored T-shirts that ended above her bejeweled belly button and tight jeans that barely covered her butt crack. Aside from her dubious looks, the bartendress had several equally dubious habits. She had studs dangling from her eyebrow, nostril, and tongue. The worst was when she picked her ear with her pinky fingernail which, like all of her fingernails, was several inches long and covered with multi-colored sparklers. When the bartendress finished scraping the filthy tunnel, she would examine the residue on the end of her nail by bringing the nail so close to her face that it made her eyes cross. It was hard to believe that I found that particular girl interesting. I guess it was her decrepitude that intrigued me.

Her name was Penelope Wiggenbottom. ("Bottom" to her friends.) When she smiled you could see the space where her two bicuspids once resided. Occasionally we would have a short conversation that went something like this:

"Bottom, I think you're fascinating."

"All men do. The French guys say my *accoutrements* are all in the right place."

"That's what they say?"

"Yeah."

"I'd like to paint you one day."

"Nude, I'll betcha."

"Nude would be fine."

"In your dreams."

The first week came and went. And then another. Still no sight of the evil Egyptian doctor. If it wasn't for my scintillating conversations with Bottom I would have been bored out of my mind. Soon I began hoping the Egyptian terrorist had moved on. Then I wouldn't have to sit on that wobbly chair in that seedy café any more watching a degenerate bartendress pick her ears. The hell with the adrenaline rush, the buzz, all that get-go crap. By the beginning of the third week the assassination had definitely lost its novelty.

It had become August 1, 1994.

It had also become steamy hot.

If I had my druthers I would have gladly gone back to goofing off on my boat with Penny. Drinking a little wine. Nibbling a slice of pizza. Taking a lazy swim in the sea. Watching the sun set. The good stuff. Then I thought, hell, someday this fucking Egyptian doctor could be responsible for my family dying a slow painful death from some biological horror. Visions of that happening sent me scurrying back to the café and the abominably intriguing bartendress with the never-ending supply of ear glop.

Then, late one afternoon, I noticed a tall woman with a small suitcase walk right by me and into the hotel.

It was Dr. Naila Omar.

CHAPTER SEVENTEEN

During the following week I diligently watched the Egyptian's comings and goings, which wasn't easy for me. I'm not very good at shadowing someone. I sluffed that course at Langley. As a rule, the person I try to follow usually tells me to cut it out within fifteen minutes or less. The Company invariably assigns other agents to do the tailing and leaves the killing to me. That's why I was shocked that we didn't have a team in place. To make matters worse, Saint Tropez isn't exactly a thriving metropolis. As a result, the one doing the following (that would be me) is unable to get lost in a crowd. This makes pursuing a target without being seen that much harder. Unless you're good. Which I'm not.

I trailed Dr. Omar for about a week. It was both a new record for me and enough time to get her daily schedule down pat. It went something like this:

She slept late, usually leaving the hotel between ten and ten-thirty. From a distance Naila Omar looked taller and maybe heavier than me, and dark. She dressed fashionably but very masculine: black leather jacket, black T-shirt, jeans, jack boots, crap like that. She always stopped at the magazine store on the port first and bought the *International Herald Tribune*, the *London Times*, a *Nice Matin*, and *Al-Haram*, an Arab newspaper.

Then she walked to the Seniquier, one of many outdoor cafés lining the harbor. She'd sit in the sun at a little red table and have a breakfast that always consisted of orange juice, coffee, and toast with butter and marmalade.

When she finished eating, Naila Omar would stay seated at the little red table, coat her face, neck and arms with sunscreen, and read her newspapers. She did that for about an hour, tilting her head up now and then for some stronger rays. The terrorist remained at the restaurant, watching the activity at the port until noon. Then she rose, tossed the newspapers in a trash bin, and walked back to the hotel. Dr. Omar stayed there for the rest of the morning and afternoon.

Around nine-thirty in the evening she left the hotel again, walked to one of the restaurants in town, and had dinner. After dinner Omar often moseyed over to the Old Port, a very quiet Tropezzian section of the village. It was where the original port of Saint Tropez was located. But the Old Port had been ruined by time, larger boats, emerging rocks, and tide changes, making it too shallow and too dangerous to use anymore. Most of the working-class locals still lived in that part of town, families that have been hanging around Trope since the headless saint the fishing village is named after floated in on a sail-less sailboat. With a dog, I think. Or a pig.

Anyway, just next to the useless Old Port was a small square called Place Henri Duvalle. Two or three nights a week, Dr. Omar walked across that square to make a phone call from a public pay telephone booth in that somnolent section of the fishing village. Then she walked back to the hotel, where she stayed until morning. Her phone calls from the pay phone intrigued me. One August afternoon I sat on Place Henri Duvalle's only bench and wrote down everything I knew about Omar's telephone calls:

(1) Though there were other pay telephone booths in the

village, all Omar's telephone calls from a public booth were dialed from that one.

(2) The pay phone was in a place very few tourists visited.

(3) All of her calls were made between ten and ten-thirty at night. (What time would that be in, say, Cairo, Damascus, Banghazi, or Ramallah? I'd have to find out.)

(4) By ten-thirty, the time she finished using the pay telephone and departed from the small square, Place Henri Duvalle was completely empty, the neighborhood was sound asleep.

I looked at my list and wondered what I had accomplished by making it. One thing was certain. Not only did I have to eliminate the terrorist, but I also had to do away with the body so that it would never be found. Otherwise, all hell could break loose. Once a corpse was discovered, there would be suspicions, clues, investigations, and, eventually, trails that would lead to my front door. This was the reason I told Boo Boo Rollins you don't shit in your nest. But what did he know, the goddamn Ivy League twat? But if the real truth be known, it was really the CIA's fault. They wanted me dead is what they wanted. God knows why. I sure as hell didn't. If not dead at least out of Saint Tropez and back in New York or Los Angeles. This mission will do that, I told myself, you just watch and see. God must have noticed I was having too much fun. "Get him outta there," He whispered to the D.O. back at Langley. "Barris is having too much fun."

Anyway, the necessity to make the body disappear gave birth to two possible plans: Plan A and Plan B. Both plans needed evaluation. Plan A called for killing the woman in her hotel room and eventually dumping her body into the sea, and Plan B, killing the woman in Place Henri Duvalle and eventually dumping her body into the sea.

Finally I concluded that Plan A, killing Omar in her hotel

room, was out of the question. First of all, I didn't know her room number (no small matter). Second, I wasn't sure I'd be able to get her room number without alerting the terrorist to a potential threat. Third, if Plan A were to work, I'd have to carry the heavy terrorist, who would literally be dead weight, wrapped in a rug or blanket and slung over my shoulder, from her hotel room down to my car parked by the hotel entrance and try not be noticed.

I reminded myself that the hotel—Dr. Omar was staying at the Bar du Lac—was located by the entrance to the port, one of the busiest sections of town. The Bar Du Lac stood by the main parking lot, the first place most of the traffic coming to Saint Tropez turned into. There were tourists parking their cars, tourists standing around scratching their heads, checking out maps, wondering where to go first. Most of the port's police loitered about the parking lot, puffing on Gauloises, checking incoming cars, and telling dirty jokes. And what if, God forbid, Dr. Omar slid out of the rug or blanket in front of a group of smoking *flics*? Or anyone for that matter? Jesus Christ, the mere thought of that happening gave me the willies.

If Plan A was bad, Plan B, killing Omar at Place Henri Duvalle, was worse. I would be carrying the dead scientist from the small park next to the Old Port all the way across town to the marina? It was a hundred times further from the Old Port to the marina than from the hotel to the marina. Omar was much too heavy to carry that far. I would collapse from exhaustion. Or worse, of heart failure.

But what if I brought my car to Place Henri Duvalle? What if I killed the terrorist in the park near the pay telephone then used my Citroën *Deux Cheval* and drove her to the port? If I did that, Plan B might work. It would be ten-thirty at night, dark, and quiet. The fact that the neighborhood would be so quiet caused a problem. A big one. The *Deux Cheval* would have every resident surrounding the Place Henri Duvalle looking out their windows. The douche bag car thought loudness made up for weakness. Its four horsepower engine at idle sounded like a Mac Truck at full throttle.

What about bringing my boat to the Old Port?

There was a narrow section of the Old Port, a sort of cove, that ended at the foot of Place Henri Duvalle. For a brief moment I thought I had a brainstorm: Kill Naila Omar, leave her on the bench, run to the marina, get Bam Bam, bring the boat to the Old Port, fetch the dead terrorist from the bench, put her in my boat, and dump her out at sea. No. Wouldn't work. For one thing, steering Bam Bam into that rocky cove in the dark of night was risky at best. For another thing, there was the noise factor. Bam Bam's two 750-horsepower engines were loud. I mean, loud. The boat, like the Citroën, would wake the entire neighborhood. And finally, leaving the dead terrorist on the bench while I ran to the port and powered back in Bam Bam was too risky.

The next day I sat at an outdoor café by the port, sipping *Perrier menthes*. I stayed there for hours, trying to decide what to do. I checked and double-checked a map of Saint Tropez. I searched for various entries and exits to and from the Old Port. I was sure everyone passing by my table was convinced I was another American tourist trying to decide what museum to visit next. Especially with my New York Yankees baseball hat on my head and maps of the area spread out in front of me. That is if they even bothered to look and think at all. I would have bet hard cash that not a soul would guess that the geeze with the cap and maps was trying to figure out how to kill an Egyptian terrorist living a half a block away.

Then, one night in August, Omar returned to Place Henri Duvalle. She was going to make one of her nightly telephone calls from the lone pay booth. I stood in the shadows of a nearby alley and watched. Omar was probably in her late thirties. She had short cropped dark hair, greased and combed straight back. That night she wore her manly black leather jacket over a white T-shirt. The T-shirt was tucked into a pair of tight black jeans. Omar had a high forehead, beady eyes, gaunt cheeks, thin lips, and wiry dark hair cut tight to her head.

I watched Dr. Omar take her phone card from her wallet and begin to insert it into the pay phone slot. And then I saw her suddenly step back. She saw something with her name on it leaning against the telephone's dial. It was an envelope that read:

DR. NAILA OMAR

I HAVE INFORMATION FOR YOU

She hurriedly put her telephone card back in her wallet and the wallet into her jacket pocket. She looked left and right, then grabbed the envelope, stuffed it into her jacket pocket, looked left and right again, then walked briskly away in the direction of her hotel. I presume that when she was safely ensconced in her room she would tear the envelope open, pull out the note, and read the following message I had carefully printed the night before:

I KNOW WHO YOU ARE. I AM ON YOUR SIDE. PLEASE MEET ME
ME TOMMORROW NIGHT AT 10 P.M. I WILL BE SITTING ON THE
BENCH BY THE PAY PHONE. YOU CAN LOOK AT ME FROM A DIS-
TANCE BEFORE YOU COME SO YOU CAN SEE I WILL BE ALONE. IF
YOU DECIDE NOT TO COME, FINE. I'LL DO IT MYSELF.

The terrorist would probably be confused; maybe even momentarily panicked. But only for a minute. It was safe to guess she had been in several tight scrapes before and would think everything through. Is this a trap? If so, what kind of trap? And who is the trapper? Is this contact an enemy out to destroy me or an ally wanting to help? Or is the contact simply *pretending* to be an ally? If the contact is an enemy bent on killing me, he or she should have done it by now, providing this person has figured out a good plan. But then maybe that's what's keeping me alive, my adversary's not knowing how to do it, how to kill me. On the other hand, what if this contact really is a friend? Quite possibly a fellow patriot from another cell. Perhaps a dedicated anti-American martyr like myself. Or maybe I've *just* been discovered and my life is definitely in danger.

Dr. Germ would have to come to a resolution that night. Tomorrow might be too late. Omar would either meet me . . . or flee.

At ten the next evening I was sitting on the bench by the telephone, wondering what Dr. Naila Omar had decided to do. At five after ten, she wasn't there. At ten after ten, someone walked out of the dark shadows that surround the little park and came to the bench.

I said, "Good evening, Dr. Omar."

CHAPTER EIGHTEEN

That evening, Saint Tropez was at its best. The twinkling lights of yachts anchored in the harbor and the restaurants on land, the accordion music seeping out of bars, the smell of crêpes sizzling on the griddle, outdoor cafés bulging with tourists, the strumming guitars of strolling troubadours, and a warm sea breeze wafting through town portrayed the little fishing village at its joyous best. All I can remember thinking as I watched Dr. Naila Omar walk toward me was: Why did I ever join the Central Intelligence Agency?

Dr. Omar sat down beside me. Well, not exactly beside me. At the other end of the bench facing me, so that she was actually sitting on her hip. She held a gun and silencer low in her lap, the gun pointed at my stomach. Her other hand was in her jacket pocket, the same black leather jacket she had worn the night before.

If looks could kill, I was a dead man.

The doctor's eyes traveled up and down my body like a spotlight. She radiated fearlessness, treachery, and self-confidence. I hoped I wasn't radiating how I felt. I was scared shitless.

"Speak," she said.

"'There's a Jew CIA killer in Saint Tropez, Dr. Omar. His objective is to eliminate you. I don't know when the Hebe assassin plans to strike, but I have a feeling it's sooner rather than later. The kike must be done away with *immediately*. He has a list of operatives, enemies of the U.S. in France and Italy. Some from your very own cell. He will kill them next. He is good. I know him. His code name is Sunny Sixkiller. Have you heard of him? I am going to kill him before he causes any more harm. I could use your help, but I will do the job with or without you."

Dr. Omar said, "Stand up."

I stood up.

"Pull your T-shirt up to your armpits."

I pulled my T-shirt up to my armpits.

She pointed her index finger downward and twirled it around as if she was stirring a cocktail. She wanted me to make a circle while I held my T-shirt up. She was checking me for a wire.

I turned around.

"Turn your pants pockets inside out, then drop your pants."

"Drop my pants?"

"Yes," she said, flashing me an expression of pure hatred, "drop your pants."

For a moment I wondered if I looked Jewish. I turned my pockets inside out and dropped my pants. I hoped none of the busybody Frenchwomen on Place Henri Duvalle square were peeking out of their windows (as they always were), and that my boxer shorts were clean. Regretfully, I didn't remember changing them that week.

"Pull your pants up."

I pulled up my pants, zipped my fly, and buckled my belt.

"Pull up your cuffs. High."

I pulled up my cuffs.

"Pull them higher."

I pulled my cuffs higher.

When she finished her inspection and was satisfied I was clean—no guns, no wires—Dr. Omar motioned me to sit down.

I sat down.

She continued to point her 9mm Beretta automatic at my quasi-potbelly. The gun was a black beauty, the Cadillac of handguns. "Nice gun," I said. "But that's just my opinion." My voice was surprisingly high-pitched.

"Shut up and answer my questions."

"Okay."

"What are your sources?"

"Internal Central Intelligence Agency."

"Can you prove that?"

"No."

"Why should I help you?"

"Your help would insure getting the job done. Getting the job done would insure you and your cell mates a longer life to accomplish your mission. As I said, if you won't help me, I'll . . ."

"What is your name?"

"Charles Preston. My friends call me Chickie. In America I am a member of the Christian Right Party. I have a small condo not far from here in Gassan. I try to live away from the United States as much as possible. My party, the Christian Right Party, has a cell on Staten Island, which is part of New York City. My party is against the Zionist demons and anyone of color." Realizing what a stupid thing I had just said, I quickly added, "Obviously that doesn't include our Muslim brothers and sisters."

Her face remained frozen, her demeanor ice-cold.

There was nothing for me to do but continue.

"We of the Christian Right are against Wall Street, federal income taxes, the city of Jew York, the *Jew York Times*, tolls and taxation, and the queer Boy Scouts of America. My cell contributed in a small way to the Oklahoma City bombing. My family—you may have heard of them, the Prestons of New Haven, Connecticut? No? You haven't heard of them? Well, my family owns newspapers and radio and television stations. We're extremely conservative. But I am the most right-wing of all the Prestons."

I stopped talking. I was winded.

The Egyptian terrorist pulled a single cigarette and a Zippo lighter from her left jacket pocket with her left hand. She lit the cigarette one-handed, put the lighter back in her pocket, inhaled, and exhaled a few times. She appeared to be thinking and finally said, "Let's get out of here."

Naila Omar got up and quickly walked away. I caught up to her. I was feeling better. It seemed I was still in business. She hadn't said anything yet to discourage me from going further. And—I was still alive.

We walked past City Hall and two noisy restaurants. We were heading toward the port. Omar and I could have easily been mistaken for a pair of tourists promenading through the streets of the famous French fishing village and not the terrorist and assassin we really were. But I bet the farm there wasn't anybody in the famous French fishing village that August evening with a heart beating as fast as mine.

Nobody.

We came to the port. Naila Omar stopped walking to light another cigarette. Through the smoke she said, "I don't believe you."

CHAPTER NINETEEN

My heart skipped three-and-a-half beats.

I said, "You don't believe what?"

"I don't believe you are who you say you are. Let me see your passport."

"I don't have it with me."

"I didn't think so."

My heart may have stopped beating altogether. I noticed her hand was still in her pocket. She was going to shoot me with the gun and silencer from inside her jacket. Right there in the port of Saint Tropez. In front of everybody—locals, ice cream and crêpe eaters, the people who chartered yachts and were presently enjoying dinner on their sterns—everybody. Internally, I started wincing, waiting for the bullet to sizzle through my belly.

"Why not?" she asked.

"Why not what, no passport? I generally haven't any use for it so I don't carry it. Good chance if I carry it I'll lose it. I've found as I grow older . . ."

"Stupid reason," snapped the doctor. "Bring it tomorrow. Bring it to the bench in the evening, the same time as tonight, at ten."

My heart started beating again.

"Come alone," she said. "I will have other associates with me. They will be hidden. If *you* bring associates, you will all be killed."

Dr. Germ turned and walked away.

The next afternoon I took Bam Bam out to sea. Far, far out. Past the point of not seeing land anymore. And then suddenly, while I was on my way, I had this incredible urge to keep sailing straight across the Atlantic to the East River. Tie up Bam Bam somewhere in the East Sixties, take a cab to Sixty-Third Street and First Avenue and walk into my cozy apartment, my playpen in the sky. Grab a piece of candy from the Edelweiss candy box and fall into my big over-stuffed green armchair. I would eat the dark chocolate covered square of marshmallow *very slowly*. What would generally be considered a three-bite treat I'd stretch to four bites, maybe even five. I'd read a good book for an hour. Fall sound asleep for an hour. Wake up. Go down the block and across the street to Gino's Restaurant. Devour a small New York steak, medium rare, not charred on top, and a side of peas mixed with onions and bacon bits.

Yowzer, yowzer, bite my trouser.

I came back to port, tied up Bam Bam and walked over to Place Henri Duvalle. I looked around, took stock, tried to figure out once and for all how to exterminate Dr. Naila Omar.

And then guess what?

I thought of a plan. It wasn't a great or wonderful plan. Actually it was a rather skimpy plan if you must know the truth. An amalgam of Plan A and B. The plan was *extremely* dangerous for me. But it *was* a plan, a way to accomplish my assignment of wasting the terrorist and making the body disappear. And then I began wondering if I had thought everything out. I mean thought it all *completely* out. It was all in the prep wasn't it? Was I prepared? To tell you the truth, I didn't give a rusty fuck if I was or wasn't anymore. I was plain tired of thinking everything out. I was just plain tired. Between you and me, it was time for me to get off the train. The sooner the better.

I went home early that evening for one of Penny's famous brisket dinners. It was delicious. When it was time to go, I got some hugs and kisses from Penny and some licks from the dog.

"Back to work?" she asked, somewhat mystified, since I hadn't been going to work—not that kind of work—for a long while.

"Yes, back to work," I answered.

Long ago my wife accepted my "other" life, with all its mysterious dangers. She made some kind of pact with her own devil. She once told me she'd rather live with me in ignorance than not at all. I made my own pact too. I promised myself never to tell Penny anything, ever. In fact, I never told Penny I was even in the CIA. It was possibly the only Company rule I obeyed to the max; never talking about assignments or any CIA activities with members of the family. It was for Penny's protection. And peace of mind, I suppose, whatever that is.

After dinner I drove back to Place Henri Duvalle, thinking the night seemed darker than most nights. I also remember thinking I should never have gone home for dinner. That was extraordinarily dumb. I should have just sat on that bench until ten o'clock that night. As it was, because of the goddamn traffic, I arrived eight minutes late! The last thing I wanted to do was allow Naila Omar to get to the bench before I did. Sure enough, she was there waiting for me, a sneer plastered on her face. Sometimes my stupidity amazes me.

She wasn't thrilled. I wondered why.

I was frightened.

The doctor's hands were jammed into the deep pockets of

her black leather jacket. I was sure the Beretta and silencer were in one of the jacket pockets. She was wearing the jacket over a man's white dress shirt, buttoned at the neck. I hate when men *or* women button dress shirts at the neck without wearing a tie. The shirt was tucked into her customary tight black jeans.

"You're late," she said.

"Sorry. Traffic. During the months of July and August the traffic . . ."

"Stand up."

I stood up.

"You know what to do."

I went through the drill one more time: T-shirt pulled up to my armpits, turned in place, dropped my pants, hiked up my cuffs. When she was satisfied and we were seated again, Omar pulled her right hand out of her jacket pocket. I fully expected to see the gun and silencer. But there wasn't a gun. Just her hand.

"The passport."

I pulled my passport out of my back pocket, then accidently dropped it. I guess I was nervous. I bent down to get it, sat up, and shot the terrorist three times in the chest.

PART III

"*My God, I'm going to blow up, my life's all wrong, everything's all wrong, I didn't mean for things to turn out like this, what the fuck is going on?*"

—RUSSELL BANKS

CHAPTER TWENTY

The following year I was back in Manhattan, a grouchy geeze and getting grouchier by the day. I was standing in line in a Starbucks coffee shop on Third Avenue, pissed at the people standing in front of me for taking so much fucking time. Paying with credit cards for a fucking cup of coffee and maybe a biscuit. Jesus Christ Almighty. That's when this guy behind me whispered in my ear, "Tell me how you got rid of the body of that Egyptian terrorist you killed in France."

I jumped twenty feet in the air.

My mind spiraled out in eighteen different directions. If Jim Byrd had been alive I would have guessed that it was him trying to scare the shit out of me. Knowing Byrd was dead made me absolutely certain the person behind me was a Muslim assassin sent to the States from somewhere in Europe to kill me; to exact revenge for killing Dr. Naila Omar. But it wasn't an enemy assassin standing behind me. It was Coulter Bean.

"Jesus, Coulter, you coulda given me a heart attack."

"Sorry."

"If I was two feet taller, I would punch you in the mouth."

"I'm glad you're a shrimp."

"What the hell are you doing in New York?"

"Lookin' for you."

"Well, you found me."

"Yeah, it's been a long time."

"I was wondering when one of you CIA punks was going to show up to investigate all the gory details. It's good to see you, Coulter."

"You wouldn't know by lookin' at you," he said.

I hugged the bastard.

He rubbed the top of my head.

"Okay, give me the details," he said. "Tell me how you pulled it off."

"Let's get our coffees first, sit down, okay? You know, behave like civilized people."

Coulter ordered two things called *grande lattes* or *lattes grande*. I didn't know how to say it or what they were. All I wanted was a cup of black coffee. After we got whatever they were Coulter ordered, we found a table. Coulter threw his top coat, sport coat, and two sweaters over the back of his chair. The chair fell over from the weight. He picked up everything and started all over again.

"Get cold these days, Bean?" I asked, wiping off the table top with a napkin.

"You forget I'm a southerner. Whatcha been doin'?"

"Wiping the table right now. Before that, nothing."

"Well, my granddaddy used to say, 'When there's nothin' to do, do nothin'.'"

"Did I ever tell you you had one smart granddaddy, Coulter?"

"He used to say somethin' else. Want to know what else he used to say?"

"No."

"Suit yourself. So," said Coulter Bean, all anxious, sitting on the edge of his seat, "tell me all the gory details."

"What's this shit I'm drinking, Coulter?"

"It's a *latte*."

"What's in it?"

"Damned if I know. So tell me."

I told Coulter Bean everything. How the only scheme I could come up with was skimpy at best. How I had to use it because I couldn't think of anything better to do. I stopped to drink some coffee.

"Let me ask you something," said Coulter Bean. "Why didn't you just shoot her one night when she was makin' a phone call in that Duvalle park?"

"And do what with the body? I couldn't grab the first plane out of Saint Tropez now, could I? Leave Penny and Willie and my home and everything? Let them be there when the police came knocking on my front door? Now let me ask *you* something, Coulter. Why did The Company in all their profound wisdom assign me to shoot someone in my own hometown? You going to tell me that?"

Coulter didn't say anything except, "Go on with your story."

"Mind if I take a sip of coffee?" I was suddenly internally furious.

I took a sip.

I told Coulter how I went to Place Henri Duvalle late that afternoon. How I took my holster and taped it under the bench with heavy industrial tape. I described taping the *inside* of the holster with smooth Scotch tape so the gun and silencer wouldn't catch and the rig would slide out easily.

"I thought that was clever of me," I said.

"Go on."

I was disappointed that all Coulter said was: Go on. Anyway, I told him I slipped my Beretta and silencer into the taped holster and split.

"Split? For how long? How long did you split?"

"For a couple of hours."

"You telling me you went away and left your gun under the bench the rest of the goddamn afternoon?"

"Yeah," I said, annoyed. "And some of that evening, too."

"What if she was watching you from an alley or somewhere . . ."

"Yeah, what if?"

"Or if some mother's toddler found it while playing near that bench earlier in the day?"

"Yeah, and if the rabbit hadn't stopped to shit, then the wolf wouldn't have caught him."

Coulter Bean stared at me for a moment, then said, "Go on with your story."

"It gets worse."

"I can't wait." He sounded disgusted.

(What the fuck was *his* problem?) "I knew leaving the gun and silencer under the bench was taking a big chance," I threw that in to placate Coulter, "but then so was everything else I did with that goddamn Egyptian. Of course I should have stayed there sitting on that bench until ten o'clock, waiting to see if she showed up. I know I should have done that, too. Any intelligent agent with a half an ounce of smarts would have done that, right? But no, I went home. And guess what happened?"

"I don't believe this," said Coulter Bean into his empty paper coffee cup.

"I got caught in a traffic jam coming back from my house!" (Was I tormenting Bean purposely now?) "A big one. A goddamn nightmare. All I kept thinking was: Why the hell did I go home?"

"Why the hell did you?"

"Penny was cooking brisket."

"Jesus, what a reason. Why do you . . . why do you take chances like that?"

I shook my head. "I don't know." (Why did I?)

"So then what happened?"

"I got to the bench eight minutes after ten! I was eight minutes late."

"She found the gun, right?"

"No, actually, she didn't. The fact that she never checked under the bench—especially when she got there first by almost ten minutes—was amazing."

"No, it was a miracle," muttered Coulter.

(Coulter was pissed.) "You're right," I said. "I guess she was so angry I was late that she probably thought of nothing else. Big mistake."

"*Fatal* mistake," said Coulter. "So what happened next?"

"She asked for my passport. She was still determined to see some kind of identification from me. I knew she would be. So when I pulled the passport out of my pocket I dropped it, reached down to get it, came up with my gun from under the bench, and put three bullets into her chest."

"The old gun-under-the-bench gambit," said Coulter, shaking his head in wonder.

"Why are you shaking your head?"

"It befuddles me that you tried that old trick."

"Why?"

"It's so old."

"Apparently it still works. Anyway, after I shot her, she just sat there staring at me. Never blinked her eyes again, just stared at me."

"Amazin'," said Coulter.

"What's amazing?" I was confused.

"I'm amazed you used the gun-under-the-bench gimmick."

"Like I said . . ."

"I know, it still works." And then Coulter said, more to himself than to me, "I'm surprised she didn't check under the bench the minute she got there."

"If she had, Coulter my friend, you would be drinking your coffee alone right now. By the way, how did you find me? I mean here in Starbucks. Why didn't you just call me or something. I know this wasn't a chance meeting."

"Been tailin' you for days."

"For *days*?" My antenna shot out all over the place. "What's the story, Coulter, The Company think I switched sides? Did they send you to find out? Is that what's going on?"

"Me tailin' you to check out your loyalties? A little paranoid, are we?"

"Well, are you checking me out or not? Yes or no?"

"No. I was just practicin'. I wanted to see if I could still put a tail on someone and not be discovered. Especially someone jittery like you. Finally got tired of doin' it and surfaced. Besides, I needed a cup of coffee."

"I don't believe you."

"Your choice."

We sat looking at nothing in particular for a while.

I mumbled, "You could hardly hear the shots."

"What?" asked Coulter.

"I said you could hardly hear the shots. Beretta makes a great silencer."

"It does," agreed Coulter Bean.

"Three little pops," I said. "Nary a curtain stirred in all the apartment windows on Place Henri Duvalle."

"Nary? Who uses nary these days?"

"I do."

"At least you noticed."

"Yes, I did."

"Unusual for you, wouldn't you say?"

"Hey, easy on the sarcasm, Bean." Coulter's asides were starting to get on my nerves. It took me a moment to get my momentum going again. When I did, I described to Coulter how the dead doctor fell against the back of the bench. "She just sat there sideways, three neat little holes through her white shirt, her looking at me as if we were still having a conversation. That's when I heard the motorcycle coming."

"You're kidding," said Bean sitting up in his chair.

"I'm *not* kidding. I almost shit my pants. I was sure it was her so-called *associates* arriving to obliterate my ass. Or a Frenchwoman heard my gun and called the cops. If the police had come, I don't know what I would have done."

"You would have been finished," said Coulter. "The CIA would have disowned you, and you would have been tried for murder in either France or Egypt."

"A Jew being tried in either of those countries ain't no trip to Hollywood," I said and sat quietly for a minute or two.

"So," asked Coulter, "the associates were comin' on motorcycles. What happened next?"

"I just sat there facing the dead doctor, moving my lips as though we were in the middle of a conversation. I had *her* Beretta in my left hand in my jacket pocket, and *my* Beretta in my right hand in between my thighs. I was wearing this green French Army field jacket I bought at the Place des Lices for twenty bucks. Best buy I ever made. Has great pockets. I can hide a howitzer in one of those—"

"The motorcyclists. Tell me about the motorcyclists, will you please."

"It was only one motorcycle, and it went right past us. In a matter of seconds, all that was left of Mr. Motorcycle Man was the sound of his engine fading slowly away and my angina doing the same thing, thank God."

"So what did you do then?" asked Coulter. "You didn't just leave her there, did you?"

"That's exactly what I did. How did you guess?"

"You're puttin' me on."

"I went to get my car."

"You've got to be kiddin'!"

"Jesus Coulter, you gotta start believing in me. It was late and dark and quiet. Nobody was around. Just the motorcycle that came and went. I crossed my fingers, hoped the neighborhood would stay that way, and took off. I left the dead doctor for twenty minutes. That's about how long it took to run down to the marina, get my car, and drive back to the bench. It was the last of the three chances I had to take to make my plan work."

"Three chances?"

"Being able to pull my gun out from under the bench and kill her was one. Leaving Omar dead on the bench without her being found for about twenty minutes was the second. And bringing my rattletrap *Deux Cheval* into the Place without waking up the entire neighborhood was the third."

"I see."

"When I returned she was still sitting there with those wide-open eyes. Just as I left her."

"Lucky," said Coulter disagreeably.

"And though my Citroën was making a lot of noise—I swear the car sounded like a world-class meat grinder, Citroëns are like that, they all sound like meat grinders—I didn't see anybody looking out any windows. I didn't look hard. I was too busy and scared to look hard."

"That's too bad."

"What's too bad?"

"You should have taken the time to look hard."

"Well, I didn't," I said irritably. "What good would it have done me?"

"You could've made notes, you know, who was lookin' at you, where they lived, what apartments they were in, or the house address if it was a house."

"And then what?"

"Killed them," said Coulter Bean, "if you had to."

"*Killed them*?! You've *got* to be kidding. You can't be serious."

"I am serious, Chuck. Witnesses can come back to haunt you, big time. What am I talkin' about? They *did* come back to haunt you, didn't they? They painted a big fat anti-Semitic death threat on the front door of your goddam *house*, didn't they?"

He's right. They did.

Somebody did.

CHAPTER TWENTY-ONE

wanted to go back to my apartment, but Coulter insisted he wasn't moving until I finished my story.

"Hell," I told him, "if I'm going to stay a while longer, I might as well get a real cup of coffee and not this *flatte* shit."

"*Latte*, not *flatte*."

"Same thing," I said. I brought a cup of regular black coffee back to the table, sat down, and said, "Where was I?"

"You came back to the park in your automobile that sounded like a meat grinder," reminded Coulter, "and the dead terrorist was still on the bench where you left her."

"Nice recap, Coulter."

"Thanks," he said, disgruntled.

I described to him how I carried Naila Omar over to my car and placed her on the front seat. "I tried to be casual, make her look like she was drunk, and I was taking her home. I put her in the front on the passenger side."

"How did you do that?"

"Do what?"

"Make her look drunk."

Coulter was becoming a definite pain in the ass.

"I threw her arm around my neck and walked her to the car. She wasn't walking, of course. Her feet were dragging. She was heavier than I thought. Still, I figured the way I was holding her, someone looking out a window would think she was drunk. What's the matter, Bean, you got a problem with me you want to talk about?"

"Why do you say that?" He actually seemed surprised.

"Because you've been all over me like a fucking hair coat."

"I have?"

"Yeah, you have."

"Sorry, Chuckie Baby. He paused and then said, "Come to think of it, I thought you're the one with the problem. Something bothering *you*?"

"Nothing's bothering me," I growled, taking a swig of my new coffee and scalding my mouth.

The coffee tasted like liquid cow dung. Goddamn, maybe something *was* bothering me. Maybe I'd been hibernating too long. Or maybe the memories of the murder in France, the anti-Semitic writing on my front door that followed, maybe all of that was taking its toll. Especially when I went out into the real world and talked about it. Or maybe I was simply becoming grumpier and more antisocial in my old age. *That*, I thought to myself, could definitely be what's going on. "Anyway," I said crossly, "when I shut the car door, the thump pushed the body down across the front seat. Her head was where I sat. When I came around and got in the car I pushed her back up as best I could. She fell over again only this time my body stopped her from going any further. She stayed there like that, her head leaning on my shoulder. We could have been lovers."

"What did you do with her?"

"I'll tell you in a minute. I need to get another cup of coffee."

"You haven't finished that one."

"It's cold."

"I thought I saw you just burn your lip."

I got up, tossed the coffee into a garbage container and went to the end of the line. I really didn't want another cup of coffee. What I wanted to do was think about Coulter. He was nettling me, giving me the creeps. Something was up. Something was wrong. Didn't know what, but something was wrong. I needed to air out for a minute or two. Maybe a break would prevent me from saying or doing anything rash. I liked Coulter. Always had. Maybe his creepiness was just my imagination. I thought about it. Tried to come up with a rationale. I came up with nothing other than maybe Coulter was right. Maybe I *was* paranoid. I bought my third cup of coffee, tried some milk and three sugars this time, threw a fourth sugar in for good measure and walked back to our table. I sat down, pulled up my seat and picked up where I left off.

"I drove home with the dead Egyptian leaning on my shoulder all the way. I parked my car in the garage, went into my house, had a cup of tea and a cookie with my wife, and went to sleep."

"You left the dead terrorist in your car?" said Coulter aghast.

"Uh-huh."

"While you had a cup of tea with Penny?"

"Yeah. I didn't say anything to Penny or she would have been worried sick. I never discuss anything I do with Pen. You know, for her own protection."

"Yeah. You're right. So you actually left the corpse in your car all night?"

"Yes, all night. My property's gated. If anyone tried to climb over the front gate or the wall around the house, he would activate a shit load of sirens, bells, and whistles. It would sound exactly like a prison breakout. They would hear the noise in Paris. Believe me, no one could have gotten on my property without me or my caretaker knowing about it."

Coulter said, "But someone did."

"Not that night. But you're right," I said, feeling embarrassed, "someone did."

"Go on," ordered Coulter.

"That night I slept with a loaded shotgun by my bed."

Coulter didn't say anything.

"So did my caretaker."

Coulter muttered something to himself.

"What?"

"I said you should have gotten rid of her body that evening."

"I *did* get rid of the body, the next morning." I hated the mood both of us were in. I should never have left my green armchair.

"Go on," said Bean again.

"I was up before sunrise and drove down to the port. Most of the fishermen had left already. There were still a few stragglers around, not many, just a few. When the last fisherman was gone and out of sight, and not a soul was on the dock, I took the corpse from my car trunk and put her on my boat. I had already stuffed her into the empty sail bag at home in the garage, so it looked as though I was lugging a sail onto Bam Bam."

"Bam Bam? That's the name of my boat. Funny, don't you think?"

"Yeah, it's a funny name. Is it a sailboat?"

"No, it's a powerboat."

"Now that's really funny."

"What's really funny, Coulter?"

"Bringing a sail onto a powerboat? Don't you think that's kind of funny?"

Damn! Coulter was right. I never thought about that. Bringing a sail bag on a powerboat. Jesus, how dumb can you get? "If anybody would have asked, I would have said the bag was full of supplies."

Coulter Bean nodded. "Thought of that just now, right?"

I didn't answer, just went on with the story. "Then I went out to sea. I left the harbor at full throttle and stayed that way until I couldn't see the shore. But I didn't stop. I kept going until I was literally alone out there. Nothing in sight. Anywhere. As far as my eyes could see. As a matter of fact, as far as my binoculars could see."

"Hold the story right there," said Coulter. He excused himself to go to the mens' room.

I looked at my coffee and took a gulp. Even with all that sugar, it still tasted awful. Before it was bitter and lousy, now it was sweet and lousy. With Coulter gone, I had time to think. The last agent I felt this uneasy about was Jim Byrd. Just before he was killed. I wondered if Coulter could be in danger.

Or was I the one who was in danger?

Coulter came back and sat down. "You were sayin' you didn't see any boats anywhere near you."

"Right. So. When I reached the spot where there weren't any other boats, I turned off Bam Bam's engines and drifted. I grabbed the canvas sail bag, tied ropes, heavy chains, and the two anchors around it, and dumped the bag into the sea. It sunk like a rock."

I recalled once again the way the canvas bag with the woman inside disappeared from view. The bag becoming smaller and smaller and smaller, fading in the blue green water, until it was gone.

Going, going . . . gong.

CHAPTER TWENTY-TWO

We walked down Third Avenue toward my apartment building. It was a bitterly cold and windy day. High above Coulter and I, a couple of seagulls glided by on wintry thermals. I wondered why they were so far inland, where they were going, and if they were married. I tossed my half-filled cup of cold revolting coffee in a trash basket and caught up to Coulter.

"That's it?" he asked.

"Yeah, that's it."

"Incredible."

"I guess so."

"One more dead terrorist." Coulter said to his dirty paper napkin while stuffing it into his empty paper cup. He tossed the cup into the next trash receptacle. "Maybe a couple of future terror plots will be foiled."

"Hope so."

"And you got away without a nick, too."

"Thank you, Jesus," I said crossing myself.

"I didn't know you were Catholic."

"I'm not."

"Didn't think so."

"Hey, Coulter," I said, all full of cheer and vitality, getting the conversation back to the Egyptian terrorist, "you know what my grandmother used to say, don't you?"

"No, what did she used to say?"

"She used to say, 'Some mistakes are too much fun to make only once.' "

I laughed, but Coulter didn't. And then, suddenly—just like that!—I knew what was bothering Coulter Bean, why he had been acting snotty all morning. I didn't know what prompted me to figure it out right then and there, but I did. It was the cocky, stupid, lazy way I had handled Omar's assassination. And the way I belligerently told my story. That's what was troubling Coulter. My potential mistakes were tormenting him. My taping a gun under the bench, leaving it there, and going home. My letting the dead terrorist sit on the bench while I took off to get my car. My not being more alert for witnesses when I shoved Naila Omar's dead body onto the Citroën's front seat. My exposing myself to being caught at the dock the next morning when I brought Omar in the sail bag to Bam Bam. My God, just carrying a sail bag onto a powerboat. My lack of proper preparation and caution, my mistakes and carelessness carrying out the mission—all of that annoyed the hell out of Coulter Bean. It angered and nettled him because any one of my mistakes could have had me arrested, which would have meant the end of my life as I knew it, or worse. My gaffes and lapses—any one of them—could have gotten me killed.

And he was right, I *had* been indolent and sloppy and could easily have ended up dead on the Place Henri Duvalle or at the port or any number of other places. I could have been killed by Dr. Omar or her associates or even the French police. There I was, thinking I was behaving like the pro I always considered myself to be, and I wasn't even close. I was a lucky horse's ass is what I was. I had completed my mission, but with almost suicidal intent, performing like a rank amature. What happened to the consummate professional I had always been in the past? I had become lazy, sloppy, and careless—behavior that was turning Coulter Bean inside out. This time I got away with it. What about next time? The teacher was pissing off his student for behaving like a student. A stupid student. Coulter, the father, had lost me, his kid—then found him—and was torn between giving his kid an angry spanking for wandering off or a joyous hug because no harm had come to him.

"You're right, Coulter, I know why you're pissed. I was really bad."

"Yeah well, forget it."

"I told you long ago it's time for me to get off the train."

"Let's talk about your other problem," said Coulter.

"What other *problem*?" I shoved my hands in my pants pockets and changed the subject. "So what about me getting off the train? Let's talk about that. Think you can swing it for me?"

"You're too good, when you want to be, to get off the train. The CIA won't let you get off the train. What about the other problem?"

"The CIA's keeping me so they can get me killed, isn't that right, Coulter?"

"No, that's totally wrong. You're obsessed about that. Tell me what happened to the front door of your house."

"Oh, *that* problem! I really don't want to talk about it, Coulter. Besides I'm sure you know about it already, or The Company does, so—"

"Talk about it," he ordered.

"Why is that part so important?"

"I just want to hear the whole story myself," answered Coulter. "From beginning to end."

"It happened a week after I dropped Omar into the Med." We stopped for a red light. The ugliness and fear of the words on my door came rushing back.

"Go on," said Coulter, impatiently.

I told Coulter I woke up one morning all bright-eyed and bushy-tailed and headed for the port to get my coffee and newspaper. I saw it as I walked out of the house. During the night someone had splash-painted the heinous sentence in big black letters across my front door:

DIRTY JEW YOU KILLED A MOSLEM WOMAN
YOU WILL DIE

"You were right, Coulter. Your witnesses did come back to haunt me. At least one of them did."

"Omar's people," said Coulter.

"Obviously."

"How did they know it was you?"

"Don't know. And they got to my front door without setting off any alarms. I don't know how they did that, either."

"Yeah, well . . ." Coulter shook his head dismally. "So what happened next?"

"What happened next?"

I stopped for a moment to grapple with the horrible memory again. I was hurting for the umpteenth time. God knows when the pain would go away and stay away. Okay, I mused, what happened next? I told Coulter Bean what happened next.

"Within two weeks I sold my beautiful château in the hills of Ramatuelle, my speedboat, my three cars, and my Harley-Davidson motorcycle. A month to the day after they painted that shit on my door, Penny and I flew back to Manhattan with our Labrador Retriever, Willie."

"That's rough," said Coulter.

"It gets rougher," I said.

CHAPTER TWENTY-THREE

Penny left me a month after we got home. Can you imagine that? She actually *walked out*! Went back to Europe. Who would have thunk it? If you were a bookie, you would have called Penny leaving me a no-bet situation. "Off the boards," as those guys say. But she split. "'Took off like a fart in a wind tunnel,' as your granddaddy would have said," I told Coulter.

It all started maybe three years before.

Maybe longer than that, I sure as shit don't know.

Penny and I were spending a lot of time gutting and reconstructing a small row house that had come on the market down in the Old Port. Only a few people know when a house in the Old Port comes on the market. The houses are handed down within Tropezzian families until all the members die off or the children have moved away and don't want it anymore. One Tropezzian tells another who tells another, until the house is sold. I was told about the house. Though not a Tropezzian, my feats on the *boule* field and my heroics regarding "saving the trees of Saint Tropez" (which I may tell you about sometime, if I don't forget) made me as close to a Tropezzian as anyone could get without being born there. So one morning I went to the bank with my friend, the French motorcycle champion Pierre Mader, withdrew $175,000 dollars, worth of French francs (the seller wanted cash), and stuffed the money into a big shopping bag. Holding the bag pressed tightly against my stomach, I sat on the back of Pierre's motorcycle while he zigged and zagged through Saint Tropez streets, eluding imaginary highwaymen at every turn until we reached the owner's house—which was soon to be my house. That was the place my wife Penny was going to decorate with antiques and furniture, the antiques and furniture she allegedly went searching for all over Europe.

The strange thing about Penny's searches was, they seemed to center in and around Zurich, Switzerland. Oh, there were side trips to London, Paris, Geneva, Madrid, and even Morocco, but mostly Zurich. Why all the flea markets and wonderful antique sales were suddenly in Zurich beat the shit out of me. Eventually, my leaden instincts began sending me weird vibes. Words like "adultery" and "cuckold" started to short-circuit my peace of mind.

One day I decided to confront Penny when she returned from her latest trip to Zurich. I would look her dead in the eyes and ask: Are you seeing another man? Are you having an affair? But wrong answers to such vile questions were too horrifying even to contemplate. So I didn't ask anything.

And time moved on.

Then came the Dr. Naila Omar mission, followed by the black paint episode on our front door. When I told Penny we were going back to the States, she looked stricken. In fact, she almost fainted. I was aware of how much she loved Saint Tropez and our old house, even the new one for that matter, but I wasn't mindful of such extraordinary love for France.

But *was* it France she loved so much?

A week after we were back in our New York apartment, Penny and I had an argument. It took place in our bedroom.

It was something we never used to do—argue—and now were doing frequently. Rough arguments. Loud and vicious ones. At one point during that fight I said, "Maybe we should get a divorce."

I was joking, though I admit it didn't sound like a joke. But if I wasn't joking, I certainly wasn't serious, either. I guess it was more like a stupid threat meant to shock. In any case, it worked. Too well.

Penny had a fit.

"Is that what you want?" she screamed. "Is that what you *really* want? It is, isn't it? You've been wanting a divorce for years, haven't you?"

I was stunned by the violence of her rebuttal, surprised by the timbre of her voice, shocked by her red and contorted face. And then it dawned on me. It wasn't the divorce I had been waiting years for, but the one *she'd* been waiting years for.

Penny stormed out of the bedroom. She stayed away from me the entire evening. That night she slept on the couch. The next day she was gone. She returned to Europe. Zurich, actually.

Zurich.

A week later I received a telephone call at home from a woman in Geneva, Switzerland. She told me in broken English that her husband and my Penny were having an affair. Had been for years. She explained that her husband owned a business with factories or stores or something all over Europe. The company's main office was in Zurich. That's where this woman's husband and my Penny would meet. Most of the time. Sometimes they met in London, Paris, Madrid, and, one time, Morocco.

The man's wife told me that she and her husband had been married for twenty-four years. They had three children: a girl, eighteen; a boy, fourteen; and a girl, eight. The wife said her family lived in Geneva because of the excellent private schools there. Her husband wasn't always home. He took many business trips. The woman began to cry. She told me the assignations between her husband and my wife had been going on for almost four years.

"Four years!" she screamed, "and you say you know nothing about this?"

"I knew nothing about it," I whispered.

"You are never suspicious?" she asked. "Almost four years and you are never suspicious?"

I didn't answer her.

The woman said she had wanted to telephone me a year ago to ask me to stop my wife from breaking up her family. "Twenty-four years married," she sobbed, "your wife is breaking up. Several years ago I threaten her I go to you. But your wife, she pleads with me, 'No. Please do not to speak to my husband about this.' She promises she stop seeing my husband if I not call you. So I not call you." The woman paused to blow her nose. "But she does not stop. I know because I pay our bills. I check our credit card bills. My husband forget this. So I know they see again each other. The last time Morocco. In the same hotel room. I check the credit card paper."

The woman brought to mind a conversation I had with Penny not that long ago. Penny had said, "I think I'll take a quick trip. I read in a magazine that there's a big sale of antiques and other great things next week."

"Like what great things?" I had asked.

"Doors," she said. "Wonderful old doors. Even jail doors. From torn-down prisons. You know with those lines prisoners make to mark off time. You know, four lines then one line through the four."

"Where's this big antique show with these great things taking place?"

"Morocco," Penny had answered.

"But then," said the woman on the telephone, "my husband tells me not too long ago your wife goes home with you to United States and I say happily to me, that is that. At last. Thank God. My prayers at my church are answered. But that is *not* that. She just come back, your wife. She come back. She in Zurich now, with my husband again. Please, I beg you, stop your wife from seeing my husband. Please. I cannot take it anymore. I telephone you because I cannot take it anymore. Please stop your wife before it too late for me. My husband and your wife stay at Hôtel Baur au Lac in Zurich. Is on Talstrasse near Buerkliplatz. My husband always stay at Hôtel Baur au Lac. Your wife is with him. Please, I beg you, Mr. Barris, please stop your wife from destroying my family."

I flew to Switzerland that evening.

I arrived in Geneva the next morning. I rented a car and drove to Zurich. I found the Hôtel Baur au Lac on Talstrasse. I checked in and foolishly looked for Penny in local stores and shops. I ran from place to place in a useless panic. I couldn't find her, so I returned to the hotel's lobby and sat there watching the entrance's revolving door. I sat for three hours before Penny pushed her way through the door and walked into the lobby.

CHAPTER TWENTY-FOUR

The two of us walked up and down the Talstrasse the entire afternoon. We sat on a bench in a small park where Talstrasse meets Bahnhofstrasse. After a while we returned to walking up and down Talstrasse. We talked and talked, or rather I talked and talked. Penny mostly walked with this stoic, angry face that stared straight ahead. I pleaded and begged Penny to come home with me. I wasn't certain why I was pleading. I had done no wrong. Besides, I always thought I would personally kill an unfaithful wife. To be a cuckold was my most horrendous nightmare. Yet there I was, pleading and begging.

I remember telling Penny, "Come home with me now and we'll be able to patch things up, go back to living happily ever after. We can see a marriage counselor or a psychiatrist or someone. We'll go together. We can work things out."

Penny pooh-poohed my suggestions.

Occasionally, Penny talked. When she did, it was mostly petty accusations and far-fetched denunciations, most of which puzzled me. Her list seemed previously prepared. She recited them as if they had been memorized. Whatever recriminations were true, were minor.

At least I thought so.

I had stopped being affectionate, she said. I cared only for my work, my writing, my TV shows, my government assignments that I never talked to her about. Ever. Why I didn't talk about it was a mystery to her. She was my wife, wasn't she? And lately I disapproved of everything she did. I disapproved of her clothes. I disapproved of her friends, at times I even disapproved of her manners. I disapproved of the minor face-lift she had and the insignificant boob job as well. (It wasn't insignificant, I interrupted. You made them *huge*!) Because of my obsession with money, she was forced to *sneak* money to her mother and on occasion to a few desperate friends. In summary, her accusations sounded like petty complaints, sour grapes, the results of a pampered married life.

On the darker side, I felt that Penny had been advised and influenced by horrid friends, "Hollywood wives" who believe that marriage was only a stepping stone to richer husbands. I grew convinced that Penny was told if she divorced me she would get millions of dollars in the settlement and then could *really* have herself some fun. Travel with her lover who sounded richer than me and didn't seem afraid to buy her expensive baubles. Perhaps, after our divorce was final, she might even marry him.

I admit I wasn't a perfect husband. I don't think anybody is. But I wasn't a bad husband, either. I think in retrospect Penny turned out to be a bad woman.

My Penny.

And I still wanted her back.

By four-thirty that afternoon in Zurich, I would have settled for Penny promising to come home, period. At any time. A week. A month. Sooner or later.

But she never did promise.

And she never did come.

"I went back to our New York apartment and my green

armchair," I told Coulter Bean, "and have been sitting in it ever since."

"For two months?"

"Yeah, that seems about right."

"Straight?"

"Yeah, straight."

"Doing what?" asked an astonished Coulter Bean.

"Reading and thinking. Mostly thinking. Rehashing where I went wrong, where *we* went wrong. It's been a blow, my divorce. I've taken it badly. I miss Penny. A lot."

Coulter didn't say anything.

"I heard Penny broke up with the Zurich man," I told Coulter.

"Oh?"

"Yeah, I heard through friends that the guy dumped her and went back to his family. I'm glad the asshole went back to his wife. She sounded like a nice woman."

"So where's Penny now?" asked Coulter.

"Penny's living in California. Someone I know saw her in a beauty parlor in Beverly Hills. Penny was supposedly over-heard saying, 'My new boyfriend's even richer than my ex-husband.' "

"Sad," said Coulter.

"Sad's putting it mildly. The thing that really bothers me, the thing I didn't understand, still don't, the thing that tore me apart for months and months is how can two people who really loved each other turn into such enemies?"

Coulter didn't have an answer.

"You know, Mr. Bean, I'm beginning to think happiness just ain't in the cards for me."

But I was wrong again.

Boy, was I ever.

CHAPTER TWENTY-FIVE

New Year's Eve, 1996.

I was in my green armchair watching Dick Clark bring in the new year on television. I couldn't help wondering how long Clark was going to keep doing that shit. I pictured him in his late seventies or early eighties, standing up there on top of that building yelling out in a creaky voice, ". . . Nine . . . eight . . . seven . . . six . . . five . . . four . . ." and a light wind blowing the poor wispy thing away, never more to be seen. Scattered like pollen seeds over the Northeast. Anyway, while Dick was doing his creaky countdown crap, I made a resolution.

Get a fucking life, I told myself. Go back to what you know best—television. Create a new game show. Get the old mojo going. Begin a comeback of sorts.

Four months later, in early April of 1997, I flew to California with a TV idea to develop. It was my first time back to La La Land in years. My new game show concept was called *Courtroom Follies*. I had traveled to Los Angeles to put the show together and see if it worked. If it did, I would try and sell it. If it didn't, I'd go home. I hired a small group of ex-employees to help me, then rented a suite of offices on Sepulveda Boulevard in the San Fernando Valley and went to work. It wasn't long before we realized that *Courtroom Follies* actually worked. In fact, it worked exceptionally well. It was funny, surprisingly spontaneous and ahead of it's time—the latter being it's only danger. It was ready to be sold. So early one July morning in 1997, I ventured forth to do battle with the executives of televisionland.

My first appointment was at the Fox Television Studios. I had visited NBC, ABC, and CBS many times in the past, but never Fox, which wasn't around when I started peddling shows. The new network was virgin territory for me, so I thought I'd try them first. As good a place to begin again as any.

I entered their main office building ten minutes early in a highly nervous state. Out-of-practice jitters, I guessed. I sat fidgeting in the programming department reception area for over an hour, staring at a receptionist who looked roughly eleven years old. Eventually, I was greeted by a flirtatious, sexually flamboyant young girl, a secretary I supposed. She offered to escort me to her boss's office, where my meeting was to take place. I might have been mistaken, but I sensed that there were other goodies she would gladly have offered if I played my cards right. I was probably mistaken. The loopy seductress walked me down the hall to my destination, pointed to a door, bowed, and, with a sweep of an arm, actually said, "Ta-da!"

The office was crowded with very small, young people. Somewhere among those wee executives was a young man named Rickey Manhattan. Mr. Manhattan had the title of Vice President of Television Programming for the Fox Television Network. He ordered the new shows. When he saw me, Manhattan jumped up from a couch or chair, I couldn't see which, said hello, and shook my hand. Rickey Manhattan was young, maybe sixteen or seventeen, had a face full of pimples and a thyroid condition, or something. His blue eyes bulged out from under his forehead. Along with being maybe five feet tall and bug-eyed, he had a pink, pale, flat face that looked as though it had just been ironed. After shaking my hand, Manhattan immediately disappeared into a huge brown corduroy sofa, covering himself with little associates as if they were sand.

It seemed that everyone who worked for Mr. Manhattan had to be smallish. Thus, there were additional Lilliputians sitting or standing all over the room, outside the door, and even in the hallway. My appearance seemed to be a sellout. Almost everyone greeted me by name, which pleased me even though they used "Mr. Barris" and not "Chuck," making me feel even more ancient than need be. I was, however, somewhat shaken by the expressions on most of the tiny executives' faces. The little twerps looked at me bewildered, as though I was some kind of legendary antique, a sort of walking Louis XIV armoire. They all seemed to know that I had done something worthwhile in the past, maybe even created a noteworthy early radio or television show, but wondered why I was standing there that morning. Had I come to pitch old re-runs or what?

I told the perplexed crowd I had a brand-new Chuck Barris television game show to sell them. I expected to hear a rolling chorus of excited "ooohs" and "aaahs," but heard silence instead. (I may have even perceived a moan or two, I'm not sure.) I explained that the program was a courtroom show, that it wasn't serious but just the opposite, it was funny. It was a *comedic* idea played for laughs. I called it *Courtroom Follies*.

"I think *Courtroom Follies* is a real winner," I said, reaching way down for some energy. "The show makes fun of all the serious court shows on television these days. It may be ahead of its time but . . ." (I chuckled) "I'll take my chances. And, by the way, a very important fact: *All the cases on* Courtroom Follies *are true*. They all actually took place, they all actually happened."

I paused to let that significant information sink in.

"Okay," I said, "a sample case we used in a practice run-through recently was the one where an elderly sugar daddy gives his young girlfriend a credit card and tells her to go to Neiman Marcus and buy herself a present. So she goes to Neiman's and purchases a sweet-fitting, rather glamourous fur coat for twenty thousand dollars. When the elderly sugar daddy sees the bill, he has a mild stroke. The young girlfriend has spent far too much of her sugar daddy's sugar."

I hesitated, waiting for the laugh.

It never came. Only several surreptitious is-he-serious glances tossed back and forth from one to another. I also noticed a few of the creatures leaning back against their couches or armchairs, their eyes glazing over, one or two of them smiling that strangely cracked smile that cartoon characters flash after being hit on the head with a mallet.

Undaunted, I continued.

"The sugar daddy wants the coat back. The girl doesn't want to give it back. The two come to *Courtroom Follies* to air their grievances. Each of them presents their case to the jury. Each has a lawyer who is a professional comic. The comic lawyers plead their clients cases to the jury, too. The comics are hysterical. I mean they're really funny. The jury consists of three outspoken celebrities. The celebrity jurists take turns telling the court who they voted for—the girl or the elderly man—and why. The celebrity jury members are extremely funny. That will always be the case, because we'll book the funniest celebrities we can find. In this particular case, the verdict was that the young girl could *not* keep the coat. She had to return it. I play the judge. Believe me, the show's a winner."

When I finished the pitch, my audience was either smiling condescendingly or engaged in hypnotic nonstop nodding. The nodders resembled toy birds whose beaks bob up and down into a glass of water.

Repellent little fucks.

"So," I said, all perky and peppy, "what do you think of the idea?"

CHAPTER TWENTY-SIX

My disastrous sales pitch at Fox had left me shattered and despondent. Also angry and pissy. I didn't bother with NBC, CBS, or ABC. I couldn't get out of Hollyweird fast enough. I caught the "red-eye" flight that left Los Angeles at 10:30 P.M. that evening.

An ancient stew with buckteeth served me dinner. What happened to great-looking stewardesses? Went the way of good food I guess. Now I had an old bucktooth hag treating me to a salad of dead weeds, a lamb chop that tasted like a baby's pacifier, and a dessert. At least the dessert was good. Hard to screw up a ball of vanilla ice cream.

After dinner, I thought about my trip to Hollyweird. My mind wandered back to the office of minuscule Rickey Manhattan at Fox Television. "So," I had said, all perky and peppy, to Rickey Manhattan and his crowd of little twerps, "what do you think of *Courtroom Follies*?"

"*Courtroom Follies* is a great title," said a small boy. "I *love* the idea of the old geezer getting taken to the cleaners by a young broad. Might have worked in '67, Mr. Barris, but this is '97. Thirty years later."

"Nice math," I said.

"What?" said the small boy, confused.

"What he means, Mr. Barris, is it ain't Woodstock any-more," said another little person. This little person had little tits.

"What's *that* mean?" I asked little tits. "What's Woodstock have to do—"

"Not so fast," said someone else.

"Excuse me?"

"The couple, the young girl and the so-called sugar daddy, they aren't *real* are they? You made them up. You rehearsed them, right?" The accuser was a huge girl, maybe five feet, six inches tall—almost as big as me—with a permanently sour expression on her face.

"No, wrong, we absolutely did *not* rehearse them. They were real. You might recall that I made it a point to say in the begin-ning of my pitch that the cases are *all real*. Don't you remember? I said that before I started."

"Stuff like that went out with those fake confrontational shows," said a weird-looking guy. "Springer, Raphael, Stern, all of those jerks had fake (he made quotes with his fingers) 'problems' on their shows all the time."

"Some still do," said somebody.

"Yeah," said the weird-looking guy. "That stuff is old-shoe now."

"All the cases on my show are *real*," I said again. I sounded as though I was whining. Or pleading. Actually more like begging.

"Nice try," said someone else.

"I thought you never did shows with fake contestants," said an old guy in his thirties. I think he was a janitor.

"I'm telling you, those two people I just used as an example were *real*. We used them in a rehearsal. It's a true story. It really happened. She bought this expensive—"

"Is that it?" asked a small turd. He wore a T-shirt that said:

Life Is Shit Then You Die. The T-shirt was under bib overalls. The kid was barefooted. Others in the room were standing up, preparing to leave.

"*Wait! I have something to say!*" It was Rickey Manhattan himself who said that. Rickey Manhattan, *the* Executive Vice President in charge of everything at the Fox Television Network. "Legend has it," said Manhattan, emerging from somewhere in the room, "you quit television when you made enough money to live happily ever after and went to France to do just that. Everybody always *says* they're going to do that, but nobody ever does. *You did!*"

"Hear, hear," said someone.

"That's right," I said, wondering where this was leading to.

"You were our hero," said Rickey, moving up to my face. "The legions of detractors said, 'Oh, he'll be back. They all come back.' But to us, your supporters, your *real* supporters, you were *never* coming back. You know why? Because you were different. At least we all thought you were."

"Right on!" came from somewhere.

"You should have stayed in France, dude," said Mr. Manhattan. "You shouldn't have come back to try to sell new shows. Now you're not special anymore. You're just greedy and egotistical like the rest of us. You lost the magic, dude."

A chorus of "Amens" filled the air.

Rickey Manhattan shot me a venomous little smirk to let me know he was finished.

"You've got a point, Rickey," I said, sadly. "Thanks for letting me in on that observation and for being so honest with me. I appreciate it. Can I show my appreciation by trying one more idea on you? I was saving this for one of the other networks. I'll be quick about it. It's real short. I promise. For old time's sake?" I held up my thumb and forefinger about an inch apart. "A quickie."

I didn't wait for Rickey Manhattan's permission. I barreled straight ahead.

"I call this one *How Low Will You Go.*"

"Interesting title," said Mr. Manhattan, his brow furrowing with anticipation for the first time that morning. "How's it work?"

I explained. "A ten-year-old boy named Billy comes on-stage with the dog he's had since he was born and the dog was a pup. It's a shaggy mutt with a zippy personality and a great smile. Four contestants are credited with a thousand dollars each and asked to bid *down.*" I paused to mention that to my knowledge there's never has been a game show where contestants bid down.

"Interesting," said an ever more excited Rickey Manhattan.

I continued. "Our host tells the contestants that the bidding will go down in fifty dollar increments. The question is: How low will the contestants go—who will take the least amount of money to shoot the dog dead in front of little Billy? Of course the winning contestant will have less money to bid down with in the next round, but at least he or she will go home with some loot for sure."

"I like it! I like it!" said Rickey Manhattan.

"Wait," I cautioned. "I'm not finished. The contestants bid. 'Nine hundred dollars,' says one. 'Eight fifty!' bids another. 'Eight hundred dollars!' says a third contestant. No one else bids. The host shouts, 'Contestant number three, you're our first round winner! You said you would blow the cute little doggie's head off in front of little Billy for eight hundred dollars! Way to go, contestant number three! Okay, here's your loaded .38 caliber Smith & Wesson revolver. Go do the nasty deed and the money's all yours!' The low-bidding contestant shoots the dog's head off, splattering its brains all over a sobbing little Billy."

For the first time that morning, I had everybody's undivided attention.

"In round two, an eighty-seven-year-old arthritic man using an aluminum walker hobbles slowly onto the stage. He's an obviously happy, nice, sweet old man. Everybody calls him Gramps. The contestants bid down to see who gets to kick the walker out from under Gramps and watch him fall down and break most of his old and brittle arthritic bones, which he does. We can hear the bones snapping with our own ears. They sound like dried twigs."

In Rickey Manhattan's office there is total silence. I have the little pissants in the palm of my hand.

"In round three, a pregnant woman . . ."

"Enough!" shouted Rickey Manhattan, boy genius.

I played deaf to the TV programming maven and pushed on. "A pregnant woman walks onto the stage. The woman is in her ninth month. She is huge. The host asks the contestants how low will they go to . . ."

"Enough!" yelled Rickey Manhattan, his arms in the air like a referee signaling that the extra point is good.

I had gone too far, hadn't I?

"I *love it!*" he screamed. "I *really, really, really do!*"

Three reallys!

I took a step closer to Rickey Manhattan, knocked my forehead against his and said, "Fuck you, Manhattan, and the horse you rode in on. The same goes for all your little dwarfs in this room. I was only kidding, you tiny turd. But if you steal that show idea, I'll sue your bony ass from here to Timbuktu."

I walked out of Rickey Manhattan's office, pinching his loopy secretary's ass as I went.

PART IV

"I don't mind being by myself.
It's being alone I don't like."
—ROBERT DOWNEY, SR.

"Never underestimate the power of loneliness."
—RICK DEMARINIS

CHAPTER TWENTY-SEVEN

At this time in my life, Judi-with-an-i Hoffman was a forty-six-year-old spinster daughter of my friend Arnold Hoffman. Judi-with-an-i is called Judi-with-an-i because that's how she introduces herself. "Hello," she says, "I'm Judi Hoffman. That's Judi with an 'i.' "

On the next-to-last evening of August, 1997, Judi-with-an-i Hoffman met a woman in Atlanta, Georgia, at the bar of the Ritz Hotel in the Buckhead section of the city. Not seeing a ring on the lady's finger, Judi-with-an-i, the self-proclaimed Don King of marriagedom, immediately thought to herself: If this woman sitting on the next bar stool isn't married, she'd be *perfect* for my father's divorced friend. What divorced friend of her father's was she thinking about?

Me.

Judi-with-an-i would later describe the woman as being in her thirties, beautiful, sexy, and *really* nice. The woman told Judi she was coming to New York that weekend. Unfortunately, Judi, who on a good day is about as bright as oatmeal, forgot to get the pertinent details—like where the alleged beauty was staying, how long she would be in New York, stuff like that.

But then two two days later, as fate would have it, Judi and the Mystery Lady met again. The two sat side-by-side on a flight from Atlanta to New York City, which only confirmed Judi-with-an-i's conviction that the Mystery Lady and I were a match made in heaven. Nothing less. During the trip, Judi-with-an-i found out the woman's name (Becky Ballard), her age (thirty-seven), her marital status (divorced), where she would be staying for the weekend (the Plaza Hotel), and her room number (728).

Judi-with-an-i told Becky Ballard she had just the guy for her.

Becky Ballard smiled and said, "Thank you for thinkin' of me, but frankly, Judi, the last thing I'm interested in at the moment is a guy."

Judi-with-an-i detached her seat belt and moved forward to the edge of her cushion so she could turn and look Becky Ballard in the eyes. "This isn't just a *guy*," said Judi, "this is your soul mate."

To this day I don't know how Judi figured *that* one out.

Judi-with-an-i begged Becky Ballard to see me if I called, because we were a couple that was "absolutely destined for each other." Becky Ballard laughed out loud this time. Judi wasn't sure if it was a good laugh or a bad laugh.

Minutes after landing in New York, Judi-with-an-i telephoned to tell me all about Becky Ballard. She called because Judi-with-an-i adores me. I've known her since she was about eight years old. I always tease and flirt with Judi, mainly because nobody else does. Judi was an irritating child from birth and unpleasant looking. Still is. That's exactly why I befriended her.

Anyway, Judi-with-an-i told me that Becky Ballard was *extremely* popular and well-liked in Atlanta. (How she found *that* out, I'll never know.) She also told me that Becky Ballard would be staying at the Plaza Hotel and gave me her room number. Judi-with-an-i begged me to give Becky Ballard a call, adding that we were "a perfect fit" and "made in Heaven" and I "wouldn't regret it."

I told Judi-with-an i that I hated blind dates. I explained that I had only had two in my entire life. Both were unmitigated disasters. My first blind date was years ago. I was matched up with a short, squat lady who sported a long and bushy Viva Zapata mustache. Her name was Yvette Israel. My sister was the matchmaker of record. The only attribute Phoebe could think of, regarding the mustachioed Yvette, was, "She's a voracious reader."

I should have fucking known.

My second blind date took place a month ago. It was worse. The girl in question wasn't worse looking. Just worse in the sense that the evening was worse. My friend, Sidney Hirschman, played Cupid. Sidney said, "She's from Kansas, she's twenty-three years old and—"

"*What!*" I had exclaimed. "I'm sixty-fucking-eight!"

"Listen, she's lithe and warm and has a perfect peaches-and-cream complexion. She might be a tad taller than you, but don't worry. She has a thing for older men. You won't be sorry."

"What's her name?"

"Fiona Pagoda," replied Hirschman.

As it turned out, the best thing about Fiona Pagoda was her name, which I loved. Fiona was lithe because Fiona was a ballet dancer. She did have a peaches-and-cream complexion, and she was tall. A little more than a tad. Fiona Pagoda was a towering six feet three inches high. (At the time, I was five feet seven. I've shrunk since then.) Fiona Pagoda and me standing side by side was an extremely appalling sight. The top of my head rested just under Fiona's breasts. The poor girl would be spending the entire evening looking down at my bald spot. Both of us wanted to strangle the bastard Hirschman. The sun was barely up the next morning when I telephoned Sidney and screamed, "What kind of sadist are you?"

"How about that complexion?" he replied. "Peaches-and-cream, right? I mean, come on."

Though I take a dismal view of women who pass out their names and hotel room numbers, this situation seemed to be different. That's because Judi-with-an-i said she had to practically get down on her knees and beg Becky Ballard for the information. "*And* I guarantee you this," said Judi, "when you see her, she'll knock your socks off."

I told Judi-with-an-i to set it up.

"When?" she asked.

"Tonight."

CHAPTER *TWENTY-EIGHT*

I arrived in front of Becky Ballard's Plaza Hotel room ten minutes early. I was quasi-excited, tempered by the knowledge that Judi-with-an-i was a dimwit. I stood there in the hallway, staring at the number Seven-Two-Eight on the door. I wanted to use the extra time to think about the potential consequences of what I was about to do.

Or not do.

If I *didn't* knock on the door and went home instead, I was assured of a pleasant evening. I would watch the Oscar De La Hoya fight on Pay-Per-View television. How bad could *that* be? On the other hand, if I *did* knock, the night could very well end up a disaster, like my other two blind dates. Not only might I suffer greatly, but I would not see the De La Hoya fight which, because I missed it, would undoubtedly be the fight of the year. True, Judi-with-an-i's hyperenthusiasm lessened the chance of a nightmare lurking behind the door of room seven-two-eight.

But not by much.

I mean, what did Judi-with-an-i know about *the little things*, traits Judi wouldn't noticed but I most assuredly would? What if Becky Ballard had body odor? Or wore cold creme that made her smell like my mother. What if she produced a thin strand of saliva that always hung between her lips when she talked or perfume that might aggravate my asthma? Or had a black tooth. Or one eyebrow that ran across both eyes. Or a high-pitched, screechy laugh. Or lots of gums and little tiny teeth, à la Meg Ryan. I mean, come on, when it came to women, Judi's eyes weren't my eyes. Not even close. I doubted that she'd notice even a black tooth, the fat dodo.

Unable to make up my mind, I continued to stare at the door, scratch my dandruffed head, and try desperately to come to a decision. And while I was doing all that thinking and suffering, Becky Ballard was watching me through the door's peephole. She would later confess to others in her sweet southern drawl, "I declare he looked absolutely adorable standin' there thinkin' and scratchin' like he was.'"

I finally knocked.

Becky Ballard opened the door, lowered her long eyelashes, and said all Scarlet O'Hara–like, "Hi darlin'. It's so nice to meet you. Come right on in."

Hi darlin'. I loved it.

She had red hair, green eyes, and soft pink lips. At least they looked soft. She spoke with a delicious Southern accent. She stood five feet four inches tall (exactly the right height) and was absolutely beautiful. Gorgeous. Sexy as I don't know what. If I could have wished for my favorite looks on a female, Becky Ballard's looks would have been the looks I would have wished for.

It was lust at first sight.

Or was it love?

"You'll have to excuse me," she said, "but I'm a *mess*. This damn hotel hair dryer blew three fuses! I made the engineer or whatever he was stand right next to me until I finished blow dryin' my hair. He just left. Could you please zip up the back of my dress?"

Becky Ballard turned so that her back was to me. So was the nape of her neck and a few wisps of red hair that hung down from the beautiful bunch she had temporarily gathered up and pinned to the top of her head. She had the sweetest neck I'd ever seen, and, at sixty-eight, I had seen a lot of necks. I'll never forget for as long as I live Becky Ballard standing there in front of me that night. Add to all of that the fact that the top of Becky Ballard's head came to the tip of my nose. I could smell her hair. It smelled great. Her figure! Her size! Her height!

We were a perfect fit!

Besides that, Becky Ballard had the cutest way of walking. When she walked, she threw one hip way out here and then the other hip way out there. Trailing behind Becky as she sashayed her cute little behind to the elevator caused me to perspire freely.

We went for one drink in the Plaza's Oak Room. While obsequious waiters fawned over us, I sweated nervous nuggets the size of hailstones across my upper lip. After drinks, we walked outside to my car. My driver, Tyrell Masella, opened the rear door for Becky, winked at me behind her back, and gave me the thumbs-up sign. Tyrell had been working for me for a lot of years. He never did that before—winked or did things with his thumbs. I made a mental note to talk to Tyrell about that wink.

When Becky Ballard was in the car and Tyrell had shut the car door, I whispered in his ear, "Love at first sight."

Tyrell smiled.

Becky and I had dinner at Nobu in Tribeca. While Tyrell drove us uptown, I gave Becky Ballard a short hesitant kiss on her lips in the back seat. It took a lot of nerve on my part. At least for me, it did. One never knew what form of temper might lurk behind a red-haired, green-eyed girl. But Becky didn't seem especially angry or surprised. It was a delicious kiss. And I was right. Her lips were soft as butter. I quit while I was ahead.

We sat at a table for two at Serendipity's ice cream parlor. We shared an ice cream sundae. While we scooped up dripping hot fudge and wet walnuts with our spoons, I asked Becky Ballard if she wanted to see my apartment. She said only if I promised to be a gentleman and behave myself.

My building's doorman, Nelson Quatman, had a lascivious look on his face as he pushed the revolving doors around. In the past, Nelson Quatman never had any kind of look on his face—lascivious or otherwise—when I came home with a new date. I made a mental note to talk to Quatman about that look.

Before I could turn on my living room lights we were kissing like two maniacal high school kids. We broke apart for only the amount of time it took me to put Diana Krall's album *The Look of Love* on my CD player. We danced through "S'Wonderful," "Love Letters," "I Remember You," and "Cry Me a River." I started fumbling with the zipper on the back of Becky's dress throughout "Besame Mucho," "The Night We Called It a Day" and "Dancing in the Dark." Sixty-eight-year-old me slipped the two thin spaghetti-straps of thirty-seven-year-old Becky Ballard's dark blue silk dress off her shoulders during "I Get Along Without You Very Well." I listened to the silky garment slide down Becky's body to the carpet and stared at the gorgeous woman naked in the lamp light from the beginning of *The Look of Love* until it was almost over. And then we went to bed.

Judi-with-an-i was right.

We were a perfect fit.

CHAPTER TWENTY-NINE

"I'm driving her *crazy*!" I told my sister Phoebe over coffee at the Whitney Museum restaurant. "Good crazy, but crazy. Sexually, I mean. *Me*, your sixty-eight-year-old bro driving a thirty-seven-year-old Southern beauty crazy! Not to be believed, right?"

"This is more information than I need to know," she huffed.

"I mean, she brings it out of me. It's some kind of attraction I never experienced before."

"I have to go," said Phoebe.

"How lucky can you get?" I asked my friend, the retired *New York Times* obituary writer, Arnold Hoffman. "Who would have ever thought that I would be *shtupping* a beautiful woman half my age thanks to *your* daughter."

"Watch your heart," replied Hoffman. "Remember what happened to Rockefeller and John Garfield."

"Which Rockefeller?"

"I forget," said Hoffman.

"She calls me an animal," I mentioned later to the perpetually pissed-off Benjamin Lorca. "She says, 'You are an *An-neeee-mal!*' I'm telling you Benny, this whole thing is a constant source of I don't know what . . . of . . . of . . . amazement, that's what. If I lose her, I'll never experience this kind of sex again."

"You're right about that," he growled.

A week later Becky went back to Atlanta. She was a fashion coordinator for a big international dress firm and had an important job to do. I wasn't sure of the details, but her responsibilities sounded very impressive. Luckily, her assignments took her to New York now and then. When Becky was in Atlanta, I would call her two or three times a day. I'd bug her about coming back, kept telling her I missed her something awful and had to see her—now! I'd told her that if she didn't come back soon I'd throw myself off my apartment terrace.

To which she would reply, "Oh, for goodness' sake."

When she did return to New York, which was about twice a month for three or four days, we'd have the best times. I'd suffer those same tinglings I recalled feeling in grammar school when I was seven and madly in love with Nancy Ketterer, age eight. I would show off for Nancy by standing on my head in her backyard. I would have stood on my head for Becky Ballard every time I saw her, if I felt I still could.

It wasn't long after we started seeing each other that I began talking to Becky about marriage. I knew it was something I shouldn't have been doing so soon after my divorce. The pain and horror of that ordeal, the terrible insecurities, the misery, and disgust were still very much a part of me. Plus, all of my new personal insecurities caused by that traumatic event continued to spread a layer of grave doubts on my love for Becky—and her love for me. I mean a beautiful, significantly younger woman claiming to worship the ground this scarred-up geezer walked on was hard for me to accept.

Still . . .

. . . being the desperate romantic I've always been and sensing true love *finally* entering my life, I talked about it anyway.

"I keep playing with the idea of us getting married, Becs," I would whisper into her ear at night after we turned off our lamps. "I obviously don't have a great marital track record," I'd say, "and probably should never think about the institution again, particularly at my age and so soon after my divorce, but here I am thinking about it."

Becky would shake her head, then say, "You're nuts is what you are. You're either a ravin' masochist or a punch-drunk romantic. As far as I'm concerned, neither condition is satisfactory. Please, let's not talk about marriage. It's way too early. Let's just enjoy ourselves. Let our romance settle in for a bit. Let's give it some time. Besides, you're still hurtin' big time from your divorce."

"But I *want* to talk about it," I'd persist, all pig-headed and stupid. "Like Laurence Shames says, 'To linger on a sad thing is as pointless as sticking your finger in your eye.' "

"Well, I *still* don't want to talk about it."

Then Becky Ballard was back in Atlanta.

Just like that!

And I was in a bad mood for days on end. No more than a week would pass before I would start up that old broken-record theme of mine on the telephone. "I miss you. When are you coming back? Huh? When are you? If you don't come back today I'm going to throw myself off . . ."

"Oh, for goodness' sake," she would say, pleased that I was so miserable without her, "ah was just there."

Eventually she would return to New York and once more all would be right with the world. We'd pick up where we left off with all our little habits and traditions. Breakfast in the apartment. Becky reading the *Post,* me the *Times.* She telling me all the gossip and me telling her the news. The two of us arguing over both. On Sundays we would take a taxi up to the Jackson Hole restaurant at Ninety-First Street and Madison for pancakes. Then we'd walk back to the apartment and finish reading the newspapers. Afterwards maybe we'd catch a film. Sitting side by side in the movie theater, we would always share a small bag of popcorn and a Coke, neither one of us taking our eyes off the screen, knowing exactly where the popcorn bag was—in my left hand between us. Now and then Becky would hold up the Coke and I would take a pull on the straw. After the film we might try getting a table at Serendipity, so that we could have a chocolate ice cream sundae with hot fudge sauce and wet walnuts like the sundae we had the night we met. During the winter, we would bundle up and I'd drag Becky out to Central Park to trot around the reservoir a few times.

It was during those trots that Becky would tell me all about her family and herself. Becky's stories concerned a time and place, and a family life, that was completely foreign to me. The Ballard roots went all the way back to the 1600s and the Church of England. Ballards were some of this country's first settlers. Some fought in the Civil War (for the South), others were generals and senators and governors (in the South). Her relatives also owned cotton plantations and slaves. A Ballard was even the mayor of Atlanta. Ballards graduated from West Point and Annapolis. An uncle of Becky's was burned on over 90 percent of his body when his PT boat—one similar to ex-President Jack Kennedy's—was blown out from under him in the Pacific. Becky's Aunt Marjorie lived in the same house the entire hundred years of her life, and had the same telephone number, too. Aunt Marjorie was a student in the twenties in Berlin and Paris, traveled by herself to China and Tibet when she was fifty, was a college professor in her sixties, and drove a dog sled in Alaska when she was in her late seventies. I was introduced to Aunt Marjorie at a large reception celebrating her ninetieth birthday party in Bowling Green, Kentucky, Becky's hometown. Aunt Marjorie was seated in a regal armchair, greeting a line of well-wishers that stretched from her living room clear out to the front lawn. People had come from miles around to see her. I came from New York. When I was finally standing in front of the woman she looked at me, smiled and said, "You're definitely not a Ballard." Aunt Marjorie was sweet. I liked her.

The lady was right about me not being a Ballard. My family's Jewish. My great-grandfather was a rabbi. My family tree goes back to Russia and Romania. My uncles were thugs and ne'er-do-wells. My aunts were complainers and old maids. The women in my family back then were so ugly they never had to hide when the local pogroms were taking place.

The Ballard and Barris families.

Two completely different cultures.

Becky's father's name was Christopher Carson Ballard, or "Kit" for short. That's because Mr. Ballard was a descendant of the famous Civil War general, Kit Carson. Becky's mother's maiden name was Rogers. Katherine Rogers. Both Christopher and Katherine were born and raised in Bowling Green. They were the same age when they met—seven. They were seventeen when they started dating. When they did, Katherine changed her name to Kitten.

Kit and Kitten.

Cutesy. But sort of nice.

Kit and Kitten Carson were married in 1948, when they both were twenty-two. The only man Katherine Ballard ever slept with in her entire life was her husband Christopher.

I think that's great.

Kit and Kitten Ballard were both seventy-one when they died. The two were killed instantly in a windy, foggy, rain-swept fifteen-car pileup on Route 40 near Montreat, North Carolina. The Ballards were on the first leg of their drive-around-the-South vacation. The Ballards perished seven months shy of their golden anniversary.

How sad is that?

At the time of the Ballards' death, Faith, the oldest daughter, was a teacher at Western Kentucky University High School in Bowling Green. She married a proctologist she met at Western named Neil Coplander. Hope, the middle sister, was a practicing veterinarian when she married Howie Wagburn. Hope also met Howie at Western Kentucky University. After graduation, Howie got a job in management working for K E&P, the Kentucky Electric and Power Company. One day Howie was working on top of a utility pole on some high-tension wires he thought were dead. Howie got himself electrocuted for his trouble. Burnt to a crisp. "Made an ash of himself," is how some Bowling Greeners put it. Now the widow Wagburn raises pigs.

Little Becky Ballard is the baby of the family, ten years younger than Faith and nine years younger than Hope. Becky's mother assured her that she wasn't a mistake, that the house had simply become too quiet when Faith and Hope grew up. Becky loved being the baby. She loved her sisters. She told everybody she was lucky. She had three mothers. And she especially loved her parents. When they died, it did something to Becky's character and personality for a spell.

Shortly after the death of her parents, Becky Ballard left Bowling Green. She was on the verge of going to Yale and becoming a doctor, but she moved to Colorado instead and attended Colorado State University. She spent her collegiate years basically fooling around. In her senior year, Becky Ballard became very pretty. After graduation she moved to San Francisco and got a job as a stewardess for the now defunct Pacific Air Lines. PAL prided themselves on their attractive stews. The Pacific Air Lines routes were San Diego, Los Angeles, San Francisco, Reno, and Las Vegas.

It was on one of these flights—the one from Vegas to Frisco—that twenty-nine-year-old Becky Ballard met thirty-nine-year-old Ned Black, who wore a large black cowboy hat even while sitting in his seat. Fact is, Black wore his large black cowboy hat everywhere he went. He was reported to have been worth a zillion dollars, though no one was quite sure who did the reporting. Legend has it that when Becky set eyes on Ned Black, she asked the age-old: Coffee, tea, or me? Legend also has it that Becky Ballard was wearing that large black cowboy hat before the plane landed. She and Ned were married a week later.

Becky never told me much about her former husband, other than his name, that he dabbled in stocks and bonds, that he was reputed to be hugely wealthy, and that he died of a massive heart attack on the one hundred and twenty-sixth week of their marriage, with his large black hat supposedly on his head. The lethal coronary took place in the Lone Star Motel nine miles outside of Las Vegas, Nevada. Ned was inside another woman at the time of his death.

As it turned out, Dead Ned wasn't even close to being wealthy. His will stated that his widow, Becky Ballard Black, would be left zilch from an estate that was mostly zilch. What little there was went to dead Ned's three kids from a former marriage.

Becky Ballard Black dropped her married name and went home. She was welcomed back to Bowling Green with open arms by her loving sisters.

CHAPTER THIRTY

December 1998.

Becky Ballard moved into my apartment just before Christmas.

We spent the holidays doing Christian things: making fudge, playing Perry Como cassettes, decorating my place with Christmas wreaths, stuff like that. We bought some angry-looking poinsettia plants whose hostile red leaves seemed to point at me all around the room. I never told Becky, but I was certain that poinsettia plant was anti-Semitic.

We even bought a Christmas tree. The night we finished decorating the tree, Becky and I walked blocks and blocks away from my apartment building, just so the two of us could look up and see the tree's lights blinking in our living room window. When we saw it, we hugged and kissed on the street. I yelled something silly like, "Ho, ho, ho," jumped in the air and clicked my heels. I was very happy.

So, of course, I started right in talking about marriage again.

Becky said I wasn't ready to marry anything, that I was only putting unnecessary pressure on both of us. I asked her how she could know I wasn't ready to get married and she said by the way I reacted to other things. She could just tell. She said I wasn't over Penny yet. She said, "You may think you're over her, but you're not. Trust me, I can tell."

I told her my friend Coulter Bean's granddaddy used to say, "Never trust anyone who says 'trust me'."

"I don't give a good goddamn what your friend's grand-daddy says, when I tell you somethin', you can bet on it."

Once again, Becky said we should just relax and enjoy our togetherness. I sensed that Becky knew better than I that I wasn't serious about us getting married, not way down deep, even though I mouthed off like I was. She made much more sense, but that didn't stop me from talking and doing things that were just plain stupid.

Like the ring.

We celebrated Becky's forty-first birthday at a posh East Side restaurant. When they brought our desserts, I slid a little blue Tiffany box across the table to her. From the moment she saw the little blue box, Becky's entire mood changed. In a nanosecond, she went from happy and carefree to angry and more angry. She refused to touch the box, let alone unwrap it. She scowled and said, "It's a weddin' ring and I don't want it."

I told her it wasn't a wedding ring.

"Then it's an engagement ring and I still don't want it." She was getting more furious by the minute.

"How did you . . . how do you know it's . . . why don't you want it?"

"Because I don't. And stop playin' games with me."

I was shocked. "I'm not playing any games. I thought you would love the ring."

"Why? Why would I love the ring? Why did you buy this . . . this . . ."

"To bring us closer together. To make our living together more of a commitment. To push me harder toward that god-damn alter. Stuff like that."

"Are you crazy? You haven't any intentions of walkin' up to that goddamn altar, as you put it. You're never goin' to marry me. Since your divorce you *hate* the thought of marriage. You don't realize that, but you do. All you're doin' is havin' fun messin' with our heads. It's safe because I'll keep sayin' no. And when the day comes I stop sayin' no, that's when you'll lay down and absolutely die. That's because you're sick. And punch-drunk. Your divorce has fucked you up. Big time. Well, head-messin', *sick* head-messin', may be fun for you, buster, but it sure isn't for me. Even though I know we're not goin' to end up together, me—the fool that I am—not only stays here, but also stays in love with you. Talk about not bein' too bright." She shrugged off a derisive laugh aimed at herself. "I've loved you from the day we met, and you simply refuse to believe it."

"I believe it."

"You don't. Way down deep, you don't. You dread the thought of gettin' married because way down deep you think I'm marryin' you for your money. What's that look on your face? You don't think so? Then explain to me why you wake up in the middle of the night two or three nights every week in a cold sweat. Go ahead. Explain that to me. Happy, stress-free people don't wake up in the middle of the night sweatin' from head to toe. You're a fool, Chuck, and if you want to know the truth, I'm an even bigger fool than you."

"You're not a fool."

"Yes, I am. Listen, I'm just somethin' to keep you company until your head clears and the pain of your divorce disappears. Time heals and when it does, you'll go back to bein' footloose and fancy-free again, and I'll be back in Georgia out of a job and too old to have a baby. *That* is why I'm a fool to stay with you."

"Don't leave me."

"I won't. Not tonight at least. Just take this ring and return it."

"You haven't even—"

"I don't want to look at it. It's probably very expensive."

"It was a romantic gesture," I said, bewildered.

"Shut *up*."

The funny thing is—Becky was right. Because one Sunday morning, maybe two months later, I was sitting in my green armchair reading the *New York Times* when I started to feel, I don't know, strange. I was having these rolling memory pains. Some of them severe at times. I was recalling Penny and the fun we used to have. I was also hurting over her loss, rehashing our walk in Zurich, replaying her apparent decision never to come back. It was like hearing I had an incurable disease and wondering: Why me? Why the fuck me?

I was suddenly and unexpectedly tired of sharing my life with someone new, someone I didn't know well. Twenty-four hours a day, seven days a week. Maybe not *someone*. Maybe just Becky. It had become a sham, pretending to enjoy my new self-imposed marital-like responsibilities so soon, duties I was definitely not ready to assume. And it was all my fault. I had asked Becky, had actually badgered her for these obligations, even pestered Becky to get *married*!

Becky put down her *New York Post* and said, "Is everythin' okay?"

Her antenna was amazing. She could sense the mood I was in if I was standing on one side of Grand Central Station and she was standing on the other.

"Is everything okay?" I repeated. "Sure, why?"

"You seem distant."

"Distant?"

"And weird."

"I never want to get married," I said. The words rushed out of my mouth like a prison break before I could stop them.

Becky didn't seem shocked at all. "You don't?"

"No, I don't."

"Why are you sayin' this now?" she asked calmly.

"I don't know. Maybe we're getting too close. Maybe it's all getting too serious."

"So what do you want me to do?"

"Move out."

"Move out?" She wasn't alarmed. Just, I don't know, resigned. Almost pre-resigned.

"Yes. I want you to move out. You know. Go back to Atlanta."

"That's what you want? You want me to go back to Atlanta?"

"It's how I feel."

"Oh. It's how *you* feel."

There was a pause.

Then Becky said, "I've been expecting this. But let me ask you something. Have you, per chance, given any thought to how *I* might feel?"

"You'll be okay."

"I'll be okay! I see. You figured that all out, have you? All by yourself? Out of a clear blue sky you tell me to move out, to go back to Atlanta, and I'll be okay. I'll be okay because that's how you figured out I would be, right? You've spent the last six months proposin' to me almost every day of the week, you even offered me an engagement ring, for God's sake, and now—just when I'm beginnin' to think maybe we *should* get married—you want me to move out! Amazin'! You know somethin', I'm not surprised. I told you I've been expectin' this. You know why I've been expectin' this? Because I've begun to think we really should be married and you can feel those thoughts inside me. That's why you suddenly want out. I knew it."

"Knew what?"

"That it was just a matter of time."

"Yeah, well . . ."

"It's not like *I've* been pressurin' *you* to get married. I haven't said a word. I've just allowed myself to fall deeply in love with you, that's all. Of course I never should have, but I did. And now look what's happened. Out of nowhere, you order me to leave. And then you add insult to injury by tellin' me, ever so wisely, I'll be fine."

"It's better than both of us being miserable for the rest of our lives," I muttered. I sounded pathetic.

I could see Becky thinking.

And then she said, "Remember the night you gave me the engagement ring and I said I'm a fool to stay with you. Remember?"

I said I did.

"I was right. I *am* a fool."

Becky Ballard spent that night at the St. Regis Hotel. The next day she moved out of my apartment and returned to Atlanta.

CHAPTER THIRTY-ONE

I'm riding around in a convertible with my old friend and living legend Dick Mr. *American Bandstand* Clark. The two of us are the same age, sixty-nine years old. It's 1999 and we will both hit the big seven-O later that year. That bothers us. A lot. It's a bright sunny day. The sky's clear and pure blue. The convertible's top is down. We're in Los Angeles and not New York. That confuses me a little. That's because I don't remember coming to Los Angeles. Anyway, we're on Vine Street, heading north toward the Hollywood Hills. Dick's driving. I'm looking at the sky. Suddenly I see paraphernalia floating down to Earth: a white starched man's shirt, brown slacks, nicely creased, a pair of brown-and-white cleated tennis shoes falling gently in tandem, their small spikes glinting occasionally in the sunshine. I bring these slowly tumbling objects to my friend's attention. Clark's annoyed. "Stop bothering me, fuckface," he snaps testily. "I want to concentrate on my driving."

And then I see an airliner tumbling to Earth. It's wings and sides are missing. I can see the pilot and co-pilot sitting in the cockpit side by side, smiling, chatting, laughing. The rest of the airliner is empty. Personal rubbish litters the seats. Obviously at one time the plane was filled with people. (Did they fall out too, like the clothes?) The airliner is going to crash a few blocks away. But where? I tap Dick on the shoulder and point to the fuselage coming down. Once again Dick doesn't seem to care. "Cut out the small talk, asshole," he says. "Can't you see there's a lot of traffic?"

We eventually arrive at my apartment. Only it's my apartment in New York. Now I'm *really* confused. I walk into the bedroom. A message has been painted across the two matching floor-to-ceiling doors of my closet. The culprit used either lipstick or red paint, I'm not sure which. There's a salutation and a message. The message has four lines. Each line is roughly five feet across. The salutation reads: "Dear Eddie." I can't read the message. The words are blurred. I try to decipher the lines, but each time I begin the blurring gets worse.

I run to the kitchen hoping to find Clark. He's always in the kitchen making something. He loves to cook. When he does cook, he's so cheap he only uses half the recipe. This time I find him making pizza; one slice instead of two. (Didn't he think I was hungry?) Thank God he's there and thank God he's making pizza, even though he didn't make enough for me. Pizza's the only thing he makes that's eatable. Of course he saves the dough from all the slices he should have made but didn't. He molds the extra dough into a ball, wraps the ball in Saran Wrap and puts the wrapped balls into my refrigerator. My fridge is completely filled with Clark's excess pizza balls. There's hardly room for anything else. Only a quart of milk and a lemon. I ask Clark to use some of the Saran-wrapped pizza balls he has stored in my fridge the next time he makes pizza so I can have some room for maybe an orange—or a few eggs. He tells me to go fuck myself.

Anyway, here I am in the kitchen, breathlessly shouting, "Dick! Dick! I've got to show you this weird stuff that's written across my bedroom's closet doors."

Dick turns around.

It's not Dick.

It's my sister Phoebe.

She and I are eating tuna sandwiches at the counter of The Luncheonette on the corner of Eighty-Third Street and Lexington Avenue.

"Let me tell you something, Chuck," she says, her mouth full of chewed food, "you treat Becky like dirt. You deserve all the heartache you're giving yourself. I'm telling you, you deserve it."

"Oh, please."

"I'm serious. Any woman who gets treated like you treat Becky Ballard would have left you months ago. *Years* ago. And never looked back. She's either a masochistic doormat, or . . ."

"Or what?"

"Or she loves you very much . . ."

"You think so?" I ask through a mouthful of tuna on rye with a touch of mayo and a slice of onion. "I certainly hope so," I say, spitting a speck of tuna on my sister's cheek. It was the "cer" in "certainly" that launched the tuna.

"When it comes to women, you're a little scumbag shit," says my sister, squinting her eyes and pointing a finger at my nose, unaware of the tuna speck on her cheek. "You lie to her. You promise you'll marry her every other week, then you change your mind. You cheat on her. You . . ."

"I'll never screw around after I'm married."

"Bullshit!" snaps my sister. She wipes her mouth with a napkin. "That's nothing but macho bullshit."

"So what's your point?"

"My point is the rocks in Becky's head fit the holes in yours."

"What's *that* supposed to mean?"

"It means you two are meant for each other. Becky's nice. She's sweet. She's smart. And she understands you."

"So?" I ask.

"So marry her!" she screams.

CHAPTER *THIRTY-TWO*

shot up to a sitting position in my bed and yelled, "Fuck!"
My digital clock glowed 6:07 A.M.
Obviously I had been dreaming.

Sweat was pouring down my face. My back was hunched in misery. I wondered why lately the first word out of my mouth every morning was, "Fuck!" And what the hell was that dream all about? I used to have a lot of nightmares, mostly when I was killing enemies of my country on a regular basis. Since the killings tapered off, so did my nightmares. But now there was this one about Dick Clark and my sister and Becky and marriage and weird writing on my bedroom's closet doors.

"Dear Eddie," etc., etc., etc.

When I was in college my mother used to call me Eddie every time I brought a bimbo home. It was her snide reference to Eddie Waitkus, a philandering baseball player on the Philadelphia Phillies back in the fifties. One afternoon Eddie Waitkus opened his hotel room door and was shot in the stomach by a wanton woman. An unbalanced wanton woman. From then on, every mother in the city, Jewish or otherwise, harped on their sons to be aware of wanton women. Especially unbalanced wanton women.

"How will I know if she's unbalanced?" I would ask my mother.

"Just don't open the door."

"What kind of an answer is that?"

"Just remember what happened to Eddie Waitkus."

Ten minutes after I brought a date home, the girl would invariably ask, "Why is your mother calling you Eddie when your name is Chuck?"

"Code," I'd answer.

"Code? Like what kind of code?"

"She's trying to tell me you're a treasure and I shouldn't let you get away."

The girl would smile from ear to ear. It always worked.

So there I was, sitting on the side of my bed, wondering what that goddamned dream was all about and why "fuck!" was always the first word out of my mouth in the morning and why, when I woke up lately, I couldn't open my eyes. They were always stuck together with some kind of sticky glop that gathered in the corners during the night. Then the glop mulched into a strange form of Crazy Glue. The glue spread across my lids, cementing them shut as tight as a bad clam. And it was getting worse with every passing year.

What the hell was *going on*?

When I finally pried my eyes apart, I reached for a pad of paper and pencil on the night table by my bed and drew the Pie of Life—my friend Arnold Hoffman's idea. The Pie of Life is a round circle divided into four slices, like a pie. Each slice represents eighteen-and-a-half years. The four slices total seventy-four years. That's the actuarial amount of time an American male is supposed to live these days. I darkened three slices of the pie with my pencil, representing fifty-five-and-a-half years. They were already history. I filled in some of the fourth slice to bring the darkened part of the pie to a total of sixty-nine years. My age. The years of my life already gone, down the drain. All that remained of my Pie, the part representing the time I had left on earth, was five years, a mere sliver. A graphic reminder that I was only moments away from the proverbial Big Dirt Nap.

Five years!

No, make that *four-and-a-half years*!

Jesus.

I stared at the drawing. A bubble of depression the size of a humongous beach ball was about to explode in my chest. The explosion would cause a flood of despair to course through my body like a volcano's hot lava flowing down a mountainside. All I could think of was diving into a swimming pool a kid and coming up for air a geeze! If that's how fast my *entire* life had gone by, how quickly would the next piddling five years vanish?

I sighed.

How sad.

Fucking Pie of Life.

What did I expect from that asshole Hoffman, for Christ's sake?

Mr. Depression.

I ripped the paper to shreds, tossed the bits and pieces into a wastebasket, and got out of bed. Once again I wondered why lately the first word out of my mouth in the morning was always "fuck!" This phenomenon was obviously beginning to bother me. It just wasn't right. You didn't have to be a rocket scientist to know something was definitely wrong. Maybe I should have taken fish oil capsules like my sister Phoebe told me to do. She read somewhere that fish oil helped mood disorders, depression, stuff like that.

That's about when I remembered that I hadn't played back my telephone messages from the previous night. Not that it mattered. I rarely received telephone messages any more. Or e-mails or faxes. I suppose it was because several of my friends and family who used to call, died. Also a number of my remaining friends weren't my friends anymore. Consequently, I trained myself not to be disappointed if there weren't any telephone messages. Still, I was *always* disappointed when there weren't any telephone messages.

There was always the possibility Becky might call.

Yes, we had gotten back together again. About a year ago. I was going nuts without her. I told her so over and over. So she put her pride in her pocketbook and moved back. A few months later we argued and Becky moved out. Then I pleaded and begged and Becky moved back. And moved out. And moved back. We were in the "back" mode now, with a slight change. Not a *slight* change come to think of it, but a *major* change. Becky wanted to get married. *Really* wanted to get married. Was insisting on it. Apparently she was fed up with the moving out and in, with the traveling back and forth, with her biological clock marching forward. I, on the other hand, dreaded the thought of being married again. I had lost confidence in the institution, in my own prowess as a husband, since my divorce from Penny. I had come to the conclusion that both the institution and my prowess sucked. I had also recently concluded that my days with Becky Ballard of Bowling Green, Kentucky, by way of Atlanta, Georgia, were numbered.

Unless . . .

Unless I could think of a ploy, a scam, *something* to keep her by my side without saying, "I do."

I reached across the night table, turned up the volume button of my answering machine and hit "play." I was startled to hear the machine announce that I had four messages! I couldn't remember the last time I had four messages.

[Message received at six-seventeen P.M.] Hey, you mean old snake, this is Becky. How are you? *Where* are you?

Gallivantin' around town with a couple of gorgeous showgirls I'll bet. Why aren't you home missin' me? I miss *you*. I *hate* when we're apart. I love you so much. Thank goodness I'll see you Saturday. About six-thirty? I'll call when my plane lands. Big kiss.

Sitting on the edge of my bed, feeling all good and happy, hearing from Becky like I just did, I stretched and accidently ripped a nasty. I seemed to be unexpectedly passing wind more and more of late, ripping nasties when I least expected to. Not long ago I was standing on a ladder extending myself full-length to push *Death Comes to the Archbishop* into a bookshelf above my head when I unintentionally ripped a particularly nasty nasty. The accident happened to be extra dismaying, since my house-keeper, Mrs. Muñoz, was standing right under my hindquarters. She had just handed me the book. And then there was the morning I sneezed and cut a real yowzer in my apartment building's elevator, which was filled with fellow tenants.

Was uncontrollable flatulence a sign of aging?

Did it get worse?

What the hell was *going on*?

[Message received at nine twenty-seven P.M.] Where are you, you cocksucker? I'm in goddamn Lenox Hill Hos-pital. Lummux Hill is a better name for this joint. The food's un-fucking-eatable. My room sucks. My nurse sucks. (Don't I wish it.) Heh, heh, heh. So I guess it's outta sight outta mind with you, right? Am I right or am I right? Remember: "The only reward of virtue is virtue; the only way to have a friend is to be one." Ralph Waldo Emerson. So, you little pissant, where are you?

"I'm here," I muttered, feeling foolish talking to the

answering machine like I was. Besides, I knew my friend Benjamin Lorca was in the hospital. A minor back operation. Lorca's wife, Gretchen Braun Lorca, called to tell me about it, said her husband would be in Room Eight-Two-Two if I wanted to visit. Now there was a marriage for you. A member of the Hitler Youth Movement when she was a child married to an obsessively religious Sephardic Jew of theatrical Spanish descent. And they truly loved each other! Go know, as my grandmother would have said.

[Message received at nine fifty-two P.M.] Chuck, this is your sister. My daughter and your adoring niece, Felicity, is having a concert tomorrow night at the Strauss rehearsal hall on Fortieth Street between Ninth and Tenth Avenues. Four Forty-One West Fortieth. Eight o'clock sharp. You better be there. Felicity wrote two of the concertos herself. This is your last chance. If you don't come tonight to support your niece, and God-daughter I might add, I will forbid anyone in our family to ever talk to you again. Bye. Oh, and maybe if you hadn't sold your company you wouldn't be sitting around your apartment morning, noon, and night feeling sorry for yourself and regretting everything you've ever done. Bye again.

It was while I was listening to my sister's message that I noticed the little green pillow. I mean really noticed it. Saw it for the first time, so to speak. It had been hanging from one of my dresser mirror nobs for years. The green pillow was about a foot long and a foot wide. It had "No Regrets" stitched in red needlepoint across its front. I stared at the pillow, lost in thought. I hit the "stop" button of the answering machine, got out of bed, walked to the bureau, took the little pillow off the nob, and held it in my hands. I was mesmerized by its message. "No Regrets." I went to my open bedroom window and threw the little pillow out with a lively behind-the-back toss that would have made an NBA point guard proud. It fell forty flights to the ground below. I returned to my bed table and hit the answering machine "play" button again.

[Message received at ten-oh-six P.M.] Chuck. It's Arnold. Did you see this morning's *New York Times* obit section? Eight, Chuck, eight! All close to our age! Gone, Chuck, including Marilyn Silverstone! Remember Marilyn Silverstone? The photographer who moved to Katmandu to become a Buddhist nun? She was seventy like us. Or almost us. Oh! And Alan Clark? Listen to this. I'll read it to you. It says: "Alan Clark is dead at seventy-one. An animal lover, Clark wanted it known that he had gone to join his Labrador Tom and the other dogs." Little weird, huh? *Gone to join his Labrador*!? Good luck, Tom, you fool. No matter, the main point I want you to keep in mind, Chuck, is that they're calling our class. It won't be long now. Life is short. The clock is ticking, Chuckie Baby. Time is not infinite. Enjoy the moment. Call me.

I got out of bed and stumbled toward the bathroom for my morning shower. On the way, I stopped to look at my copy of Munch's painting, *The Scream*, that hung next to my bathroom door. That particular Munch painting has always fascinated me. I love the painting's orange and red slashes of sky mixed with the swirling blue, white, and yellow sea. The boardwalk with the two men in the background and the weirdo in the foreground: his hairless, skull-shaped head, the round white circles that are his eyes, the two black dots for eyeballs, the two smaller dots beneath the eyeballs for nostrils, and a large round oval for a mouth. His hands cupping his skull where his ears should be. He appeared to be screaming, "AAAAAAAAAA!"

I stepped into the shower, turned on the cold water, cupped my ears, and yelled just as I imagined the weirdo would have done in the painting. "AAAAAAAAAA!"

The wingless airliner appeared before my eyes!

CHAPTER THIRTY-THREE

I t was still early in the morning. A little after seven. Except for mountains of green garbage bags, the city streets were empty. Visiting hours at the hospital didn't begin until nine o'clock. It was 7:21 A.M. when I slithered past the unmanned reception desk. I glowered angrily at two frowning security bozos wearing blue blazers with the highly creative corporate name—Atlas Protection—stitched on their pockets. While the pair of Neanderthals tried to figure out what came after frowning I was gone. I now had a clear shot at the elevators. I walked to them as if I owned the place. I took one to the eighth floor, found Eight-Two-Two, and tiptoed into Benjamin Lorca's room. My friend was laying on his back, his hands clasped together on his chest, the sheet pulled up to his chin. He smelled of rubbing alcohol and urine and looked like a corpse. For all I knew he could have been dead.

"Come to pay your obligatory visit?" grumped the corpse.

I jumped. "You startled me. I thought you were . . ."

"Dead? You wish."

"I do not."

"Well, tough titty, asshole, I'm not dead."

Benjamin Lorca. Actor. Legendary larger-than-life cocksman of yore, fading former ladies' man of the footlights, holding on with bloodied fingertips to those delectable memories of succulent breasts and rosy behinds, bygone days when Lorca was a dashing scoundrel with a gigantic lust for life. That morning the legendary cocksman of yore didn't look much like a cocksman of anything.

"How do you feel, Ben?"

"How do I feel? How do I look? That's how I feel."

"You look like cow dung."

"That's how I feel. Like cow dung. Why are you here? Did you come to insult me? Is that why you came?"

"I'm here to lift your spirits."

"You think telling me I look like cow dung is lifting my spirits? My wife made you come, didn't she?"

"No she didn't."

"Did you bring coffee?"

"No."

"Why not?"

"I forgot."

"'No mask like open truth to cover lies. As to go naked is the best disguise,'" boomed Lorca.

"What's that from?"

"*Death of a Salesman.*"

"I didn't lie to you," I said. "I told you the truth. I simply forgot."

"About what?"

"Your coffee."

"Fuck off," snarled Lorca.

He turned his back to me and stared at the opposite wall. His faded green hospital gown had come apart. I saw the actor's rounded shoulders, pimply back, and wizened wrinkles where his ass used to be. Not an appetizing sight.

After a few minutes, Lorca said to the wall, "I'm hungry. The food's un-fucking-eatable in this joint."

"You told me."

"When?"

"On my service. You left me a message."

"Well it is," he said petulantly,

"Sorry to hear that."

I was mesmerized by the back of Lorca's head, the mussed and thinning strands of hair, the pate that appeared to be surprisingly balder than I remembered.

Lorca suddenly turned. "What are you looking at?"

"Nothing."

Self-consciously, Lorca fondled the top of his head with his fingers, then spoke with wide hostile eyes and a nervous laugh. "Nothing! Ha! Ha! That's funny. That's very funny. Nothing. Ha! Ha! Ha! So that's why you came to my sickbed, is it? To make fun of my late-in-life-baldness? Like you're God's gift to women?"

I ignored Lorca's snide remark. I recalled my friend the ex-obituary writer Arnold Hoffman telling me how he always used to write off Lorca's scathing repartee to a carefully engineered persona. The growly macho lion. The seething Andalusian lover with gallons of hot Spanish/Sephardic/Jewish blood coursing through his veins. The big bad bully who, underneath it all, was nothing but a fuzzy panda bear with a heart of gold. "Fuzzy panda bear my ass," Hoffman had said. "Lorca's a prick."

It's true, Benjamin Lorca was a prick. And not easy to be around. But for some metaphysical reason I could never explain, I loved the son of a bitch. Also, if I badgered him long enough, he would eventually come up with good advice.

"They're going to fuse two discs together tomorrow morning," whined the actor. "It's going to hurt like hell. Who knows, my heart may give out from the anesthesia. I beg of you, Chuck, grant a friend's last wish. Before I meet my maker, go to the deli at the corner of Lexington and Seventy-Seventh and get me a cup of *good* coffee. *Please.*"

"Okay. Okay," I said, leaving the room.

On my way to the elevator I heard Lorca bellow, "And a toasted bagel with a schmear."

Outside, the sun was up in its entirety.

I didn't need my windbreaker, but wore it anyway. The city smelled good, too. The air hadn't filled yet with the toxic fumes that spewed out of cars, taxis, buses, and trucks. For a surprising moment, everything was sweetness and light. I stood by the curb in front of the Lummux Hill Hospital entrance, enjoying the moment, getting my bearings. And then a cab came to a screeching stop directly in front of me. The driver leaned out his window, looked up and said, "Uncle Sam wants you, muthahump. Get in."

It was The Duck.

CHAPTER *THIRTY-FOUR*

"**F**uck you Duck *and* the cab you rode in on."

"Get in or you're dead meat."

"Hey Duck, the last time I saw you and your rotten cab was in Los Angeles, what, in the seventies, wasn't it? You were a world-class lowlife then, and obviously you still are."

"I said get the fuck in the cab. I promise you, muthahump, your life depends on what I'm going to tell you."

I got in The Duck's taxi.

The Duck and his taxi smelled like they always had—awful. And he still looked like he used to look—revolting. Stringy hair down to his shoulders, a pockmarked face pitted from scratching festered chicken pox sores when he was a kid, his nose a cocaine faucet constantly dripping snot on his chest. The Duck always had several diseases to boot, a modern-day Typhoid Mary. Typhoid Scumbag. That's what his nickname should have been.

When I lived in Los Angeles, The Duck was my CIA contact/messenger boy. He brought me my Company orders fresh off the presses. Back in those days, The Duck seemed to derive great pleasure from throwing monkey wrenches into my personal life. I'd be on a wonderful date with a reservation at a romantic restaurant. My date and I would be approaching the restaurant's entrance and, lo and behold, there was The Duck's taxi. He would taunt me by waving my airline tickets out of the cab's window, ordering me to leave at once for some godforsaken place in the world. Or I'd arrive at the Dorothy Chandler Pavilion for the opening night performance of a famous ballet troupe direct from Leningrad, with the most beautiful female doctor in all of cancer research–land on my arm, and who do you suppose would be standing near the will-call window? The fucking Duck. And what would the bastard be doing? He'd be waving those goddamn airline tickets in the air, a cigarette dangling from the corner of his mouth, one eye squinting from the smoke, grinning up a storm. The more The Duck sensed he'd screwed up my life, the happier he was. So now, over twenty years later, I'm back in The Duck's cab.

"You know I don't have to do this shit anymore, Duck. I'm retired. My killing days are over."

"Fuck they are," he said grinning.

The Duck's taxi contained more trash than a city sanitation truck: empty soda cans, used Kleenex, cigarette butts, a dirty tampon, and a half-eaten Goldenberg's Peanut Chew candy bar. The cab's interior wasn't any different then the one The Duck used to drive in La La Land. It may have been the same trash.

The Duck smiled into his rearview mirror. "Scared the shit out of you when I pulled up, didn't I?" The Duck had an infuriating smile.

"Where're we going?" I asked, attaching my seat belt.

"Patience, fuckface." He looked at me through the rearview mirror again, grinning like one of those huge man-of-war lizards.

The Duck was enjoying this.

He pulled away from the curb, burning rubber as he did. (He *would* burn rubber.) He drove up the street a block to Park Avenue, turned left and tore down Park for nine blocks. At the southwest corner of Park Avenue and Sixty-Eighth Street, The Duck came to a screeching stop. He parked in a red tow-away zone, shot me a glance through in his rearview mirror, squished his cigarette into dust in a butt-filled ashtray, hawked an oyster out his window, and said, "Simon Oliver's fuckin' dead."

"That's old news, Duck."

Years ago I received my marching orders from this guy Simon that Oliver. He was a big deal on The Company flowchart. In fact, that he was normally too high up to personally be in charge of an agent, especially me. I wasn't a full-fledged CIA operative. I was a hired gun, a lowly stringer-assassin. I was convinced Oliver was a rabid anti-Semite. I truly believed he personally picked me to run in order to get me killed. I never knew that for sure, but I felt it in my bones. Anyway, I disliked Simon Oliver almost as much as The Duck. News of Oliver's death didn't move me very much when I had heard it a year ago. Still didn't.

"Tell me something I *don't* know, Duck."

"The new guy who took over for Oliver's a real cocksucker." The Duck meant the dirty word as a compliment.

"Why are you telling me this?"

"The new guy wants you to do a job."

"What's this new guy's name?"

"Not for you to know."

"Bullshit, Duck. You don't know his name do you? Still out of the loop. Same as you were on the West Coast, right? After all these years, they still won't let your sorry ass in, will they? Forever the messenger boy. And a Yalie to boot. Shame on you, Duck. You're a disgrace to your alma mater."

He sat staring out of his front window, seething.

"Let me ask you something, Duck. This new boss who you don't know the name of because nobody ever tells you anything, you think he understands what the word 'retirement' means?"

"I guess not," said The Duck through the rearview mirror, burning me with his eyes, lighting up a new cigarette.

"Ever hear of that new Executive Order #12333? The Presidential order that bars government sponsored assassinations. Don't see any reason for me to hang around The Company anymore, do you? So, I'm quitting, Duck."

"Yeah, sure."

"You don't believe me?"

"Like I said," The Duck was speaking with a hint of superiority in his voice, "they want the hitter for this particular job as far removed from The Company as possible, someone nobody knows or remembers, somebody the target wouldn't expect comin' at him from any angle."

"That's what they want, someone *as far removed* from The Company as possible?"

"Yeah, that's what they want."

"You don't know phrases like *as far removed*, Duck. The powers-that-be made you write those words down in the palm of your hand with a Sharpie, didn't they?"

"Don't fuckin' push me, Sixkiller."

"Show me the palms of your hands."

"I said don't push me."

"Golly gee-whiz, I certainly won't, Mr. Duck. You smell *real* bad, so get to the point."

"*You're* the fuckin' point. You're the one they want to do this job."

"No shit, Santa Claus. Why else would you be here? Hey Duck, do me a favor. Tell the powers-that-be that when I wrote to tell them I'd retired, I meant it. I wasn't playing games. I'm retired and I plan to *stay* retired. Bye, Duck."

"You don't fuckin' listen, do you? This new guy, he's a mean muthafucker. He doesn't take no for an answer. You back outta this, he'll make it so someone fixes you real quick. Believe me when I say that, buddy-boy. *Real* quick. Hey, I already volunteered for the job. I told them I'll not only waste you, but I'll dump your dead ass in the Jersey marshes free of charge. Nobody'll ever know you existed, I told them, mainly because nobody knows you exist now."

The Duck thought his last remark was so witty that he laughed for almost a minute. That made him cough like the consumptive he is. Which, in turn, brought on another barrage of lugie spitting out his open taxi window.

When all the noise quieted down, I said, "Fuck you, Duck."

I don't know why, but The Duck always brings me down to his level. Well, maybe not down *that* far, but pretty far down.

He said, "I'm crossing my fingers you'll pull a Pasadena."

"As a matter of fact, Ducky Boy, I'm pulling a Pasadena right now."

I yanked on the cab's door handle. It didn't budge. It was locked. One of those locks only the driver can release.

"Let me out, Duck." I sounded as though I was begging. I felt foolish, even embarrassed.

"When I'm ready," he said into the rearview mirror. The Duck was beaming. He was stoked. He was definitely in charge. "On Friday," said The Duck, "the day after tomorrow, buy an *International Herald Tribune* and go to the fucking hotdog stand behind us at noon."

I turned and saw the vendor a few feet away. His pushcart was on the corner under a large orange and blue umbrella. The umbrella had BEEF SAUSAGES, HOT DOGS, and PRETZELS printed in large red letters around it.

"Lean against the building just around the corner on the Sixty-Eighth Street side," said The Duck, pointing his finger, "as close to the corner as you can get, and read the newspaper. Hold it so someone can see it's the *Tribune*. A man will come to you and introduce himself as Barclay Robb. Listen to what he says." The Duck took a hit on his cigarette, flicked the butt out onto Park Avenue. A glob of spit followed after the butt.

"You going to open the door now?" I asked.

"By the way, Sixkiller, the boys at The Company wanted me to pass on to you a little message. They wanted me to remind you, you owe them."

"I *owe* them?"

"Yeah, that's the message."

"*What* do I owe them?"

"Just that you owe them."

The Duck unlocked the rear doors.

I pushed the right rear door open and started to get out, stopped and said, "Oh, and one other thing, Duck. Give this note to whoever you give notes to these days." I scribbled out something on a small piece of white paper and slid it into the money slot in the bulletproof plastic that taxis use to separate the front seat from the back. When The Duck reached three fingers into the slot to grab the note, I punch the slot down as hard as I could, catching his fingertips.

"AAAAAAAAAA!" he howled.

The falling airliner fuselage I dreamed about went by my eyes again.

Furious, The Duck whipped his head and shoulders around to the right, his left hand quickly moving toward his left hip.

"Don't even think about it, Duck," I said reaching for my .38 Smith & Wesson, tucked into my pants at the small of my back. "I'm using hollow points, jerk-off. They smart something awful."

The Duck froze.

"Besides, dumb ass," I said, climbing out of the taxi, "I don't think it would be smart, playing with guns out in the open on the corner of Sixty-Eighth Street and Park Avenue, do you?"

The last I saw of The Duck was him sucking on his fingers and reading my note that said: "Asshole." When I stepped out of the taxi, I left the right rear door wide open. The Duck was forced to leave his cab and come around the taxi's trunk to shut the back door.

"Muthafucker!" he shouted at me.

My back was to The Duck as I walked away. He couldn't see my smiling face. I waved my index finger at him and headed back to the hospital. I made a mental note to begin carrying my .38 Smith & Wesson tucked into my pants at the small of my back.

CHAPTER THIRTY-FIVE

Forty-five minutes later I entered the hospital again.

I carried a brown paper bag containing two paper cups of steaming black coffee and a bagel smeared with Philadelphia Cream Cheese. It wasn't nine o'clock yet and visiting hours still hadn't started.

On the way to the elevators someone yelled, "Hold it, busthter!"

It was a woman, a senior citizen maybe in her seventies. She was a volunteer hospital receptionist who had apparently just come on duty. The woman was short and squat and redolent of Ponds Facial Cream. Her hair was frizzy, her eyeglasses thick as Coke bottle tops. She wore a green hospital smock over a nondescript dress. Her feet were stuffed into a pair of flowered bedroom slippers. Her name-tag read: A. WEINGARTEN. The woman talked with a crotchety lisp.

"Visthiting hours hasthn't started yet," she barked angrily.

"I'm Benjamin Lorca's brother," I said with authority. "I just flew in from Hollywood."

The woman wagged her right forefinger in my face. "No you're not."

"I'm not what?"

"Misthter Lorca'sth brother."

"What makes you so sure?"

"Becauseth you don't look the leasthst bit like Benjamin Lorca. Heth's tall and hanthsome and you're neither."

"He *used* to be tall and handsome," I said, miffed. "Not anymore, lady. Have you seen him lately? No? Well, he's shrunk. Significantly. Not only that, but he's gotten bald and wrinkly. Looks pretty close to me now. Please telephone him. He's expecting me. He'll confirm that I'm his brother."

With a look that could marinate tomatoes, the aging receptionist telephoned Lorca's hospital room. "Excuseth me for bothering you Misthter Lorca, but a short man who looksth nothing like you isth here at the reception dethsk claiming, get thisth, that heth's your brother!" The woman started cackling nervously, but stopped abruptly when she (and I) heard Lorca's reply, which was, "DOES THE COCK-SUCKER HAVE COFFEE?"

A. Weingarten was so startled she dropped the receiver.

I pointed to the brown paper bag in my hand.

Shaken to the quick, the lady picked up the receiver and said, "Yesth thir he hasth the coffee."

"THEN SEND THE LITTLE PRICK UP!"

"Ye-yesth, thir," said A. Weingarten, seriously disturbed, holding the receiver a foot from her ear. The half-blind volunteer's face was all squinched up with fear and loathing.

I returned to Lorca's room and sat in the same chair. I removed the lid from one of the paper coffee cups, unwrapped the bagel, and gave the coffee and bagel to Benny.

"Where the fuck were you?" he asked.

"Getting your coffee."

"Takes an hour to go half a block down the street?"

"It wasn't an hour. There was a line. Here's your coffee and bagel."

"Putz," muttered Lorca.

"Hey, Benny, quit giving me these putz and asshole asides of yours will you please? They're getting on my nerves."

"I love you, Chuck," said a suddenly contrite Benjamin Lorca. "You're a good friend, but sometimes you're a major pain in the ass." Lorca smiled, signaling he was now in a good mood. "So, how's your little girlfriend from Nebraska?"

"She's from Kentucky. That's one of the reasons I wanted to see you. I wanted to ask you . . ."

"See? I told you," snarled Lorca, visibly falling back into his funk. "Didn't I tell you? You didn't come to offer me succor and comfort. You came to bleed information from me, you bloodsucking maggot."

"Cool it with your persona, Benny. I need you now. You're one of my closest friends. You've got to help me figure this out. What are friends for?"

"To give succor and comfort to the dying. Not to suck their blood like a fucking leech."

"You're not dying."

"I'm sorry I brought the subject up," said an irritated Lorca.

"What subject?"

"Your girlfriend from Missouri."

"Kentucky. You do that just to needle me, don't you?"

"Do what?"

"Say the wrong state."

"What a pleasant visit *this* is," growled the actor.

"I'm running out of time, Benny. I have this feeling Becky's going to stop seeing me and go back to Atlanta real soon, unless . . ."

"Yeah? Unless? Unless what?"

"Unless I marry her."

"She's threatening you?"

"Not really, but . . ."

"No marriage, no pussy, is that what she's saying?"

"Noooo. She's saying no marriage, no more seeing each other."

"JESUS CHRIST, THEN LET THE CUNT GO!" boomed Lorca.

"Watch your fucking mouth, Benny. I'm not kidding anymore. I may end up marrying Becky, and I don't want to lose our friendship over your filthy fucking mouth."

We didn't speak for a few minutes.

"You whine like I don't know what," grumped Lorca. "Can you hear yourself whine?"

"It's my heritage," I said. "I don't *want* to let Becky go."

"Why not?" growled Benny.

"I'll miss her."

"Because?"

"Because she's young, and fun to be with, and beautiful, and she loves me, and we have great times together, and . . ."

"So if she's so great looking and loves you so much, what's the problem?"

"I'm scared."

"Of what? Of her?"

"I just told you. Of *marriage*. I don't think I'm good at it. I thought I was a good husband to Penny. So what did she end up doing? She cheated on me, committed adultery, is what she ended up doing."

"I'm talking to a cuckold," laughed Lorca. "That's rich."

"It's not funny, Ben. And what's so rich about it? As far as I'm concerned, a woman who is unfaithful to her husband, or a man to his wife, is the worst thing that can happen to married people. It ruins each for life. How fucking unfair is that? How low is that? You know the *main* reason I don't want to get married?"

"No, what's the main reason?" asked Lorca, rolling his eyes in boredom.

"I don't want to go through another divorce." I broke out in a cold sweat, thinking about the junkyard dogs Penny and I had for lawyers. Their tactics of creating fear and hatred between Penny and me, trying to scare the shit out of us (and succeeding) so that we would both agree to anything just to return to a life of peace and quiet. "Never again," I told Benny. "I vowed when my divorce was final, I'd never ever marry again."

"So do your vow."

"I'll miss her too much."

"Enough!" shouted Benjamin Lorca. "This may be my next to last day on Earth, for God's sake."

"What do you mean your last day on earth?"

"I could expire from the anesthesia. Let's talk about something else instead of going around in circles with your god-damn love problems. That's all we do, you know, when we talk about Becky, just go around and around in circles. Well I'm fucking fed up with your goddamn love circles."

"So," I said, chastened, "what do you want to talk about?"

"Me!" yelled Lorca.

"I don't really have time to talk about you, Benny. I've got to make up my mind soon. I'm down to my last sliver."

"Sliver?"

"My last five years," I said. "You know, Hoffman's Pie of Life?"

"I hate Hoffman's Pie of Life. Pie of *Shit* is what it is."

"I hate it too. I wonder why I keep drawing it. All it does is make me depressed."

"*More* depressed," muttered Lorca.

"It keeps reminding me how fate has left me."

"Yeah? How *has* fate left you?"

"Divorced and alone in my quasi-golden years."

"Don't pawn that crap off on me," said Lorca, gently lifting his side and farting.

"What crap?"

"That alone crap."

"Yeah? Well, who the hell do I have?"

"Who do you have? Let's see, you have your mother and father . . ."

"My mother and father are dead."

"Your mother too? I didn't know that. When did she die?"

"Seven years ago."

"Yeah? Okay, okay. So then how about your sister and brother-in-law, what the hell's their names? You still have *them*, don't you?"

"I rarely see Phoebe and Herman."

"Is that my fault? You blaming me for that? Okay, who else do you have? You have your driver Tyrone and your secretary Mrs. Plotz."

"Tyrell and Mrs. Poltz, and they're *employees*, for Christ's sake."

"I know *that*," said Lorca, peeved.

"What I'm talking about," I said, "is not having a loving wife, or children, or grandchildren. That's who I expected to spend my quasi-golden years with, not with my driver and my secretary."

"The hell with the golden years, quasi or otherwise. Besides, you're only seventy . . ."

"Not yet."

". . . and I'm seventy-two. In eight years I'll be *eighty*, for Christ's sake!"

"You'll never make it," I mumbled.

"I heard that. Thanks a lot." Lorca rolled on his side tugging his sheet with him, presenting me once more with his exposed ass. It still wasn't a scrumptious sight.

"You've got to help me figure out what to do, Ben."

"Figure it out yourself."

"Hey Benny, did you hear the one about the dumb blonde who comes to a river? She wants to cross it but doesn't know how. And then she sees this blond woman across the river, so she yells to her, 'How do I get to the other side?' and the other blonde yells back, 'You *are* on the other side!'"

"Ha. Ha. Ho. Ho. Ho. That's a good one. Oh. Oh," moaned Lorca. "Oh God, oh Jesus, it hurts. Ha. Ha. THAT'S A DIRTY FUCKING TRICK, MAKING ME LAUGH WHEN YOU KNOW IT'S GOING TO HURT, YOU MOTHERHUMPING COCK-SUCKER! WHY'D YOU DO THAT?"

"You were beginning to annoy me," I replied.

"Do you need anything, Mr. Lorca?" asked a nurse crossly, appearing like magic in Lorca's doorway. She was an extremely large nurse and super muscular for a woman her age, which was probably about fifty. The nurse, her face as starched as her uniform, had an extremely commanding voice. She stood with her hands on her hips, oozing an I-don't-take-shit-from-anyone attitude. She cleared her throat and said again, "Do you *need* anything Mr. Lorca?"

Lorca lifted his head up and turned toward the door. "No, thank you," he said meekly, a befuddled expression on his face.

"Then I would appreciate it if you would kindly keep your voice down. Others along the hall can hear your lewd outbursts." The nurse glared at Lorca, did an about-face and left the doorway.

"Cunt," whispered Lorca, laying the back of his head down on his pillow.

"I didn't give three shits about turning forty or fifty, or even sixty, Benny," I said, attempting to change the subject, "but seventy's got me spooked."

"*The days of our age are threescore years and ten; and though men may be so strong that they come to fourscore years: yet it is their strength then but labor and sorrow; so soon passeth it away, and we are gone,"* bawled Lorca in his finest thespian voice. *"Much Ado About Nothing,* my boy."

"I've never been sure whether it was threescore or fourscore."

"What difference does it make?" said Lorca staring at the ceiling. "They're calling our class, Chuck."

"Arnold Hoffman just said the same thing."

Lorca didn't move his head, just his eyes rolled toward me. *"What,* pray tell, did the putz Hoffman say?"

"Arnie left me a telephone message last night. In the message he said, 'They're calling our class, Chuck.' "

"Fuck Hoffman. What does *he* know?"

"I'm all messed up, Benny."

"Aren't we all."

"I'd give anything not to feel this way. I'd just like a little peace of mind."

"You mean a little piece of ass, don't you?" said Lorca giggling, pushing the index finger of his right hand in and out of a hole he made with the thumb and forefinger of his left hand.

"That's not funny."

"I thought it was," mused Benjamin playing with the remains of his bagel and cream cheese. When he finished, Lorca bunched up the crinkled sheet of Reynolds Wrap with its smears of cream cheese and bagel crumbs on it, jammed the wad into his empty paper coffee cup, and handed the cup to me.

I tossed it into a wastebasket across the room.

"Nice shot," said Lorca agreeably.

"Thanks. I really like Becky a lot, Ben."

"You want to know what the bottom line is?" said Lorca, farting. "The bottom line is, you're too old for her. That's what's causing you two to fuss. She can't stand herself for falling in love with an old *putz* like you."

203

"I don't know about that," I said softly.

"'I'm too old for her,'" orated Lorca, "'but because of my immaturity I have a boyish charm. Woody Allen. Sometimes that sick fuck is actually funny'."

"Yeah. I like Woody Allen."

"I'm telling you, Barris, you're too old for her."

(Maybe he was right. Maybe I was too old for Becky Ballard.) "Hey Benny, I have to go. So tell me, what's your last words on the subject?"

"Last words?! You ask me for my last words?! I'm heading for the fucking operating room and you have the unmitigated gall to talk about last words?? Jesus H. Christ, you crazy or something? You know how superstitious I am. Jesus H. Christ. Use *advice* for Christ's sake. Say, 'What's your *advice*,' would you please?"

"Okay, what's your *advice*?"

"You want my advice? Okay, schmuck, here's my advice: Don't let her get away."

CHAPTER THIRTY-SIX

Two days later at noon I walked up to the hot dog stand on the corner of Sixty-Eighth Street and Park Avenue. I ordered a doggie with mustard. His dogs and pretzels were world-class. There was always a line for the stuff: cabbies, private-school students, construction workers, CEOs, truck drivers, homeless people. A good hot dog leveled all classes.

I stood in line and paid for my dog, grabbed a few napkins, and walked around the corner. I bit off one end of the hot dog, then the other (my favorite parts), tucked the *International Herald Tribune* under my left arm and leaned against the building's Sixty-Eighth Street side. I concentrated on eating the rest of the hot dog as slowly as possible. This is never an easy task for me. I usually wolf down a hot dog in maybe a minute and a half. I noticed after I finished eating the dog, which was about a minute and a half later, that I had dripped a small blotch of mustard on my windbreaker. I wiped the blotch off with a paper napkin and tossed the napkin toward the wired trash receptacle standing on the corner maybe twenty feet away. It was a long throw, so I really aimed.

I missed.

I returned to leaning against the building. I held my news-paper up so someone could see it was the *International Herald*

Tribune. I made out I was reading, but I wasn't. I was thinking how, at age seventy (almost), I was *still* hanging around street corners waiting for some jerk-off from the Central Intelligence Agency to arrive and tell me how, with very little effort, I could get myself killed.

When will it end?

And it was such a nice day, too.

A warm breeze was blowing sweet gusts of fresh air down Park Avenue forcing young school girls to hold their short plaid skirts down and elderly women to grasp their little hats. A dog walker excused himself as he came by with the big guys: the Labs, goldens, rotties, and setters. He was followed by his partner with the little guys: the terriers, spaniels, cockers, Boston Bulls, and Jack Russells. All of that to the music of tree branches brushing new leaves against each other. It truly was great to be alive. I wanted to keep it that way.

"Mr. Sixkiller?"

The sound of my code name woke me from my reverie with a start. "That's me."

"Barclay Robb," said a tall, distinguished-looking gentleman I immediately despised. It was the way Barclay Robb said "Barclay Robb" that made me dislike him so. If not despised or disliked, then at the very least wary. Very wary.

Barclay Robb was in his early sixties and wore his pure white hair parted in the center, causing two fluffy wings to flow backwards from his forehead. He dressed in a gray banker's three-piece summer suit, dark blue dress shirt, and bright yellow tie. He held a mahogany cane with a curved sterling silver handle. (There had to be a long, thin, sharp sword inside the cane. There just had to be.) I was sure by Robb's expression that he wasn't fond of me either. He said, "Get your things in order."

(The man gets right to the point.) "What things?"

"You know what things. Passport, shots . . ."

"Shots?" I asked.

"Cholera, yellow fever, smallpox, hepatitis, tetanus, polio . . ."

"Where am I going that requires such an extensive assortment of shots?" I asked, quickly adding, "That is, if I decide to go."

"Middle East," answered Barclay Robb.

"I've never had to take cholera, smallpox, or yellow fever shots for the Middle East before."

"Were you ever sent on an assignment to the Middle East?"

"I've been there."

"On assignment?"

"No."

"I didn't think so. In any case, Sixkiller, it's good to have those shots," said Robb, smiling. He had an evil smile. I didn't know which smile was worse, his or The Duck's. "And Sixkiller, as to whether you do or do not decide to go, I'm sorry to say that the decision is not yours." He didn't sound the least bit sorry. "You will go whenever and wherever summoned. I've also been instructed to pass on to you this message: 'You owe us'." He smiled that fucking smile again. No doubt about it, the smile was evil.

I straightened up to my full five feet six and a half inches, pulled back my shoulders and said, "That's the second time this week I've heard that *you owe us* crap, Robb. Perhaps you can explain to me the meaning of 'you owe us.'"

"I'll be glad to, Sixkiller. There are four basic reasons. The Company believes that you are in debt to us in some form or other. Hence the term, *'owe us'*. Reason number one goes way back to July of 1979. Your fiasco in Canada and the East German Spy."

"For Christ's sake, Robb . . ."

"You failed in your mission."

"I know I failed, Robb, but I was tired, beat, done in . . ."

"Be that as it may, that was your first transgression."

(Transgression! Give me a fucking break.)

"Reason number two took place in November of 1995, when you went to Cuba. I believe that you were sent there to eliminate a Haitian who was spying for Iraq."

"Yeah, yeah, the Haitian. Another one-in-a-million snafu."

"Seems, Sixkiller, you suffer from an abundance of one-in-a-million snafus. The Haitian, a Cuban/Soviet spy, was making his way from Haiti to Miami Beach, but had the misfortune to be scooped up by the Coast Guard during a boat raid. God knows what he intended to do when he got to Miami Beach. Remember the episode, Mr. Sixkiller?"

I nodded.

"Your target was incarcerated in a U.S. holding camp at our Guantanamo Naval Base there."

"More like a concentration camp, if you ask me."

"It is my understanding that you traveled to Cuba to eliminate him, make it look like a prison fight, I believe, something like that. In any case, it didn't matter how you accomplished the mission as long as you did. You failed and returned home."

"He escaped, for Christ's sake. He knew I was there. When the guards opened the gates to let a CNN crew into the camp, the guy took off. He must have been tipped, or it was just bad luck for me."

"The Director doesn't excuse bad luck."

"Yeah, well . . ."

"And where exactly could he have taken off to?"

"If you had ever been to Guantanamo, Mr. Robb, if you were standing outside that gate of the prison compound, you would have been able to see quite clearly where he went. The simple answer is Cuba. That's where he went."

"Is that right?"

"Yeah, Cuba."

"If I remember the terrain correctly, Sixkiller," said Robb, reveling in the knowledge that he had been to the Guan tanamo Naval Base, too, "in order for the target to get off U.S. territory and into Cuba, he would have had to climb down a jagged cliff, swim across a narrow but dangerous strait of water with deadly currents, and then climb up an equally jagged cliff on the other side of the strait. If he got that far without being picked off by U.S. sharpshooters, or if he wasn't killed by falling off either cliff, or drowned swimming across the treacherous strait, he would have been out of U.S. territory and into Cuban territory and most likely captured by a Cuban patrol and returned, if he wasn't bitten by a poisonous snake first."

"But he would be free."

"If he got to Havana or some large city before being apprehended."

"Yeah, but free," I repeated.

Robb chortled pleasantly to himself. "And you're telling me that's what the target did? Managed to conquer all those hurdles and get away?"

"That's exactly what the target did. I watched him do it."

"Whatever," sniffed Barclay Robb, dismissing the matter by slowly closing then opening his eyes. "Bottom line is, you did not complete your mission. Once again you returned home a failure. That was two."

"How was I able to complete a mission if . . ."

"The third infraction . . ."

"Oh, now it's an infraction. What happened to transgression?"

". . . the third infraction was when you were sent to Gaza in December of 1995. You were posing as a stringer-photographer for the Associated Press, I believe. You remember that assignment, I'm sure."

"Yes, I remember."

"You remember that you were unsuccessful again in your efforts to eliminate a target. This time a Palestinian. Once again you came home a failure."

"The Palestinian was a nice guy. I got to spend a little time with him and his family. He had great kids and a wonderful wife. Everybody loved him and . . ."

"Obviously, the decency of the target is not for you to evaluate," declared Barclay Robb harshly, "nor is it expected to encroach in any way on his or her elimination. You also know as well as I do that in our organization our failures are public and our successes are secret."

"What the hell's that supposed to mean?"

"The D.O. did not take kindly to your dereliction of duty in Gaza. You embarrassed him. Every major clandestine service in the world heard about your Gaza fiasco." Barclay Robb brushed a speck of lint off the front of his suit jacket. Not taking his eyes off his brushing, Robb said, "I might add, neither did I take kindly to your dereliction, either."

"Neither did you? Who the hell are you, Robb? What's your title? Are you my Case Officer? My boss? What?"

"I am none of the above," he hissed angrily." In the new set-up, Case Officers deal completely with foreign U.S. agents, not agents based in the States. Case Officers report to the assistant D.O. and on occasion to the D.O. himself. You are not an agent, Sixkiller. You are a paid assassin. None of the above applies to you."

"What does? Who do paid assassins report to?"

"Actually, we do not have any hired assassins. Not any more. There are none on our records."

"None on your records? What am I, a nonperson? Here, touch me. I promise you, I exist."

Barclay Robb exhaled his annoyance. "The fact that paid

assassins are not carried on our records does not mean they do not exist. Am I going too fast for you, Sixkiller?" Mr. Robb didn't wait for an answer. "You are a relic of the Cold War, Sixkiller, a prehistoric creature. I and a few others are in charge of those of you who remain active."

"You mean those of us who remain alive. So how did they hear? How did every major clandestine service in the world hear about my Gaza fiasco, as you put it?"

"Because of the damage your beloved target caused the Mideast peace process."

"What damage?" I muttered softly.

"The Palestinian gentleman you befriended and subsequently choose *not* to exterminate was a terrorist, a leader of Hamas. He masterminded the bombing of two buses in Jerusalem and one in Tel Aviv that killed a great number of Israeli fathers who were also nice guys and good family men, and many nice Israeli mothers and nice Israeli children."

"He was an enemy of Israel, not America," I said lamely, looking for a rock to slide under.

"How do you know he wasn't an enemy of America? Did he tell you where his next targets were going to be? Did he mention New York? Philadelphia? Los Angeles? Did he speak of smallpox in those cities? Anthrax in those cities? God knows what diseases in their reservoirs. Did your friend in Gaza tip you off to any of those secrets? Didn't he let you in on any of his plans? He didn't? Then what good was your new friendship? Think of all the lives you would have saved, Sixkiller, if you had eliminated that one Palestinian *before* he masterminded the blowing up of those buses. So, Sixkiller, in the future, refrain from your personal evaluation of terrorists and your goddamn conclusions as to whether or not they should be eliminated."

"Okay, okay," I said, duly chastised.

Neither one of us spoke for a bit. Robb switched his briefcase to his other hand, attempting to curtail his anger as he did. I watched a pigeon pecking at something on the pavement.

"So," I said with false cheer, an obvious glutton for punishment, "what's the fourth reason, or infraction, or whatever the fuck you're calling them now?"

"Recall if you will," said Robb, still quietly infuriated, "the afternoon of your marriage to Penny Pacino. In November of 1980, I believe. At the Beverly Hills Hotel in Beverly Hills, California, correct?"

"Correct."

"Nineteen years ago?" he asked, knowing full well it was.

"More or less," I answered.

"Do you remember that afternoon? I mean remember it *clearly*? You and Penny Pacino had just been married. The two of you were leaving your post-wedding party and walking out of the hotel through the main entrance. You were heading for your waiting limousine, I believe. There was a sizeable crowd of well-wishers lining both sides of the red carpet. The well-wishers were throwing confetti and rice. And then, according to *your* report, halfway down the runway to your limousine you saw something rather startling, did you not?"

I did. Halfway down the runway I saw the gun. A Walther PBK, the perfect assassin's weapon. It dangled from a man's hand. I saw a gold ring on the little finger of the hand holding the gun. I remember the ring clearly. I remember the little finger too. It was sticking straight out as if the man's hand was holding a tea cup and not an automatic.

"There was a contract on your life that day," said Barclay Robb, "to be consummated sometime during the afternoon of your wedding. We heard about it down at Langley early that morning."

"You were with the CIA back then?"

Ignoring my question, Robb continued, "It was my understanding that if the assassin had missed the opportunity to exterminate you at the wedding, he planned to catch up with you later that day or night and finish the job. In other words, the Soviet assassin was instructed not to leave Los Angeles until you were dead. We extracted the Russian from the crowd of well-wishers just as you passed him. We took him away and eliminated him."

"How do you know all this? I mean, how do you know that's what the Russian was going to do?"

"He told us," said Barclay Robb.

"He *told* you?"

"Yes, the assassin told us."

"How do you know that?"

"I interrogated him."

"*You* did!" I had to think about that for a few seconds. "So where is he now?"

"He's dead. I shot him."

I was instantly shocked.

And unexpectedly impressed.

"After you shot the shooter," I asked, somewhat humbled, "why didn't the Russians send in another guy to get me? Certainly they had a team in place."

"Let me see if I can explain this to you," said Robb as if I were some kind of dunce.

"Give it a whirl," I snapped back all smart-alecky. Couldn't seem to like this guy if I tried.

Barclay Robb, impatient and turning surly, began. "The initial effort to take you out on your wedding day was in retribution for your successful elimination of the two Russian agents Kirby and Slasky in Paris. The would-be assassin at the Beverly Hills Hotel was Major Valerie Kasilov. George Slasky was reputed to be Kasilov's best friend. Kasilov disliked you intensely. You killed his best friend. Major Kasilov was old and past his usefulness to the KGB. That's probably why the Russians let him try. When he failed, the Russians decided that any further attempt on your life was basically a waste of time. Certainly not worth the life of a *good* assassin. The truth is, Mr. Sixkiller, you simply weren't worth it."

"I guess I owe you some sort of thanks."

Barclay Robb brushed another speck of something from the right shoulder of his suit coat with his left hand to show his disdain for any expressions of gratitude from me. I was right from the get-go. Robb detested me. "Your four botched assignments and the fact that the Agency saved your life is why you owe us."

"Yeah, well—"

"And I didn't even count your Agular assignment," said Robb. "The first one."

"Okay, what's next?" I asked, straining for a touch of cockiness.

"Your assignment's being put together as we speak. We'll keep you informed."

I muttered thanks and started to leave, stopped, and said, "Mr. Robb, may I ask you a couple of questions?"

Robb nodded.

"If I was such a fuck-up, why are you sending me on another assignment? Am I expendable? Like Major Kasilov?"

"No, we don't think you are expendable. Quite the opposite, Sixkiller. This is a tough assignment. We all believe that when you're at the top of your game, you're the best. We think you can be at the top of your game when you have to. That's why we are sending you on this mission."

"And what if I don't feel like going? What if I decide to hang up my Beretta and silencer this afternoon?"

Barclay Robb left me standing where I was and walked to

the hot dog stand. He bought a hot dog for himself, didn't even ask me if I wanted one, waited until the vendor put mustard on it, wrapped the dog in a napkin, then walked back to me. He started to take a bite of his hot dog, stopped, and said, "That, Mr. Sixkiller, would be a *deadly* mistake."

"Either way you look at it, Mr. Robb, it's a deadly mistake." I started to leave, then stopped again, turned around, and said, "You lie, Robb."

He chewed a bite of dog, swallowed, and said, "I lie?"

"Yes, you lie. I *am* expendable."

CHAPTER THIRTY-SEVEN

I t was early evening on Saturday, April 10, 1999.

I would be seventy in less than two months.

My town car pulled up to the Krispy Kreme doughnut shop on Third Avenue between Eighty-Third and Eighty-Fourth Streets. The sign in the window wasn't flashing. I was deeply disturbed by this. When the neon Krispy Kreme sign in the window flashed HOT DOUGHNUTS, doughnuts were available just out of the fryer. I loved the whipped cream-filled doughnuts best. The whipped cream ones were good on the natch but when they were hot they were remarkable. The hot ones literally melted in your mouth. They become a delicious glop of molten sugar and dough.

"Goddamn it," I growled, "the sign's not flashing hot doughnuts."

"It's too early," explained my driver, Tyrell Massella, while double-parking in front of the store. "It's only six o'clock. The hot ones don't come out till ten. Ten to midnight. You know that, Mr. Barris."

When I walked up to the counter, the first thing Laverne, the Krispy Kreme girl, said was, "I can't get used to that beard, Chuckie Baby."

"It's not a beard, Laverne. I just haven't shaved for a few days. You sure you don't have any hot ones?"

"You don't see the hot sign flashing, do you? It's only six o'clock. You know the rules, Chuckie Baby. Let me get you your cream-filled. And listen to me . . ."

"What?"

"Lose the beard."

"She's right," said my driver.

"What?" I wasn't listening to Tyrell. I was distracted by the wonderful smell of the doughnut shop. That and new-car smell are my favorites. Though I guess you can't ignore the smell of a new baby's neck, either. That's a good one, too. "What did you say, Tyrell?"

"I said Laverne's right. Lose the beard."

"It's not a beard."

"Then what is it?"

"I forgot to shave."

"It makes you look older, and older is not what you want to look," Tyrell said.

"It's not going to be a beard."

At the time of this conversation Tyrell Massella had been my driver for a ton of years. I love him and his family. Tyrell's father, Tony Massella, was white and Catholic. He was a huge muscular Sicilian who worked as a chef in a black restaurant in Harlem called Sugar's Afro-Italian Café. The restaurant specialized in fried chicken lasagna. That's where Tony met his wife Bernice. One night at the Massella dinner table, Tony died of a massive heart attack. His head fell into his plate of pasta mixed with shrimp and swordfish.

"If he had a choice of a way to go," said Bernice, "that would be it."

Me, I'd prefer falling into a plate of two fried eggs and a slice of country ham or a batch of fried chicken gizzards, but who cares what I'd like to fall into.

Tyrell's mother, Bernice Massella, is rather hefty and very

black. She used to be a waitress at Sugar's. After Tony died she quit the Afro-Italian Café. Now she spends most of her time singing in the Amsterdam Baptist Church Choir on One-Hundred and Thirty-Third Street and Amsterdam Avenue.

Tyrell's gigantic like his father and sort of beige colored because of his parents. A big Derek Jeter. He's an award-winning cook and a minor league opera singer. He used to be a great athlete, too. Almost played professional football for the Pittsburgh Steelers back in the one-for-the-thumb days. An injury he never speaks of put him out of pro ball. He drove a garbage truck instead.

Eventually Tyrell worked as a chauffeur/bodyguard for mafioso biggie John Gotti. (Tyrell likes to think he's a good-looking, tan version of Gotti.) Tyrell also sang with an amateur opera company and won blue ribbons for his lasagna. It was always a toss-up whether Tyrell Massella was a better driver or a better cook. As far as I'm concerned, his Italian dishes are world-class. Not only is his lasagna the best but so are his sausages and meat balls, and his cannelloni and chocolate cake. They're all out of this world. I don't think there's a chef in Italy that comes close to my driver, Tyrell Massella, Renaissance man himself when he's at his culinary best. Ironically, what Tyrell enjoys eating most is a balongna sandwich on white Wonder Bread with mayonnaise, washed down with a can of RC Cola. His favorite dessert, to the best of my knowledge, is a Goo-Goo Cluster.

Tyrell's married to a woman named Tulip. Tulip Massella resembles Tyrell's father in that she's very white. But that's where the resemblance ends. Tulip Massella is petite and very Italian. On Sundays, Tyrell and Tulip ride matching Harleys. Well, not exactly matching. Tulip's bike is a smaller version of Tyrell's. They also have matching multicolored dragon tattoos dedicated to each other on their left arms. The tattoos run from shoulder to elbow. Tyrell's dragon on his huge arm looks like the monster it's supposed to be. Tulip's dragon on her skinny little arm looks like an angry puppy dog.

The way Tyrell and I got together was kind of strange. I had done some work for John Gotti in the past. (You'd be surprised how often the Mafia and the CIA work together.) Gotti saw the instant affection Tyrell and I had for each other, so The Don said, "He's yours." Not that Tyrell was an indentured servant or anything like that. Tyrell didn't have to come. He could have stayed with Gotti. But Tyrell and I had this sort of intuition thing going. We knew we'd be great running buddies and good friends. So Tyrell came to work for me and the rest is, as they say, history.

Back to that drizzly April evening in the Krispy Kreme store.

Tyrell and I were standing at the counter when he said to me, "The beard changes your face, Mr. Barris. Makes you look like a real dickhead, which you are obviously not. Know what I'm sayin'?"

"It's pathetic."

"I wouldn't go *that* far," said Tyrell. "The beard's not 'zactly pathetic, jes' not your thing."

"I'm not talking about the beard, Tyrell. What I meant was, it's pathetic that Laverne doesn't even have to ask me what I want. She *knows* what I want. When a Krispy Kreme employee doesn't even have to ask what a customer wants, that's pathetic."

"Why, Mr. Barris? Why's that pathetic?"

Tyrell Massella started working for me twenty-seven years ago. He'll be fifty-five soon and refuses to call me anything but Mr. Barris. Sometimes Snakeman. But never Chuck. For the life of him, the man can't get his tongue around the word Chuck.

"I'll tell you why Laverne's knowing what I like is so pathetic, Tyrell. It's pathetic because it means this doughnut shop has become an integral part of my life. A man of my age and means should be having dinner at home every night with a cook and butler. But no, I hang out here with Laverne at a Krispy Kreme shop."

"But you hate cooks and butlers," said my driver, "and you like Laverne and hangin' around here."

I paid for the doughnuts and coffees.

We found a table for two.

"The same at Ray's Pizza," I said to Tyrell, wiping the dirty table top with a paper napkin. "The guy at Ray's Pizza, what's his name . . ."

"Tommy."

"Yeah, Tommy, he knows I take a little dressing with my salad to go. Not a lot, just a little. I don't even have to ask."

"So?"

"So? So that's really lame, Tyrell."

I went to the counter to find more paper napkins, pulled a handful out of the metal dispenser, and returned to the table. I wiped the top again and sat down.

"And another thing," I said. "I can't seem to make a decision anymore. Lost the knack. Used to be good at it. Like when I decided to sell my company, I sold it. Bam! Just like that! Remember? But not anymore. Now for some reason or other, I can't decide dick."

"If you excuse me for sayin' it, but you never *could* decide dick. Not the little things. Could always decide them big things but never them little things. What kind of decision can't you make now? Give me a 'zample."

"I can't make up my mind whether to marry Becky or—"

"Or what?"

"Or, I don't know what. I'm really confused. I mean, where am I going to find someone as beautiful as Becky who's . . ."

". . . I know, I know," said Tyrell, "who's thirty years younger and all that other stuff."

"I'm boring everybody to death with my nutcase neurotic indecision over Becky, I know, but . . ."

"But what?"

"But where am I going to find another woman that sick?"

"Sick?"

"Yes, sick. Don't you think she's got to be sick to find an old fuck like me attractive?"

"Well, come to think of it, maybe the woman's a *little* sick." Silence.

"No, but let me ax you somethin'."

"Ax away, Tyrell."

"You ever think of datin' slightly older women, say in their fifties?"

"Baggage," I snapped.

"Baggage?"

"Older women, women fifty and over, all have baggage. Ex-husbands, married kids, snot-nosed grandchildren. Baggage."

My driver moaned, exasperated. "Do you love Becky?" he asked, suddenly all serious and Sunday-pulpit looking. "I mean *really* love her?"

"I'm crazy about her. I worship they ground she walks on."

"But do you *love* her?"

I added another packet of sugar to my coffee. "I like her," I said, stirring. "We haven't put in enough time together for me to love her yet. But, like I said, I like her. *A lot.*"

"I always thought you believed in love at first sight."

"Never. Smitten at first sight, yes. Infatuated at first sight, yes. Even lust at first sight. Most definitely yes. But love at first sight? Never. You've got to put in time to fall in love with someone. You know, go through some ordeals, bond, that kinda shit. You I love, but we've been together for a long time. And we've been through some heavy-duty stuff, too."

"But you told me the night you met Becky, 'It was love at first sight?' Didn't you say that to me that night?"

"I said that?"

"Yeah, you said that."

I shook my head. "I don't believe I did."

We concentrated on our doughnuts for a few minutes.

And then Tyrell said, "Can I ax you somethin' else?"

"What, for Christ's sake?"

"Somethin' botherin' you?"

"No. Nothing's bothering me."

"*Bulllllshit!*" said my driver. "Come on, you can tell me."

I took a deep breath and let it out. "I saw a guy from the CIA today at noon."

"No shit!"

I nodded.

"What'd he want?"

"They want me to do a job."

"What!" yelled my driver, sitting straight up in his chair.

I shrugged. "Yeah, they want me to go somewhere."

"You don't *do* that stuff anymore, Mr. Barris."

I shrugged again.

"Jesus, don't they know you don't do that stuff anymore? Don't they know you ain't done that shit for . . . for . . ."

"Maybe twenty years."

"Not really," said my driver, the only human being in the entire world I ever confided in. I figured if someone came looking for Tyrell, he'd be able to take care of himself. "You forgettin' them trips you took to Canada . . . an' Gaza . . . an' Cuba . . . an, what was the other place? Four, five years ago? What *was* that other place, the last place you went to?"

"Haiti."

"Tha's right, Haiti, when you went in wiff the muthafuckin' Eighty-Second Airborne on invasion day."

"Yeah, yeah. But those were quickies."

"Mexico City?" said Tyrell. "How 'bout Mexico City. Twice!"

"Long time ago. Before we even knew each other."

"Those other jobs weren't so long ago. Canada and them places," said Tyrell. "Canada was just a few years ago. You never told me about that Canada job. How come you never told me about that one?"

"The Canadian job was embarrassing."

"To who?"

"To me."

"Why?" asked Tyrell.

"Because, for the first time, I was scared."

CHAPTER THIRTY-EIGHT

I n 1997, I flew into Burlington, Vermont, rented a car, and drove north to North Darby. The highlight of the ride was a Country & Western song I heard on the car radio called "If I Had a Brand New Liver."

> *If I had a brand new liver*
> *I could keep drinkin' my sorrows away.*

North Darby was a small, depressing mill town a few miles from the Canadian border. Even the grass was gray. Over the years the mill's main business, whatever it was, evaporated and the young people of North Darby moved away. By the time I got there, North Darby was populated with the elderly and the infirm.

Just out of town, to the north of North Darby, was a sorry excuse of a river whose name I either don't remember or never knew. It might have been a roaring waterway decades ago, but in 1997 it was mostly just a trickle. The trickle separated the United States and Canada. A battered old bridge connected the two countries, North Darby on the U.S. side and a town called Beebe on the Canadian side. There wasn't any barrier on either end of the bridge. Nothing. Not even stop signs. Terrorists, drug pushers, deserting servicemen, illegal arms traders, errant husbands, wayward teenagers, and God knows who else crossed that small dilapidated bridge from one country to the other every week of the year for as long as anyone could remember. On that day in July, I started to cross that bridge to look for an East German terrorist not too far away.

The terrorist, an alleged ex-Braader Meinhof Gang member, left Germany for Canada several years ago. He was traced to Beebe. I was told that the German had been responsible for helping blow up a U.S. consulate building in Munich in 1994. He and two others took twenty-four hostages and promised to kill one an hour unless ten Palestinian terrorists waiting to stand trial in Berlin were released from a Kraut prison. The German government thought the terrorists in the U.S. consulate were bluffing. One of the hostages was a young American woman who had come to the consulate to get a visa. The American woman was Jewish. When the first hour had passed, one of the terrorists dragged the American woman outside onto the embassy's balcony so that everyone could see, and shot her in the back of the head. The shooter wore a ski mask. Only his eyes were visible. The Germans caved in, freed the Palestinians, and provided a plane to fly the three terrorists to safety. The man hiding in Canada was supposed to have been the terrorist that killed the young American woman. I was told he was positive that he was ancient history. Figured international law enforcement agencies had forgotten all about him. In a month or so he planned to return to Europe and cause new problems.

I was glad to get the assignment. I hated that piece of dung hiding out in Beebe. Shooting the woman the way he did made my skin crawl. Unfortunately, it also reminded me of the women I killed. I guess there's not much difference between what the terrorist did to that woman on the balcony and what

I do. Still, the women I killed were killers themselves. *That* makes a difference, doesn't it?

Other than the fact that the East German terrorist hiding out in Canada was a cold-blooded murderer, I knew very little about him. I had no idea what name he was going by or even what he looked like. I was told I would find everything I needed to know on the other side of the disintegrating bridge. A packet of information would be in a rain-faded green metal mailbox on a slanted wooden pole exactly one mile from town on the main road to Beebe. The mailbox was old. It hadn't been used in years, other than as a possible dead-drop for someone else. The barely visible house number on the box was supposed to be 3702.

I arrived in North Darby in a foul mood. I was fed up with killing people for the CIA. This assignment didn't help matters. I began to think about things I never used to think about before, like what right did I have to take another human being's life? Lately I couldn't sleep nights without having nightmares. But, luckily, I forget them immediately. Except one. I had a nightmare recently that I remembered with the clarity of a religious vision.

It was about me chasing a mysterious, demented Palestinian terrorist who was responsible for plotting the bombings of three Israeli grade schools. Twenty-two children, ages five to ten, had died. A vicious killer, this one. I couldn't wait to take him down. I went to the terrorist's address in Hebron and entered the dusty, mud-splattered house. No one was home. Then I heard a sound in the hall closet. It was obviously where the terrorist was hiding. I walked up to the closet door, pointed my Uzi at it, practically shot the door away, opened what was left of it, and stepped back. The dangerous terrorist I thought I had killed was actually a pretty blonde eight-year-old girl. She fell out of the closet onto the floor like an old umbrella.

God, I hated what I was doing.

And to think I could get killed in the process! I never used to think about getting killed. The thought rarely entered my mind. But that day in North-wherever-the-fuck-I-was, the thought entered my mind big time.

I realized I was getting punch-drunk. No, more like scared. Actually, terrified. I was about to walk across a broken-down bridge that traversed a leak they called a river into Canada to kill yet another enemy asshole for my country. If the asshole didn't kill me first. I decided I had had enough. It was time to get off the train.

Or was it?

Perhaps the best thing I could do would be to simply end it all. Jump off that godforsaken bridge. Put an end to my regret-filled existence once and for all. I looked over the bridge's side. The dry riverbed wasn't that far down. If I jumped I'd just break a leg or something stupid like that. Maybe that's why the thought entered my head. I knew if I jumped I wouldn't kill myself.

I decided not to jump.

I decided, instead, to go to church.

I would liked to have gone to a synagogue but the chances of finding one in a town like North-wherever-the-fuck-I-was, was slim to none. I found a Catholic church a few blocks from the bridge. The church—Little Saint Loretto—was small and made of red bricks. Inside was the usual musty smell of dirt-poor religion, the usual parishioner on her knees praying, the usual depressing darkness of an unlit house of worship, broken by the sprinkle of twinkling yellow candles on either side of the church. I took a thin wooden stick from a metal container and lit it, using one of the burning candles. I chose a candle of my own and put my flaming stick to its wick. When my candle was lit, I got down on my knees and prayed.

This is what I prayed.

I thanked God for sparing my life so far and beseeched Him to continue to do so. I thanked Him for finally making me smart enough to realize the futility of the life I had been living, at least the CIA part. I also thanked Him for trying to make me come to my senses and quit before I became severely injured, or worse. I promised God I'd make a deal with Him. For his continued protection and kindnesses, I would stop doing things He disliked, like killing people. I told God I was an atheist myself, but that if He *did* exist, I knew He wouldn't like me very much if I continued to go around taking other people's lives. Even if they were evil people. I felt sure He wouldn't like it. I mean, my assassinations were obviously encroaching on His territory.

I told God I really felt uneasy asking Him for favors—me not even being Catholic. But since I was right there in one of His branch offices, I'd only ask for one or two. I prayed that God would please let me know in some way which team to bet on in the up-and-coming World Series. You know, some kind of Epiphany, if that's what He called jolting answers that came out of the blue to sports questions. I tried to explain that I sure could use His help in the World Series, being that I was a hundred and twenty-five smackeroos in the hole with my bookie, the most I'd ever been down. Also, I asked if He could grant me the willpower to stop chewing unsweetened chewing gum. All that saccharin and imitation flavoring couldn't be good for you. Not if someone was chewing ten packs a day, like I was. One thing for sure. I'll bet old God never had too many requests like mine that year.

Anyway, sitting in that Catholic church in North Darby was comforting. Like I said, even though it wasn't my God, it was nice to pray to someone's God. I especially hoped this Catholic God was knowledgeable about baseball, bookies, and willpower. I wasn't sure if He was, but what the hell, it was worth a try. I stuffed some dollar bills into the prayer box and walked out of Little Saint Loretto Church.

I walked across the street and sat down on a bench in the town square. As I sat there, a foreboding filled my chest. I've had really lucky days, I thought to myself, days where I should have died and didn't. Maybe today's the day I *will* die. Maybe today is the time to get off the train.

I never did kill that East German terrorist.

I think I was afraid.

I went home instead.

CHAPTER *THIRTY-NINE*

Back to the Krispy Kreme doughnut shop.

"Wow," said Tyrell excitedly, "so you quit the CI-fucking-A!"

"Not really."

"Meanin' what?"

"Meaning I didn't keep my word to God, mainly because He didn't keep His word to me. He didn't send me any hints about the World Series, or help me stop chewing gum. I still chew ten packs a day. Anyway, it was all academic."

"Meanin' what?"

"Meaning the CIA didn't accept my letter of resignation."

"No?"

"No. It seems they don't cotton to quitting."

"So, like, what'd they say?"

"They basically said, you just keep working, sport, or you're a dead man."

"Tha's what they said?"

"Tha's what they said. More or less."

"Listen," said Tyrell, "to this day I don't know why you kept doin' what you did, makin' all them trips. You said you was finished with the goddamn CI-fuckin'-A back there in eighty-somethin' when you got back from Mexico City."

"Mexico City was in the late seventies, Tyrell. I didn't even know you then."

"Okay, when you got back from somethin' back there in the eighties, you said that. Way back then you said you was finished. An' I was glad 'cause you was one crazy muthafucka back then. I didn't think you was ever goin' to be straight again. And then jes' when I think you gettin' you act together—bam! You in Gaza. Know what I'm sayin'?"

"I know what you're saying. I got bored, Tyrell. So I went on a few little excursions. N.B.D."

"Okay, okay, no big deal, but you kept your finger in when you should have pulled it out. Know what I'm sayin'? Anyway, you're happier these days than I ever seen you. Specially with Becky an bein' away from all that CI-fuckin'-A shit like you been. I mean when you with Becks, you lookin' *good*. You lookin' *happy*. You *actin'* happy. Why you wanta go back now?"

"I just told you. I don't. It's them. *They* want me to go back. They say I owe them."

"Who says?"

"*They* do. The CIA does."

"Owe them what? What the fuck you owe?"

I didn't say anything.

"Well screw 'em," said my driver. "Jes' refuse to do anythin'. Jes' plain refuse."

"Didn't I just tell you I'm a dead man if I try to quit?" I took a deep breath and blew it away. "Shit, Tyrell, why don't you listen to what I'm saying once in a while?"

Tyrell looked away from my face and stared at the wall. He was sulking. I guess I hurt his feelings.

"Jesus, Tyrell, they'll kill me if I don't do what they want me to do. See, I'm not officially in the CIA. I'm what they call a freelance assassin. A hired gun. They don't have to obey company rules, especially when it comes to me. I'm not on their books. I don't exist. I've explained all of that to you before. Anyway, they . . ."

I jumped out of my chair.

My cellular phone was vibrating. The vibrations always scared the hell out of me. But cell phone rings scared me more, so I chose the vibrations. I grappled for the phone in my pocket, got it out, opened its lid, and pulled up its aerial.

"Hello? Hi, Becky! Uh-huh. Uh-huh. Uh-huh. Sure. Okay. You want to meet here at Krispy Kreme? I'm with Tyrell. Yeah, I'm at Krispy Kreme having a cup of coffee and a doughnut. I only had one. Honest. Only one. So far. Want to ask Tyrell? Okay where, then? Where? You're fading. Yes, that's better. Okay, Madison and Eighty-Sixth. When? Fifteen minutes? Great! What? So, if you have something important to discuss, we'll discuss it. I promise." I turned my head and shoulder away from Tyrell and mumbled, "I love you too." I turned around, closed the cellular telephone and put it back in my pocket.

"You don't have to be afraid or embarrassed to say words of endearment to Becks in front of me," said Tyrell. "You don't need to mumble those things."

"I wasn't mumbling . . ."

"*Bullllllshit* you weren't. Why you lie to me?"

We sat there thinking for a bit. I can always tell when Tyrell's thinking about something important by the expression on his face. And the way his brow furrows up. Finally, he spoke. "Listen, can I ax you somethin'?"

"Ax away."

"Why don't you get yourself a good, you know, marryin' agreement."

"You talking about a prenuptial agreement?"

"Yeah, right, one of them things and jes' marry the woman already. I mean a *really* good agreement. Get you lawyer Mort what's-his-name . . ."

"Mort Rosenblum."

"Right, an' make him get one of those marryin' agreements things up for you and then marry Becky. If it don't work out,

232

hell, get yourself a dee-vorce. No big fuckin' deal. Know what I'm sayin'?"

"I don't want any more dee-vorces in my life, Tyrell."

"Maybe you won't have to get a dee-vorce. Maybe the two of you will be happy as clams."

"I'm not sure."

"Why?"

"She gets angry at me a lot."

"Who don't."

"Over little things."

"You sure they little things?" asked my driver. "You sure you not drivin' Becks crazy an' thas' why she's gettin' angry at you? Seems like from what you tell me you drivin' that woman crazy."

"I'm not driving her crazy."

"How do you know? From what I can tell, Becky has two choices—hang in there or drop you ass. I predict she goin' to drop you ass. Know why?"

"Why?"

"'Cause Becks can't keep hangin' in there foever. She can't keep runnin' back and forth from Atlanta to New York fo' the rest of her life, tha's why. Sooner or later she's gonna get tired of all that. So's her company gonna get tired o' her takin' so many days off to come see you. Becky'll quit you for her own good before she goes belly-up fiii-nancially *and* eee-motion-ally. Besides, sooner or later she's gonna want to marry someone and settle down so she can quit travelin' and have a kid. Also, Becky loves you, an' . . ."

"You really think she loves me?"

"*Yeah*, she loves you, course she loves you, but the woman can't keep lovin' on someone forever without gettin' a little bit of honest-to-God commitment back. Know what I'm sayin'? If you don't make an honest woman out of Becks, you gonna drive her either back to Atlanta or to the loony bin, one or the other."

"You know something, you might be right about that."

"I *know* I'm right about that," insisted Tyrell.

We both sat quietly, thinking.

"On the other hand . . ." said Tyrell.

"On the other hand? On the other hand *what*?"

"On the other hand, how long you two been goin' together now?"

"Two years this August."

"Well then," said my driver, "if you *really* loved her, you would have married her by now."

"What are you saying, Tyrell?"

"What I'm sayin' is I think you should leave her." Tyrell straightened up in his chair and smiled.

"*Leave her*! You just told me to get an airtight prenuptial agreement and *marry* her."

"I changed my mind."

"You know something, Tyrell, you're some piece of work. You say one thing you're absolutely sure about, then the very next minute you say the opposite. And you're absolutely sure about that too! Some help you are. You say I drive Becky crazy? Well, you drive *me* crazy. Besides, I can't leave her."

"Why not."

"She makes me happy."

CHAPTER FORTY

I saw Becky Ballard from my car window.

She was standing on the southwest corner of Eighty-Sixth and Madison. She was wearing a light tan raincoat over a white T-shirt, jeans, and brown loafers. To protect her from the April drizzle, she held a child's yellow umbrella that had Babar the Elephant's picture on it. A Burberry rain hat sat on top of her head, barely covering her long red hair.

"Jesus," I said to Tyrell out of the side of my mouth, "she sure looks good."

"You ain't jes' bumpin' your gums."

Tyrell opened the door for me and I hit the ground running. I dashed across Madison Avenue, dodging cabs and cars like a toreador. I waved my arms trying to catch Becky's attention.

"Here I come!" I yelled, all smiles, feeling *good.* "Here I come, Becky!"

When I arrived, I gave her a big kiss on the mouth.

"Hi, darlin'," she said. "I missed you so much. I always do. It's downright pitiful. How were the doughnuts?"

"Good."

"Were there any *hot* doughnuts?"

"No. It was too early."

"I'm glad. It's just as well. I would have ruined my appetite.

Know what I'm in the mood for? I'm in the mood for a *good* hamburger. Let's go up to Jackson Hole. We can walk. It's only drizzling."

"We can walk and talk. You said you wanted to talk." I wondered why I reminded Becky about her wanting to talk to me. Nine out of ten times *wanting to talk* meant talking about marriage.

"I do," said Becky Ballard. "I do want to talk."

We strolled north toward the restaurant. It was at Ninety-First Street. Jackson Hole had great hamburgers and pancakes, depending who was cooking them.

The drizzle turned to a light rain. I took the umbrella from Becky and held it over her head.

Becky put her arm through mine. "Do I feel like a ten-pound pot roast hanging on your arm like this?" she asked softly, smiling. "You told me about a girl you once dated who always put her arm through yours and you said that time she did, said she felt like a ten-pound pot roast hanging there."

"You'll never feel like a ten-pound pot roast to me, Becky Ballard."

"I love you, Chuck."

"I love you, too," I lied. I liked Becky a lot, but when the subject started to veer toward love, I became confused.

"You look like such a *man* tonight," said Becky. "But lose the beard. Makes you look too sinister."

"I'm not growing a beard, Becky. I just haven't shaved for a few days."

"Promise me you'll shave it off."

"Okay. I promise."

"When?"

"Tonight."

Becky smiled. "Will you also promise to make love to me as soon as we get to your apartment?"

I nodded, a little excitedly I might add.

"Tell me. I want to hear you say it."

"I promise to make love to you."

"When?"

"Tonight, as soon as we get to my apartment." I realized I was more than a little excited.

"Cross your heart?"

"Cross my heart."

"Then cross it," she said.

I crossed my heart with my finger.

"Chuck, do you *really* love me?"

"I really do."

"How much?"

"Very much."

"Who? You love *who* very much?"

"You."

"So say my name."

"Becky."

"Say the whole damn thing."

"I love you very much, Becky." (Maybe I did.)

"There," she said, "isn't that better? Don't you like to hear your name when I tell you I love you? Isn't it better when I say I love you, *Chuck*?"

I smiled. "Yes, it's better."

Becky stopped me from walking any further and kissed me all over my face. I was always happy as a clam when Becky kissed me all over my face. And I loved the idea that we were going to have wild and woolly sex when we got back to my place. I took the umbrella from Becky, opened it, and began dancing on and off the curb up the street toward the corner of Eighty-Ninth and Madison Avenue. Twirling the umbrella over my head, I shouted, *"Singing in the rain, just singing in the rain . . ."*

"Did you think about me when I was gone, Chuck?" asked Becky, frowning, hurrying to catch up.

"Absolutely. I think about you all the time . . . *what a wonderful feeling, I'm happy again . . .*"

"Have you been thinking of a marriage date, honey? That's what I want to talk to you about. A date. I think the time has come for the two of us to set a date. Please stop singing."

". . . *laughing at clouds, goin' on by. Nothin' to fear, there's rain in my eye . . .*"

"We have to *talk*, Chuck," said Becky Ballard, walking then trotting then walking then trotting. "We really do. I can't keep up this commuting stuff much longer. Can't afford to, actually. I'm losing too much time at the office. Pretty soon I'm going to lose my job. The commute is affecting my work, too. It really is. Please stop singing and listen to me. It's important."

"So stop commuting," I said, "and stay in New York with me." I went back to singing and twirling the umbrella.

"And what do you suppose I'll use for money?" she asked.

"I don't understand."

"If I live with you, what will I use for money?"

"I'll support you."

"Sure you will," she said laughing, but not really laughing. "When you get tired of me and throw me out like you did last year, then what? I'd have to look for another job, and good jobs like mine are hard to find. I can't keep doing this forever, Chuck. It's not like when we started out and I was thirty-seven. I wasn't sure then if you would ever marry anyone, but I could wait. I had time. Now, it's different. I can't keep waiting. I was forty last month. Pretty soon I won't be able to get a job *or* have a baby. I'll be too old for everything. Look at me!" she said, taking hold of my chin and pulling my head around so she could look me in the eyes. "I'm serious!"

I nodded. Put a serious expression on my face.

Becky took the umbrella from my hand, closed it, pushed its wooden tip into my stomach, then gently forced me back against a storefront. "You used to ask me to marry you every other day. Now when I finally feel secure with you and want to get married, you keep stalling, Why is that, honey?"

I wondered why that was.

Becky said, "I know why. You don't have any intentions of marrying me, that's why. You don't, do you?"

The falling rain had made Madison Avenue glisten. Passing taxis and cars hissed when they drove by.

"You don't, do you?"

"I don't?"

"See?"

"See what?"

"Your non-answer is an answer. You couldn't say, 'Yes, I do. I have every intention of marrying you,' could you?"

"Come on, Becky. Lighten up."

"If you had your way," she said, angry, her green eyes flashing, "you'd want to be commitment-free and just make love every night, wouldn't you? Just fuck until your prostate blew a gasket. Sooner or later you'd send me back to Atlanta and that would be that. It would just be a matter of time, wouldn't it?" Becky handed me the umbrella. She placed both hands on her temples, closed her eyes, and shook her head like someone who just heard that a loved one had died.

That's when I started wondering how our different moods, both Becky's and mine, could change so quickly. A few minutes ago we were looking so forward to seeing each other and now we were mad. It was probably my fault. Like Tyrell said, I drove her nuts.

"I should have known," Becky said to herself, getting all teary, talking to the wet sky. "I should never have come back. Why do I keep coming back? Why do I keep falling for his bullshit?" Becky started crying. "I can't *stand* this anymore. Why are you *doing* this to me?"

"I was only singing," I said in a small voice.

Becky uttered I don't know what—an enormous wail, I guess—and said, "What's missing from our relationship that makes you keep hurting me so? What am I doing that's tormenting you? All I do is love you more than life itself. How bad is that? You seem to enjoy my loving you. You seem happy when you're with me. So tell me, what am I doing wrong?"

A small crowd had gathered. They seemed equally perplexed. They wanted to know the answer to Becky's question, too.

"Tell me," wailed Becky, "tell me and I'll try to fix it. Tell me before we lose each other."

"Something's missing," I said quietly, ill at ease, my stomach all queasy.

"*Something's missing from what?*" asked Becky, flabbergasted.

"From our relationship."

"Oh, really?" said Becky. "Like what?"

"Like *that!*" I shouted, pointing across the street.

Becky turned to look.

So did the crowd of pedestrians.

CHAPTER *FORTY-ONE*

The rain hadstopped. The city was quiet.

"*What?*" asked Becky, looking in the direction of my finger but not seeing.

"*That!*" I said.

"The church?" she asked.

"It's not a church, it's a synagogue. Madison Avenue Synagogue."

Becky Ballard was confused. "What *about* the synagogue?"

"I have to go there."

"Why?"

"To come of age."

"Excuse me?"

"I must come of age. The synagogue is where I can do that."

"Come of age?"

"It'll help me get rid of my problem."

"What problem?"

"*You* know what problem," I said, lowering my voice, not wanting the spectators to hear any more than they had to.

"I *don't* know what problem. Please tell me what problem you're talking about."

"Marrying you." I spoke in a whisper. "Before I marry you, I must come . . ."

"What? I can hardly hear you. You're whispering."

I pushed my lips inside her ear. "I said before I do anything like get married, I must come of age. I must find some kind of faith, some kind of identity. When I saw the synagogue just now, everything became clear as a bell. Lack of faith is what's holding me back. Lack of any kind of spiritual identity is stopping me from marrying you. I need a spiritual connection to something. *Anything.*"

"Oh, for God's sake . . ."

I straightened up and said, "I'm godless, Becky. I'm a religious pygmy. I simply don't have enough faith to get married."

The spectators quickly dispersed. Religious discussions are traditionally poor crowd-pleasers.

"Get real, Chuck."

"I don't, Becky. I don't have enough faith to get married. But if I come of age, I will."

"Will what?"

"See the light."

"Puh-lease," moaned Becky Ballard. "If I had a brain in my head, I would catch the next plane back to Atlanta."

I continued undaunted. "My new faith will give me the confidence to make our marriage work."

"Will you please get serious, for Christ's sake."

"I *am* serious, sweetheart."

"You are not. You're just trying to figure out some ruse to keep us together without you having to get married."

Her prescient assumption momentarily rattled me to the core. But I persevered. I took Becky's hand and started pulling her up Madison Avenue toward the Jackson Hole Restaurant. "You don't understand, Becky. Not believing in some higher being doesn't allow me to believe in *myself*. If I can truly find some sort of spiritual identity, I know I'll find peace of mind. I'll be able to think maturely and positively be secure enough to marry you. You're a woman who can marry because you have faith in your religion. You're a Methodist, right?"

"Right."

"And you believe in Methodist stuff, right?"

"Right."

"You believe in God too, don't you?"

"Yes, I do."

"Don't you see, Becky, I don't believe in anything. Not Judaism, or God, or Heaven, or Hell. I don't even believe in mothers. I don't believe in *anything*. I have to believe in something before I can become a man, and I have to become a man before I can become a husband." I liked what I was saying. It sounded good.

"But you *are* a man," said Becky, wavering. "You're more man than I can handle."

"In my faith, I'm not."

"Not what?"

"A man. It's a Jewish thing."

"A *Jewish* thing? *What's* a Jewish thing?"

"I was never bar mitzvahed. I have to be bar mitzvahed."

"What's your being . . . what's the words . . ."

"Bar mitzvahed.

"What's that?" asked Becky.

"It's a religious ceremony."

"What's being bar mitzvahed got to do with our getting married?"

"When you get bar mitzvahed, at the end of the ceremony, the rabbi says, 'Today you are a man.' You're supposed to be bar mitzvahed when you're thirteen. I was never bar mitzvahed. I've never become a man. Not in the eyes of my religion and, who knows, probably not in my psyche, either. I've got to become a man before we're married. It will be good for my head and good for our marriage."

"That's bullshit and you know it." Becky's bark was becoming worse than her bite.

"No, it's not, Becky, it's the truth. I swear to God it's the truth."

"You say you don't believe in God?"

"I don't."

"What's God have to do with anything you're saying? I just don't understand."

"Yeah, well—"

"How long will it take?"

"How long will *what* take, sweetheart?"

"Your coming-of-fucking-age?"

"It's complicated. It may take a while. I'll find out as quickly as possible."

"I'm going to give you this one last wedding postponement, sweet pea. Who knows, you may be right. I certainly don't know. Right now I'm totally confused. What do I know about Judaism and bar mitzvahs and . . . and the rest of the shit you've been spewing? Not a goddamn thing. What I *do* know is how afraid you are of marriage. So maybe this bar mitzvah thing makes sense. It doesn't to me, but maybe it does to you."

"You bet it does to me, honey!" I said, all perky and peppy, full of renewed life and . . .

"But I promise you by everything that's holy, Chuck Barris, whether you believe it or not, *this is it*! One more postponement and it's bye-bye Becky. Are you listening to me?"

"Yes," I said, thrilled to pieces, "I'm listening to you."

PART V

"Sensible plans are often abandoned but senseless ones
hardly ever."

—STEPHEN VIZINCZEY

"You cannot find a peril so great that
the hope of reward will not be greater."

—PRINCE HENRY OF SPAIN, CIRCA 1419

CHAPTER *FORTY-TWO*

When I walked into the office of Rabbi Axel Angel, senior rabbi of Madison Avenue Synagogue, he was talking on the telephone with his back to me. As I approached his desk the rabbi extended his arm and, without turning around to see who he was signaling, held up a large index finger in my direction. The finger might well have been a street sign that said: **Walk no further!**

I was furious.

The ill-mannered boor didn't even face me! He just gave me the finger. I debated whether to leave or stay. If I left, I'd have to start all over again at another synagogue. Either that or forget about the ruse. If I decided not to pursue the ruse, I might as well say good-bye to Becky Ballard. She would quickly detect, once and for all, that I had no serious intentions of walking down the aisle with her and would promptly leave me. Good-bye soft pink breasts, smooth white thighs, fun nights, companionship, laughs, a pal, good times. Hello renewed hypochondria, bitterness, solitude, boredom, four-wall claustrophobia, deep unhappiness. Free but lonely. Not a great trade-off. It wasn't much of a debate, either.

I stayed.

Standing in the middle of the rabbi's office, I couldn't help hearing what he was saying on the telephone. That's because the rabbi obviously *wanted* me to hear what he was saying on the telephone.

". . . and you'll have a wonderful time, Leonard, I promise you. I have a crew of six, two beautiful stewardesses, a legendary cook, a captain, and two other crew members to help the captain. They're all there for you, Leonard, to help meet your every need. How long? Four nights. We pick up the yacht at Istanbul and sail to Naples. The food's delicious, the weather beyond belief. There'll be a small but very influential group on board. Very, very, very influential. Three verys, Leonard. I'm sure you know most of them. Len Garment, Nixon's old compadre, Heather Reisman, and Jerry Schwartz. You know them, the two Canadian zillionaires. And speaking of zillionaires, quite possibly David Geffin. Let's see, who else? Oh, the Weinstein boys, Harvey and Bob and their wives. Bob's the nice one. And let's see, Ed Pressman and his wife Annie. Young Andrew Lazar and whatever beautiful dish he's taking out these days. Big Buzzy Clagett, the Kentucky racehorse breeder and . . ."

There was a sizeable pause.

"Yes, yes, I know you're a busy man, Leonard. Yes. Yes, I know you have other things . . . yes, Leonard. Thank you, Leonard, thank you. You'll get back to me, right? Thank you, thank you. Thank you, Leonard. Good-bye Leonard. And thank . . ."

The rabbi stared at the telephone receiver in his hand. He seemed torn between the remote possibility that maybe the guy named Leonard didn't hang up on him, that he just might still be on the other end of the line waiting for the rabbi to continue—or—bowing to the inevitable, the guy named Leonard actually did the unspeakable and hung up on him. Looking seriously chastised, the rabbi put the receiver down and walked around his desk to greet me. He was brooding.

"Sorry," he said, obviously still annoyed and distracted at being cut short by the guy named Leonard. "And you are . . ."

"Chuck Barris."

"Chuck Barris!" he chirped. "Of *course*, Chuck Barris. Who else could you possibly be?" He giggled—hee, hee, hee—covered his mouth with the palm of his hand. "I'd have to be blind not to know a Chuck Barris when I see one. Well, it certainly is a pleasure to meet you, my dear Chuck Barris. How are you? Please have a seat. Sit on the comfy couch. I'll sit here on the hard chair next to you." The rabbi smiled. The smile was quite wide. I saw an assortment of overwhelmingly large capped teeth. "Can you imagine, my dear Chuck Barris, a solid half hour on the phone with *the* Leonard Goldberg. Do you know Leonard Goldberg? I'm sure not. Not many people do. A very private person. Very private."

"I know Leonard Goldberg."

"You *do*?" The rabbi appeared stricken. But rallied yet again. "One solid half hour. Would not let me hang up. Absolutely would not. Leonard Goldberg. Huge movie mogul. Very, very, very rich. Three verys."

"I know Leonard Goldberg," I repeated. "We're old friends."

"You *are*?" The rabbi paused, dismayed. "Well, I bet you didn't know that Leonard's still a congregant here. See? You didn't know *that*, did you? His family have been members for years. The Goldbergs love me. Wendy, in particular. They live in New York now."

"They do? I thought the Goldbergs lived in Beverly Hills."

"They haven't *always* lived in Beverly Hills, for God's sake," Rabbi Angel said crossly, annoyed with me. "The entire family is from New York." Then he giggled again. Hee, hee, hee. The giggle was out of place. Too high-pitched for such a large man. The rabbi sighed, charmed to the gills by his own charisma. God knows why. "The man would not let me hang up," he said yet again. "You're from B.H., too, aren't you?"

"B.H.?"

"Beverly Hills."

"I'm originally from Philadelphia but now I live in . . ."

"So you want to be bar mitzvahed."

"That's right."

Rabbi Angel was still noticeably ruffled by Leonard Goldberg's curt dismissal on the telephone, mainly because the disgraceful scene occurred in front of me. This was causing the clergyman trouble locating and holding onto a proper attitude. His mood swings were getting in the way. In the short time I spent in Rabbi Angel's office, I witnessed downcast depression, bubbly enthusiasm, unsuppressed irritation, and a fit of high-pitched, slightly feminine giggles.

Meet Rabbi Bipolar Macho Fairy.

The obviously disturbed cleric was a tall, broad-shouldered man with a full head of dyed puke-yellow hair parted in the middle. He wore a smart black suit, an off-blue oxford shirt and a yellow rep tie that tried desperately to match his hair. It was the same outfit I noticed the rabbi wearing in the many framed photographs of himself taken with various celebrities of stage, screen, television, radio, industry, and politics that were hanging on his office walls. The rabbi and Tom Hanks. The rabbi sandwiched between Presidents Ford and Nixon. The rabbi and Ronald Reagan. The rabbi and Charlton Heston, Billy Graham, Jerry Falwell, Governor Pataki, Mayor Giuliani, and Oliver North.

"Is this who I think it is, Rabbi?" I said pointing to a picture in the rabbi's bookcase.

"My dear friend Louis Farrakhan."

"I thought he hated Jews."

"Slanderous gossip. In any case, let me say this. I *loved* your TV shows. I did. As God is my witness." The rabbi raised his right hand. "I'm not just saying that to flatter you."

"Thank you, Rabbi Angel."

"The *Price Is Right. Family Feud.* Little masterpieces."

"They weren't my shows, Rabbi."

"Really? How do you like my office?"

The rabbi's office was cold, garishly furnished, and grossly pretentious. The walls were covered with large, ornately framed, repulsive paintings. Oversized and nauseating sculptures stood on small tables. An enormous oil painting of an old hag with a large head of died purple hair, obviously the rabbi's ugly mother, covered the entire wall behind the rabbi's desk.

"Cozy," I lied.

"Thank you," replied Rabbi Angel smiling, revealing yet again his mouthful of super-white Chiclets. "I knew you'd say that. Decorated it myself. All the paintings were done by my wife, including the big one behind my desk. She did that too. A self-portrait. My daughter Rachel made the sculptures. So tell me, dear Chuck Barris, why do you want to get bar mitzvahed? Certainly not for the pens and pencils." The rabbi put his hand in front of his mouth and giggled—hee, hee, hee—to let me know the pen thing was a joke. "You probably own dozens of the best already." The rabbi slapped my knee. "And not for the cash presents from your aunts and uncles. I *know* you don't need the money. Your reputation precedes you, my dear friend. But then," added the rabbi in a sort of reverie, "I guess one can never have enough of that filthy lucre, *n'est pas?* Or be too thin. Isn't that the saying? You can never be too rich or too thin? So, dear Chuck Barris, why do you want to be bar mitzvahed . . . at your age? Or did I ask you that question already?"

"You did."

"Did you answer it?"

"No."

"Why not?"

"I—"

"You seem somewhat older than the usual bar mitzvah boy. May I ask how old you are?"

"Guess."

"Fifty-five."

"I'll be seventy soon."

Rabbi Angel was completely nonplussed about his wrong guess. "And why do you desire to be bar mitzvahed at . . . uh . . . seventy?"

"Not yet."

"Not yet?"

"I'm not seventy yet. I'm *almost* seventy."

"Oh, for God's sake. Okay, okay, *almost* seventy," barked the rabbi, visibly irritated. "Why do you want to be bar mitzvahed at *almost* seventy?"

I told Rabbi Angel that I came from atheistic Jewish parents who knew nothing about Judaism. "Nor did they care to know. I've never had any religious training. I've never had any religious *anything*. You see, Rabbi, I'm looking for faith in something. I want an identity."

"I see," muttered the disinterested rabbi, who didn't see at all. "So, it's not a knowledge of Judaism you're seeking." He began rummaging in his pockets looking for something.

"I don't know, maybe it *is* a knowledge of Judaism. Maybe it's something else. All I know is, I must have something to grasp on to, something I don't have now. Whatever it is, I hope it takes the place of this never-ending feeling I have of loneliness and depression." There was an unfamiliar note of clarity in my voice. "I want to have faith in *something*, Rabbi Angel. I've begun a quest to find my identity, a quest to find myself. I need to come of age, so to speak." I wondered if I was laying it on a bit too thick.

"Uh-huh," murmured the rabbi, stifling a yawn.

Perhaps not.

"On second thought," said Rabbi Angel, taking his hands out of his pockets and clasping them on top of a crossed knee, "I do believe one can become too thin. Anorexic, you know? Don't you think so? You *are* Jewish, aren't you?"

"Of course I'm Jewish." (Dumb fuck.)

"You can try and renounce your Judaism all you want, my new friend, but . . ."

"Who said anything about *renouncing* anything?"

". . . God forbid a million times, if the Nazis ever took over these United States they'd send you to the gas chamber just as fast as they'd send me. You can do all the renouncing you want, the Nazis won't give a farthing."

(Give a farthing?) I gathered my belongings together. This loonbird rabbi should have been committed years ago. I was outta there.

"I'm sorry, Rabbi Angel, I have an appointment and I'm late. I have to go."

Fuck the scam.

CHAPTER *FORTY-THREE*

That night I was working in my den, writing up a storm, when in walked a bunch of my old girlfriends. A whole passel of them, maybe five or six. One of them explained that they had all been out celebrating being my roommate at one time or other, though not anymore. They were all wearing party hats with brightly colored streamers hanging around their necks. Some were blowing New Year's Eve horns, while others whirled those little cricket things around and around. One girl plopped herself into my armchair. Three made themselves comfortable on my daybed. One looked at the titles of the books in my bookshelves and another wiggled in between me and my computer and sat on my lap. I didn't know the names of any of the women in the room except the one on my lap. Her name was Doris. My ex-girlfriends were all chattering and giggling, carrying on almost as though I wasn't there. I was confused. I was also definitely not enjoying their company.

Then into my den walked Becky Ballard.

She looked crushed.

I was mortified.

I tried to explain to Becky that I wasn't responsible for the activity she was witnessing, nor did I ask the girl on my lap to get on my lap.

Becky held her hands over her ears like the character in *The Scream*. Her eyes welled up. Then huge tears began sliding down her cheeks. I felt miserable, but I couldn't seem to do anything about it.

Next thing I knew I was in one of those old small Morris Minor automobiles, trying to get it started in the middle of a raging blizzard. The Morris Minor was filled with snow. I had to dig out the brake, clutch, and accelerator pedals with my bare hands. The accelerator seemed miles away from the ends of my feet, as if a huge giant of a man had been driving the car before I got into it. I felt around the dashboard until I found the starter button. I pushed it and the engine coughed once or twice, then came to life. I drove down to the corner where Becky was waiting in the snow storm for me. She was wearing a light summer dress and sandals. She held her arms tightly crossed on her chest, her fingers gripping her shoulders. Becky opened the door on her side of the Morris Minor. She brushed away the snow on the passenger seat, got in, and shut the door.

"You must be freezing," I said.

Becky smiled a wispy smile.

"Off we go," I said.

"Off we go," said Becky.

"You seem strange," I said.

"Strange?"

"Yes, and distant."

"How 'bout that," she said.

And then I started talking about some girl named Doris to my sister Phoebe. Phoebe had suddenly materialized in the back seat of the Morris Minor. Every time I mentioned the girl named Doris, my sister laughed insanely. I looked at her through the rearview mirror, somewhat amazed at the intensity and pitch of her laughter. She was embarrassing me.

"Who is Doris?" asked Becky Ballard calmly.

"Doris?" I said, alarmed.

"Yes. The girl you and your sister are talking about."

"Let's see, who is Doris?" I mumbled.

"Yes, who *is* Doris?" asked my sister smirking.

"Doris is our cousin," I told Becky.

"Yes, Doris is our cousin," said my sister unable to control her hysterical howling.

"You both think I'm stupid, don't you?" said Becky.

"She thinks we think she's stupid," said my sister, laughing helplessly, unable to control herself.

"Well, I'm not stupid," said Becky Ballard. "The two of you are stupid." She opened her door and walked into the blizzard.

I followed her with my eyes until she became a little black dot. Then Becky disappeared entirely and out of the sky came the empty airliner with the two giggling pilots. It was heading straight for me. I closed my eyes, cupped my ears with my hands and screamed, "AAAAAAAAAA."

My scream woke me up.

My head was buried deep into my pillow.

My entire body was damp.

For some reason or other I was also panic-stricken.

CHAPTER FORTY-FOUR

"I was sure you had changed your mind and decided not to be bar mitzvahed," chirped Rabbi Axel Angel with unexpected good cheer. "I'm *thrilled* you came back."

"I completely forgot about a meeting I had yesterday," I fibbed. "I apologize for leaving so hurriedly."

"We all forget. Where were we? Oh, I remember. I was about to ask you when you wanted to get bar mitzvahed, my cherished new friend? And approximately what size affair do you want?"

"Isn't it too early to be discussing the size of the affair?"

"Not at all. You'll be bar mitzvahed before you know it."

"I don't want to be bar mitzvahed before I know it."

"For you," exhorted the rabbi, flashing his Chiclets, "I suggest, in fact, I *insist* the ceremony be held in the cathedral."

"There's such a thing as a Jewish cathedral?"

"Cathedral. Sanctuary. Same thing. The service is exquisite and I officiate."

"Great. How much money are we talking about, rabbi?"

"The cathedral ceremony with me officiating? Twenty-thousand dollars."

"I see. Is there something less expensive?"

"Absolutely. The sidewalk in front of the temple," joshed

Rabbi Angel, guffawing. "It'll cost you twenty-five dollars. Of course, I won't be your master of ceremonies."

"I'll take it."

"I was joking," snapped the rabbi.

"So was I. Your rates are expensive, Rabbi Angel."

"We're not finished. Remember, Chuck, you'll have to join the temple before you can be bar mitzvahed here."

"How much?"

"Three."

"Three hundred?"

"Three thousand."

"Dollars!?"

"*Oui*. And you'll have to purchase two seats in the cathedral. That's mandatory if you're going to be a member."

"How much?"

"Two."

"Two thousand dollars?"

"*Oui* again. Where do you live?"

"The Cheltenham Towers on East Sixty-Second Street."

"How many square feet?"

"How many square feet?"

"In your apartment."

"I don't know."

"Guess."

"Maybe fifteen hundred square feet."

"Precious Charles, dear new friend, would you believe me if I told you that I am going to build a synagogue on Madison Avenue, not far from here, that is going to be twenty thousand square feet *dans chaque direction*? That's French for in every direction."

"In every direction?"

"Yes, in every direction, so that those who live in mansions like so many of our congregants or insignificant apartments like yours, all of you can come to me and worship with room to spare! That's going to be our slogan: 'Spread your arms out to God with room to spare in the Sterling Silver Synagogue!' " The rabbi made this proclamation standing up, arms spread, eyes heaven-bound.

"The Sterling Silver Syn . . ."

"Merely a catchy phase. Weren't you in movie production, too?"

"No, just television."

"No matter. Invite as many of your celebrity friends as you want. It's your party. The more celebrities the merrier. Our cathedral holds fifteen hundred worshipers. Black tie, of course."

"Rabbi, you're making my bar mitzvah sound like some kind of fund-raiser."

"*Au contraire, mon ami.* Black tie, *oui.* Candlelight, *oui.* A nice substantial orchestra, *oui.* A sizeable donation to the temple if one so desires, *trés, trés, trés, oui. Trois trés!* Fund-raising, *no.*"

"What's the difference?"

"The difference between what?"

"Sizable donations and fund-raising?"

"Semantics. And Chuck, hold off giving your speech until the dinner afterwards. Works like a charm. And you'll have to hire limousines, of course."

"Limousines?! For *what?*"

"To transport your many guests from our cathedral to the restaurant of your choice. Look who I'm telling what to do. I'm sure you know how to give a whiz-bang, boffo Hollywood party better than I do, coming from Tinsel Town and all that. You must have given hundreds of them."

"I never gave a whiz-bang, boffo anything."

"And though it may sound presumptuous of me, Charles, I am going to suggest that you choose an excellent hotel because an excellent hotel, generally has an excellent trendy restaurant. Your guests, I might add, will think more memorably of the occasion *et vous aussi*. I have a few suggestions if you need them. In any case, dear friend, that's where I would give your speech. At the restaurant." The rabbi changed his sitting position, fondled my knee, and said, "Like it so far?"

I changed my sitting position moving my knee out of reach. "Like what, rabbi?"

"Please. Call me Axel. The plan. Do you like the plan so far?"

"Well . . . Axel . . . I don't know. First of all, I question . . ."

"When?" asked the rabbi.

"When?" I repeated.

"When do you want to be bar mitzvahed?"

I suddenly remembered Becky saying, "I'm going to give you this one last wedding postponement, sweet pea, but I promise you by everything that's holy, this is it! One more postponement and it's bye-bye Becky."

"When do I want to be bar mitzvahed?" I repeated.

"Yes, for Heaven's sake, when . . . do . . . you . . . want . . . to . . . be . . . bar . . . mitz . . . vahed? We're not exactly deciphering an Einstein equation here."

"After I learn what I'm supposed to do, I suppose." I couldn't explain to Rabbi Weirdo that I needed time. The entire scam's *raison d'être* (as the Rabbi would have said) was to give me more time with Becky Ballard. The longer I spent learning how to be bar mitzvahed, the longer I'd have with her.

"When's your birthday?" asked Rabbi Angel.

"June third. That's when I'll be seventy."

"That's when you should be bar mitzvahed. On your birthday."

"But that's . . ." I counted rapidly in my mind . . . "that's what? That's less than a month away."

"We can do it," said the rabbi encouragingly.

"I can't do it that soon. I just can't."

The rabbi didn't hear me. Or chose not to. "Okay, dear friend," he said, jovial as all get-out, "let's make it July fourth. We'll do a patriotic bar mitzvah. We'll have lots of red, white, and blue bunting and . . ."

"NO! NO! THAT'S TOO SOON!" I shouted. I guess I spoke louder than I intended to.

"Temperance, my son."

(Temperance?) "Listen, Rabbi . . ."

". . . Axel . . ."

". . . Axel . . . I don't want to rush it. I don't want to miss anything. I want to learn everything and digest everything. This is more than just a bar mitzvah for me. It's . . . it's . . . it's my *coming-of-age*, that's what it is, and it's important I do it right. Let's have the ceremony on my *next* birthday."

"That's too far away," snapped the rabbi, not jovial anymore.

"My half birthday?"

"Still too far away." The rabbi was starting to sound borderline angry. "Don't worry, we'll make the event very, very, very breathtaking. *Three* verys. Yes, we will. I promise you it will be a glorious evening to remember. You betcha! Streamlined to your needs. Short and snappy. Rabbi Tawil and I will do the Hebrew portions. We'll be right up there on the *bemah* with you."

"The where?"

"The *bemah*. It's the stage, for Christ's sake. Anyway, you'll like Rabbi Tawil. Nancy Tawil. A fine woman. Looks exactly like Sandra Bullock. You'll memorize your prayers. You'll only have a few. Maybe a sentence. You'll do the abbreviated or crash version, the one I designed especially for dummies and duhs. A week of practice, my marvelous new friend, and by golly you will sound like you've been doing bar mitzvahs all your life."

"It's not important to me to sound like I've been doing bar mitzvahs all my life, rabbi."

"Axel."

"Axel. What *is* important to me is that I have a full-blown religious ceremony. No shortcuts. No abbreviations. I'm *not* in a rush. I have nothing but time. I want to learn what I have to learn the right way, slowly but surely. I beg you, my *next* birthday."

"Absolutely not."

"Think about it."

"No! I will *not* think about it. I don't *want* to think about it. I'm going to London, Paris, and Rome, then sailing up the Turkish coast from Istanbul to Genoa for the boat show. The show is during the month of June and I do not want the problems of organizing your cockamamy bar mitzvah to ruin my good time or make me miss the boat show. I want to leave here unencumbered and your *fercockta* bar mitzvah will encumber me. Nuts to that."

(Nuts to that?)

"By the way," said the Rabbi, all merry again, "have you ever been to the boat show in Genoa? Magnificent. Best sailing ships and yachts on display in the world. You'll never see any better. Genoa's a port, you know. Most of the boats at the show, dear Chuck Barris,—well maybe not *most* but certainly a goodly number—are in the water. Gorgeous. Absolutely gorgeous. And the food." The rabbi touched together his thumb and forefinger then gently kissed them. "Is there anything better than Italian cuisine? In *Italy*! Nothing, am I right?"

I said he was right.

"Of course I'm right. The boat show's usually in October. This year they're holding it in June. A trial."

"Interesting," I remarked.

"And if you think, my friend," the rabbi was becoming

angry again, "if you think I'm going to miss this incredible trip to Europe with my rich friends for a new congregant's bizarre decision to be bar mitzvahed at seventy . . ."

". . . almost . . ."

". . . you are most definitely mistaken."

"I certainly don't want to cause you any problems, rabbi."

"Don't worry, you won't. I won't let you. By the way, I put some money in Lycos Industries yesterday and today the stock doubled! Well, it *did*! Isn't that just amazing? Understand, dear friend, that I cannot do it myself."

"Do what?"

"Tutor you. Give you your Hebrew lessons. As much as I want to, I just can't. Workload and all that. And then I'll be away. I'm sure you understand. Let's see, then, who will your tutor be?" The rabbi pulled out an expensive leather pocket secretary from somewhere inside his suit jacket. "Who will get to teach my dear Charles his Hebrew lessons?" The rabbi turned pages in his leather book that rested on his knees, stopped, placed a well-manicured fingernail on a page, thought for a moment, then said to me, "May I have the enve-lope please." The rabbi giggled shyly.

"You were mimicking the Oscars, weren't you rabbi?"

"Right!" he yelped, all fuzzy with happiness that I under-stood his little quip. Then, tapping his temple with the same well-manicured fingernail, declared, "I am a genius. I've picked the perfect Hebrew teacher for you. He's a bit of a tyrant and short-tempered, with a smidgen of unpleasant body odor, but then aren't they all?"

"Aren't who all?"

"Hebrew teachers. Mine was. Wasn't yours an angry smelly little tyrant?"

"I was never bar mitzvahed."

"Of course. How amnesic of me. Well, little friend, they all are. Take my word for it. Despotic villains exuding distasteful stinkies. Tradition, it seems. Okay, tell you what I'm going to do. Today is what?" He checked the expensive leather pocket secretary on his knees. "Today is the eighth of May. Okay, you're bar mitzvah will be . . . let me see . . . it will be . . . on . . . on . . . Thursday the nineteenth of August! A *mazel-dickey* day! Did you know Tuesdays and Thursdays are very lucky days? They are. That gives you three months: May to June, June to July, July to August. A little more than three months from today. A compromise, *mon ami*. I'm firm but fair. *N'est pas*? You'll despise your teacher but he's good. Very, very, very good."

"That good?"

"Three verys," said the rabbi.

"What's his name?"

"Who?" asked Rabbi Angel.

"My Hebrew teacher."

"Shmul. Shmul Sussman. Thank you for coming, precious new friend."

I guessed the meeting was over. "Thank you for seeing me, Rabbi Angel."

"Axel," he said.

"Axel."

I walked out of the idiot's office smiling from ear to ear. The ruse continued.

At least for three more months.

CHAPTER FORTY-FIVE

T hat night Becky Ballard turned on her side and faced
me. Her right arm was folded so that her chin rested on
the palm of her hand. I was on my back, my hands
behind my head, looking at her. Though completely spent, the
sight of her naked body, her musky smell, her erotically
crooked smile caused my johnson to—

"Don't even think about it," she said.

"How could you tell?"

"Your eyes."

"What about them?"

"They're very blue."

"Meaning . . ."

"You want to do it again. Well, forget it."

"Why?"

"Because I want to talk about something important."

"What?" I asked, a feeling of dread beginning to wander
around inside my chest.

"The wedding."

"What about it?" I said, my voice cracking.

"We have to start making plans."

"I have to get bar mitzvahed first."

"So? Have you and the rabbi finally decided on the date of

the big event? I should think after all those meetings you would have a date by now."

"I do," I said, nodding vigorously, though I don't know why. Nerves, I guess. When I spoke, I sounded as though I had strep throat. "August nineteenth. It's a Thursday. Thursday's a *mazel-dickey* day."

"It's a *what?*"

"A good luck day. Tuesdays and Thursdays are good luck days. *Mazel-dickey* is Yiddish for 'good luck.'"

"Good. Let's see, that's just four, no three! . . . That's only three months away! My God, why didn't you tell me before?"

"I just found out today. Anyway, we have time. Three months is plenty of time."

"Maybe for you, but not for me. If you're getting bar mitzvahed August the nineteenth, then we're getting married one week later, that was the deal, and one week is . . . exactly . . ." she was checking the little calendar she kept by her side of the bed ". . . exactly . . . August twenty-sixth! Why are you sweating?"

"I'm not sweating."

"What do you mean you're not sweating. You're dripping. Is something wrong?"

"I feel a bit queasy."

"Bullshit, you're fine. You're sweating because our marriage is just around the corner. That's the reason you're sweating, isn't it? Well, that was our deal, sweet pea, so sweat away. We're getting married on the twenty-sixth of August, end of discussion, period."

"I know that was the deal, but . . ."

"Don't give me any buts, honey," she said cheerfully. "I've been patient. God knows I've been patient. Let me tell you, I wouldn't have waited this long for the King of England, let alone a creaky old Jew with no ass. The reason I did's because I love you so much."

"Yeah, well . . ."

"But now I can finally see the light at the end of the tunnel. *Finally*!" Becky sat up, pointed a finger at me and pretended to be angry. "So don't you try and pull any funny stuff, mister." She clasped her hands together and looked at the ceiling. "Thank you, Jesus."

"Yeah, well . . ."

"August twenty-sixth. My, my, my. I'm going to have to start making lists right now." Becky reached for the brown leather Hermès notebook and its accompanying gold mini-ballpoint pen I bought her. They were laying on the night table by her side of the bed. When she stretched for the notebook, her naked bottom showed above the sheets. It was a very cute sight.

"What kind of lists are you going to make?" I asked.

"Lists of what I have to do. First and foremost I have to buy a wedding gown."

"A wedding gown?!"

"Of course. A beautiful white gown."

"White! White's for a virgin. You were married. You're not a . . ."

"Chuck, you get married in white, you go to funerals in black. *And our rings*! God, I almost forgot our wedding rings."

"Obviously you didn't."

"Simple gold bands. Just simple gold bands."

Becky kissed me smack on the lips. I didn't remember Becky Ballard ever being so excited.

"We have to be prepared for every contingency, honey."

"Like what?" I asked, my blue eyes turning gray.

"Like our wedding invitations! We have to order tons of wedding invitations."

"Tons? Why tons? How many people do you . . ."

"And silverware of course. And dishes!" she yelped. "And

crystal! Where's the place with the wonderful crystal? It's on Park Avenue, isn't it? Or is it Fifth Avenue? No, Park. My God, there's so much to do."

I suddenly panicked. A great expenditure of money for something that wasn't going to happen was looming on the horizon, and the horizon wasn't that far away. I didn't count on the ruse costing me any big-time cash and then—bam!—a sudden gathering of potential bills. Just like that! "Becky, I thought we were going to have a really simple—"

"Now wherever did you get *that* idea, sweet pea? When we get married there's not going to be anything simple about it. You know why? Because it will be a glorious day for both of us. I know you're scared shitless, but that's only natural. You're still shell-shocked from your divorce. I know you love me and I love you. We'll be soul mates joined together in the eyes of God. In *my* church, marriage is a holy sacrament." She took my hands in hers, looked me in the eyes and said, "I love you so much. We're going to be very, very, very happy."

" 'Three verys,' as Rabbi Weirdo would say."

"It's going to be wonderful, sweet pea. Oh, don't let me forget the sterling silver marriage certificate holder."

"The *what!*"

"A sterling silver marriage certificate holder. A friend of mine has one. They're a really marvelous memento to have. In fifty years it'll become a family heirloom."

"Great. I'll be a mere hundred-and-twenty."

"Silly boy. I'll still love you no matter how old you are."

I began thinking that it might not be the worst thing in the world if I got out of this relationship sort of like, now.

"I'm sooooo excited!" whooped Becky Ballard, tweaking my dick.

Then again, maybe not.

CHAPTER FORTY-SIX

later that night, I left my bed and Becky, tiptoeing into the kitchen. I made a peanut-butter-and-jelly sandwich and fetched a carton of milk from the refrigerator. I held the sandwich in one hand, the carton of milk in the other, and leaned against a counter. In the quiet of those early morning hours, I decided to dictate into a small handheld audio tape recorder a list of the pluses and minuses of marriage to Becky Ballard.

And so I put the carton of milk down and began.

"I kind of know," I said into the audio tape recorder, "that if I give Becky a lot of love and make her feel real secure, she'll be as sweet as sugar, which is a definite plus. Tyrell said that Becky's really the love of my life only I am just too blind to see it. Maybe he's right. He said Becky was like a rose bud and that if I watered her every day with lots of love and affection she would blossom into a beautiful sweet flower, which was pretty poetic stuff considering the poet's Tyrell Massella. Or was it Ben Lorca who said that? It doesn't matter who said it. What matters is, the saying makes sense. The way I figure, give *anyone* lots of love and security and chances are, they'll blossom. Even me. Anyway, if all that stuff's true, it's absolutely another plus. And then there's Becky telling me how much she loves me about twenty times a day and that she worships the ground I walks on and thanks God every night for leading her to me. More pluses.

"But," I said into my audio tape recorder, "there are some major minuses, too. I always wonder way down deep if Becky *really* loves me. Or is she just trying to nab a fairly wealthy husband before she becomes too old for competition? I guess that's the curse of being a rich unmarried geeze. And then there's the problem of me not going to an office anymore. You know, staying home writing most of the time. I'll be with Becky twenty-four hours a day. Seven days a week. Twenty-four-seven as they say. At my age? With my habits? And my relentlessly inconsiderate attitude toward other people's proclivities and addictions, particularly if they don't coincide with *my* proclivities and addictions. I mean, I *like* being grouchy and smelly. I *like* being ornery and uncompromising. I've lived long enough to earn those rights *and* the right to wear stinky underwear and spit on the street. Now isn't the time to start making concessions. At least I don't think so. Another minus or two.

"Oh, and one other thing," I said to the audio tape recorder. "A *big* thing. Becky has a dog. It's name is Beatrice. She's an overweight, depressed Whippet with psychological problems. Becky saved Beatrice from being gassed at some Atlanta, Georgia, dog pound. Becky's told me a thousand times how she and Beatrice are inseparable, how dogs know instinctively who saved their life and grow super-attached to their savior. Beatrice will move in with us after Becky and I are married. It isn't a debatable subject.

"Now that's a *big* minus.

"Dogs in the country are one thing. Dogs in the city are something else entirely. The thought of Beatrice coming to live in our tiny apartment keeps me sweaty at nights. I envision my once cozy bachelor pad overrun with water bowls, doggie beds, doggie rain coats, doggie booties, vials of doggie medicines, boxes of doggie treats, giant bags of kibble, various leashes, and God knows what else. After every rain storm, even after a drizzle, I can see the dog's four paw prints appearing all over my rugs and couches and armchairs. As far as I'm concerned, walking a dog in the summer is bad enough. Having to go down forty flights to the street every time Beatrice has to pee-pee ain't a bag of laughs. And that's not the worst of it. The worst is going to be having to *clean up* after her. In winter, when it's freezing, walking a dog becomes intolerable. And cleaning up after it is *especially* intolerable. That's what you have to do if you live in New York—clean up after your dog or it's a five hundred dollar fine. Not in Paris. Not in London. Not in Tokyo. Not in Calcutta. Only in New York. And what if the dog has diarrhea? Great way to start the day, right, scooping up soupy dog shit before breakfast? Hell, if I won't follow my *relatives* around collecting their bowel movements in zipper cellophane bags, why in God's name would I trail after a fucking dog?

"And finally, if I *do* marry Becky, it will probably be nothing but trouble. Me, at my age with my shriveled-up dick, married to a young sexy woman thirty years my junior? It'll only be a matter of time before she does the same thing Penny did, run off and have an affair with some young macho dude with a woody the size of California. Except the affair won't stay behind my back for long. It never does. It'll only be a matter of time before a 'good friend' tells me—"

I turned off the audio tape recorder, rewound it, and listened to what I had dictated. When I finished, I thought about what I had just heard. So how did the pluses and minuses add up?

Damned if I knew.

And then the next day, just like that, Elke Metz walked into my life.

CHAPTER FORTY-SEVEN

"**E**lke Metz," she said extending her hand.

"Chuck Barris," I said shaking it, wondering if she was Rabbi Sussman. I mean, maybe they switched rabbis.

She had a firm handshake.

We met on a warm day in May in front of a classroom on the street floor of the Madison Avenue Synagogue. I was wearing an old T-shirt, blue jeans, and scuffed-up Nikes. She had on a conservative white blouse that managed to project a full bust, a blue tight-fitting skirt, white half-socks, and white sneakers. She carried a light blue cardigan sweater over her arm. Elke Metz was either in her late twenties or early forties, I couldn't tell which. Her face was definitely interesting. More than interesting, now that I think about it. Much more. More like sexy. No, more like erotic. Her looks were similar to those European women whose faces sometimes can appear downright carnal. She wore her brunette hair to her shoulders with deep blue eyes and full lips that seemed wet. Maybe her lips weren't really wet. Maybe it was the lipstick. She even had a slight accent which only added to the . . . the . . . I don't know what. I didn't think she was a rabbi.

Unfortunately, Elke Metz wasn't exactly my size; not a perfect fit. I've always believed that the girl should be smaller than the boy. The girl's temple should press against the boy's ear when they're dancing. Otherwise the relationship may be troublesome. On the other hand her size seemed a mute point, standing there looking at Elke Metz as I was in that moldy synagogue hall.

"Excuse me," I said, "I must have been daydreaming. What did you say?"

"I said why do you want to be bar mitzvahed?"

"For various reasons," I answered, and then thought for a moment. "How did you know I wanted to be bar mitzvahed?"

"Aren't you old to be a bar mitzvahed?" she asked.

"How old do you think I am?"

"Sixty-nine. Why do you want to be bar mitzvahed at sixty-nine?"

"Like I said, for various reasons." Again I was puzzled. "How did you know my age?"

"You look sixty-nine," she answered.

"I do?" I was slightly confused, though I wasn't sure why. "And why are you here?"

Before she could answer my question, we were distracted by an old man shuffling toward us in the hall. I realized as he came closer that the old man was really a young man. He stood in front of the classroom door, his hands fumbling in his pants pockets.

"I'm looking for my keys," he muttered. "I am Rabbi Shmul Sussman, your Hebrew teacher. Sorry I'm late."

I smiled.

Elke Metz nodded.

Rabbi Shmul Sussman was thirty-four or five, plump and short. He wore a yarmulke bobby-pinned to his sparse pate. The wisps of hair that were still on his head were strawberry blond. The rabbi dressed as though he once was very cold and never wanted to be cold again. Ever. Though it was May,

Sussman wore a yellow plaid long-sleeved woolen shirt under a maroon short-sleeved sweater. The sweater had two rows of tiny boats on it. One row of boats was sailing across the rabbi's concave chest, the other row over his convex stomach. Baggy corduroy slacks, socks, and sneakers rounded out his ensemble. The rabbi was unsmiling and apparently quite introverted. He also was redolent of something very unpleasant.

Rabbi Sussman unlocked the classroom door and led the two of us into a depressing room made gloomier by its dark brown melancholy walls. The walls were covered with deep bookshelves, the shelves filled with dusty old books whose spines were either torn or broken. There were cardboard cartons all over the floor containing torn window shades, hangers, old empty spiral notebooks, picture frames, used fly paper, and file folders discolored with age. The three lamps scattered about the room had shades whose fabric was brittle as dead leaves. Twenty-five-watt bulbs barely illuminated the tables that the lamps sat on, let alone the room. Most of the ambient light fought its way through the windows streaked with dirt from previous rainstorms. A musty smell, undisturbed it seemed for centuries, was thick and ubiquitous. The smell reminded me of moldy bread.

I walked to a window and tried to open it but couldn't. So I looked out of it instead. It was still a nice day with a pleasant breeze. Children, grown-ups, tourists, shoppers, and dogs walked and ran happily about on the pavement below. Every living creature seemed to be smiling and carefree. Even the pigeons strutted around cheerfully. I was envious and slightly panicked. I became short of breath wondering why I had chosen to spend the next three months in a gloomy mildewed and decaying room where my only joy would be looking out a dirty window at jubilant people, birds and animals enjoying fresh air and sunshine. How, I wondered with growing anxiety, did I allow myself to be incarcerated in this slightly upscale dungeon? Why did I voluntarily place myself in the arms of a small, round, introverted, and angry rabbi who reeked of baby shit? Because, I told myself, I am trying to hang on to a pink-skinned, sweet-smelling Kentucky widow, that's why.

And so, at age (almost) seventy, I began the trials and tribulations of fucking Hebrew School.

CHAPTER FORTY-EIGHT

The days came and went.

I sat there in that dank and smelly classroom endlessly pronouncing letters from an alphabet that looked as though it had undergone shock treatment. I repeated those letters to a Hebrew teacher better fitted to be a capo at Auschwitz.

One day I was trying to pronounce the Hebrew letter "B" or *Bet*. "Beh," I said mirthlessly. I could tell I was wrong because Rabbi Shmul Sussman was glaring at me. He was also tisking his tongue, jiggling his house keys in his hand, shaking his leg, and changing his position in his seat. He used all those irritating examples of body language when he was pissed. And he was always pissed. The rabbi's patience and temper were short and his anger severe, especially when you couldn't pronounce a Hebrew letter he had already explained, like *Bet*. It was a crime he didn't tolerate lightly.

In our class of two it was never the bizarrely fascinating Elke Metz who suffered the rabbi's wrath, it was always me. Shmul would cock his head, close his left eye, contort his mouth into a nasty sneer, bend the sneer up toward his closed eye, suck his teeth, wind up, and drill a scowl right through my forehead. Shmul would end his tantrum by spraying some spittle-filled invective at me and then order me to pronounce the infamous letter again.

When the rabbi wasn't throwing temper tantrums he was trying very hard to be precociously sage. Sussman seemed to be in a hurry to grow old, to become a wise elder spouting prophetic truisms, rather than relax and be the young dumb ass rabbi he really was. Shmul's pompous philosophies, I would quickly learn, were completely indecipherable, his teaching uncomprehensible.

Not long after I began Hebrew School I discovered a procedure that would replace the study of heinous Hebrew letters with the discussion of subjects I discovered (to my surprise) I wanted to learn; important ideas concerning faith, identity, and life after death. At least receive some religious input regarding these subjects, subjects I had never taken the time to learn. Life after death was much more fun to probe than learning how to correctly pronounce an inverted "C" with a dot in the middle or an upside-down "L." The problem of suckering the insufferable rabbi into a theological discussion was twofold. One was getting him to talk about anything other than Hebrew letters. The other was having to listen to his theological answer, if—that is—you had successfully lured him off his vile letters. The rabbi, I was quick to discern, didn't know dick about religion.

Anyway, this is how I would divert the rabbi. "Shmul," I would say, "I have a confession to make."

"This is not a Catholic church," he would reply. "This is a Hebrew school. We don't listen to confessions here. Pronounce the next letter."

"I don't believe in God, rabbi. I don't believe in Heaven. I don't believe in Hell. I don't believe in *anything*, theosophically speaking."

"Theosophically speaking. Get him. Pronounce the next letter."

"Rabbi, I think the Bible's a book of fairy tales, myths, and legends. I don't believe a word of it. I mean if God created everything, then who created God? You've got God talking to Moses and Moses talking to God. Come on, give me a break. If these guys really talked to each other, shouldn't there be little bronze plaques nailed up on various buildings and streets all over the Holy Land, saying: **God Spoke To Moses Here About The Ten Commandments** or **This Is Where Moses Parted The Red Sea, and . . .**"

"Mr. Barris . . ."

"Tell me, Rabbi Sussman, who named Adam and Eve? If they didn't have a mother or father, then who called Adam, Adam and Eve, Eve? And what authority decreed it was an apple and not, say, a pear or an orange? Who saw all this? It doesn't say, does it? And what's all this stuff about souls, and Heaven, and Hell? I think when we die, we're just plain dead, don't you? Like a dead leaf or a dead twig. Dead as a flattened-out cat or possum on the highway. Dead as a dead ant or a dead daisy or a dead elm tree. Dead as roadkill. I'm not thrilled that I feel this way, rabbi, but I do."

"What's your question?"

"My question is what happens, rabbi, when you die? Where do dead things go? Do dead things just become dirt like leaves and twigs? What happens to dead cats and dogs after they're gathered up by city sanitation departments and thrown on bonfires at city dumps? What happens to dead gazelles after they're eaten up by lions and tigers? What happens to the lions and tigers when they die with the dead gazelles inside their bellies? What happens to people after they get thrown in a hole in the ground? Is that it, Shmul? Is that we have to look forward to? A hole in the ground? Becoming mulch? Like dead leaves and twigs? All this training and education and knowl-edge, all of our rocket scientists and our brain surgeons, all our advances in diabetes and in vitro fertilization in the heads of magnificent research people. What happens to all of those people? Do all of them just end up a handful of mulch? Same as a squashed raccoon on Route 66? What happens to us after we're cremated? We're just a jar of ashes, aren't we? All that stuff about our souls going to Heaven or Hell is bullshit, isn't it? What's a soul anyway? And what the hell's Hell? It's all crap, isn't it Shmul? It means nothing, doesn't it? When you die, it's just plain over, right? Am I right or wrong? We really do end up nothing more than a skull and some bones or mulch or goddamn ashes. All any of us have to look forward to is The Big Chasm, right Shmul? The Big Void, The Big Dirt Nap. Isn't that right, rabbi? It's exactly the same as before we were born, isn't it?"

Rabbi Sussman thought for a while, then said, "Too many questions."

CHAPTER FORTY-NINE

O ne day I interrupted the class to say to the rabbi, "Shmul, can you please tell me why Judaism is so unlike all other religions."

Rabbi Sussman breathed a heavy sigh of displeasure, then said, "Why Judaism is so *unlike* all other religions?"

"Yes! Why do we have so many versions of the same thing?"

"Why do we have so many versions of the same thing?"

"Yes, so many versions of the same thing. Some Jews wear different clothes. Some Jews say different prayers. We even have different synagogues."

"*What* different synagogues?" barked the testy rabbi.

"Very Orthodox synagogues. Conservative synagogues. Not so Conservative synagogues. Reform synagogues. *Really* Reform synagogues. It's like the joke . . ."

"We don't have time for jokes, Mr. Barris," insisted the rabbi.

". . . about the Jewish guy who buys himself a Lamborghini sports car and wants to put a *mazzuza* on the dashboard for good luck. He goes to the orthodox rabbi and says, 'I just bought a Lamborghini. Can I put a *mazzuza* on the dashboard?' The orthodox rabbi says, 'What's a Lamborghini?' The guy says, 'It's an expensive Italian sports car.' The orthodox rabbi says, 'You want to put a *mazzuza* on a sports car? You out of your mind? Don't be ridiculous. You don't put a *mazzuza* on any kind of automobile, let alone a sports car.' So the guy goes to the conservative temple and tells the Conservative rabbi, 'I just bought a Lamborghini and I want to put a *mazzuza* on the dashboard. Is that okay?' The Conservative rabbi asks, 'What's a Lamborghini?' The guy says, 'It's an expensive Italian sports car.' The Conservative rabbi says, 'You nuts or something? You don't put a *mazzuza* on a sports car. You can put a *mazzuza* on a *regular* car, but not a sports car.' So the guy goes to the Reform synagogue and tells the Reform rabbi, 'I just bought myself a Lamborghini and I wondered if it was alright to put a *mazzuza* on the dashboard.' The Reform rabbi says, 'What's that?' The guy says, 'A Lamborghini?' The reform rabbi says, 'No. I know what a Lamborghini is. It's an expensive Italian sports car. What's a *mazzuza*?' "

Elke Metz laughed out loud. She never laughed at anything.

"*Enough*, Mr. Barris!" snapped Rabbi Sussman. "You're taking up entirely too much of my time with stupid theological questions and dumb jokes. Pronounce the letter 'R.' "

"Wait, Shmul. Before I do the letter 'R,' I want to ask you about life after death again. Could you please explain Judaism's theory regarding life after death? Is there such a thing as life after death? I mean, if there is, do we come back as another human being or do we come back as something else? An alligator perhaps? Or a sloth? I would hate to be a sloth. I would hate to be an alligator, too, for that matter. I mean, who figures out what we come back as?"

"Mr. Barris . . ."

"And Heaven? What about Heaven? Exactly what *is* Heaven? You never said. Do you have any idea what Heaven is all about? I'm serious, Shmul. I mean, what's the *Talmud* say about life after death? Come on, rabbi, you're not going to sit there and tell me . . ."

"Mr. Barris, enough!" shouted the red-faced rabbi.

Later that night Becky and I were seated at a corner table at Nello's restaurant on Madison Avenue between Sixty-Second and Sixty-Third Streets. Becky was having a lobster salad. Me, a bowl of vegetable soup.

"You bait him," said Becky Ballard.

"No, I don't."

"Yes, you do. From what you tell me, you bait him. He's *not* an idiot, Chuck. He's a religious man who is trying his best to teach an extremely tedious subject to an obstinate student. You're going out of your way to drive the poor guy nuts."

"He had a nose hair today that must have been five and a half inches long. I am *not* trying to drive him nuts."

"Yes, you are. You're rude and obstinate to him. You've disliked him from the day you met him and you've never let him up. Apparently, it's hard for him."

"What's hard for him?" I asked

"To communicate."

Becky was serious. She became even prettier than she normally was when she was serious.

"I'll bet when you were a little girl you took birds home with broken wings and nursed them back to health."

"I'm serious, Chuck."

"Hell, Becky, he never explains anything I can understand. He speaks gobbledygook. He's demented and delusional. He makes me ask myself why I am doing this. Why am I wasting my time learning crappy Hebrew letters from a little turd like him?" I realized immediately that I had just uttered maybe the two stupidest questions of my life. I knew it the moment the words left my big dumb mouth.

"I'll bite," said Becky, "why *are* you learning crappy Hebrew letters? Have you forgotten? Didn't it have something to do with finding your manhood or your faith or something like that?"

"Of course I remember," I stammered. "I have to learn Hebrew letters so I can recite aloud the prayers I have to say when I'm bar mitzvahed."

"So give the guy a break. You know, cut him some slack. He's probably very sweet."

"Sweet!?"

"Yes, sweet. And shy. Give him a chance. I'll bet he surprises you some day."

"Surprises me?"

"Yes. Gives you a hug or something."

"That'll be the day."

Becky Ballard smiled, then said, "How does the rabbi treat your classmate?"

"He loves her," I answered irritably.

"What's her name?"

"Elke Metz."

"Tell me about her."

"Well, like I said, her name is Elke Metz and . . ."

. . . and that's all I really knew. Elke Metz was an enigma to me. I had no idea where she came from or where she was going. She was pretty some days and some days she wasn't. She was young but maybe not that young. Was she engaged? Married? She never spoke of her personal life and I never asked. I never had time to. Instead I talked about her to my friends and family. I said to Arnold Hoffman, "She's extremely intelligent. I think. I haven't really talked to her that much. But I get this feeling she's brilliant."

"Did you know that Milt Rosen died," replied Hoffman. "Our age, Chuck. You knew Milt. The master of the zinger. And Harry Hoffman. No relation, thank God. Hoffman was the world's greatest collector of light bulbs. I read it in the *New York Times*. They're calling our class, Chuckie Baby. I keep telling you that, but you don't seem to be listening."

I told Sidney Hirschman, "Some days she comes to class and her looks knock me out. I mean they effect me so much it's almost disturbing. And then some days she's a real plain Jane. Is that possible?"

"Is her skin like peaches-and-cream or not?" he asked.

I explained to my sister while walking on Madison Avenue after we finished lunch how I thought I was becoming more and more attracted to Elke Metz.

"Attracted how?"

"Sexually."

"I don't want to talk about this."

"Why not?"

"Because I don't," she said and walked away.

One afternoon our Hebrew class ran long. It was early evening when Elke Metz and I walked out of the synagogue and onto Madison Avenue. The night was unseasonably warm. I carried my light sport jacket over my arm. Elke asked if I wanted to walk a bit. I thought it was a great idea. Becky was in Atlanta and I would be going home to an empty apartment. We strolled toward Fifth Avenue. Elke Metz appeared to be more talkative than I had remembered. She said, "You seemed so angry at Shmul today."

"He drives me nuts with his unintelligible God and Bible dissertations."

"I stopped believing in God and the Bible when I was seven," she huffed angrily. Then, quickly back to her sweet self, said, "I know you were trying not to be cross, but you couldn't seem to help yourself. It's a reaction to loneliness."

"How do you know that?"

"I majored in psychology in college. Are you lonely?"

"I'm not sure." I was when Becky wasn't around, but I didn't want to get into that.

"You must have had an unappreciative mother."

"Unappreciative?"

"Not to see the *genius* in you."

"Me a genius? Please."

"I've read your books. I love them."

"Thank you."

"I don't usually watch game shows on television, but yours are incredibly clever."

"Thanks again, that's really nice of you to—"

"Do you know what I call you behind your back?"

"What?"

"Leonardo da Vinci Barris."

I was instantly embarrassed.

"Just remember, 'Should my voice fade in your ears and my love vanish in your memory, then I will come again.' "

"That's extremely poetic," I said, lying through my teeth. "Did you make that up?"

"No. It's from *The Prophet* by Kahlil Gibran."

The lousy Gibran stuff didn't diminish the loveliness of that spring evening nor Elke's wet lips.

"How do you keep your lips wet like that?" I asked.

"It's my lipstick. It tastes good, too. Want to taste it?"

I tasted the lipstick. She was right, the lipstick tasted good. I tasted some more lipstick. We were kissing under a street lamp on Fifth Avenue by the zoo.

"Would you be kind enough to take me home?"

"With pleasure," I answered, feeling a tingling in my testies.

Like high school.

Elke Metz's apartment was somewhere in SoHo, or the Village, I wasn't sure. I don't know that area of Manhattan very well. It was a basement apartment. You unlatched a small wrought-iron gate and walked down a few steps to the front door. The place was small and uncomfortable looking. Elke's living room was sparsely furnished. Just the bare essentials. As

I looked around, something tweaked my concern though I wasn't sure what it was.

Elke brought me an opened can of Bud Lite. She had an opened can in her hand, too. I wondered if she owned any glasses. "Tell me about yourself," she said.

"You tell me about yourself," I said. "We've been going to the same class every day for a month and I hardly know anything about you."

"So," she said, "what do I know about you?"

"You know my age."

"I know other things too," she said.

"Like what?" I asked, noticing I was holding my breath, abruptly alarmed, though I wasn't sure why.

"I know that you are handsome."

I exhaled. "Well . . ."

"And you're shy, and sweet to everyone, except maybe Rabbi Sussman." She smiled, sat down beside me on the couch, and pulled her legs up under her. "May I ask you a question?"

"Sure. What?" I asked, a trifle alarmed again.

"Will you sleep with me tonight?"

Elke turned and looked at the open door that led to her bedroom and the rumpled bed I saw not that far away.

Quickly disturbed, I said, "I've got to go home."

"Why?" asked Elke.

"Well . . ." I sighed.

Actually I didn't know why, I just knew I had better go home.

On the way to my place I remembered what it was that bothered me looking around Elke Metz's living room. There weren't any framed photographs of family or friends. Just like Harry "Boo Boo" Rollins's place.

CHAPTER FIFTY

And then on the last Saturday in May, at eight-thirty in the morning, Rabbi Shmul Sussman telephoned the Madison Avenue Synagogue to say he was sick with food poisoning and unable to teach. Elke and I, sitting side by side in our one-armed hard-backed desk chairs, high-fived each other and smiled.

No Hebrew School today! How great was that?

"Listen," I said, spur-of-the-momentish, wondering if Elke was angry with me for not sleeping with her and leaving so hurriedly earlier that week, "it's only nine-thirty. My driver's parked around the corner. Let's take a drive somewhere. Let's drive to West Point. It's a nice drive. I can show you around. The weather's a little threatening now, but that could change and—"

"Let's go," said Elke.

It was a gray morning, strangely cold for May. The temperature was in the low fifties. It was windy. The sky was heavy with rain clouds. Route 9W that traveled through the New Jersey and New York Palisades was covered from asphalt to tree tops with a heavy mist. I could hardly see the gray-green shrubs alongside the highway. The foggy weather didn't stop my driver Tyrell Massella from moving the town car along at a decent clip. He diligently kept his eyes on the rearview mirror, primarily to look for state troopers and secondarily to see how I was getting along with the new lady.

I was sure Tyrell disliked Elke Metz. It was the vibe I got. One of those hated-her-on-sight things. My driver and I were usually in concert on situations such as liking and disliking a new woman in my life. I was somewhat confused and disturbed by Tyrell's apparent resentment toward Elke. I frankly couldn't see anything to dislike about her. Other than being a bit odd, she had all the other attributes of a winner. I mean, she was bright, I think. And I was pretty sure she was interesting and cheerful. And Elke was definitely pretty—almost angelic-looking in her clean white T-shirt, clean white jeans, and spotlessly white sneakers. Yet she definitely wasn't an angel, though I have no idea why I was certain of that.

I, on the other hand—heathen that I was—wore an old Army jacket, a two-week-old sweatshirt and rancid jeans with a chocolate smudge on the thigh. I didn't plan to take a trip that morning with sweet and pure Elke Metz or I would have worn more appropriate clothing.

"Isn't the mist and drizzle beautiful?" she sighed.

"Yes," I lied, preferring sunshine over that shit any time. And then I surprised myself by asking, "Are you married?"

Tyrell swerved the town car ever so infinitesimally.

"No," she answered calmly.

"Neither am I," I said too quickly.

"Are you about to propose?" she asked, smiling.

"Me? No. No! I was only . . ."

"Curious? I'm curious, too. Was that very pretty Western woman I saw you with recently your girlfriend?"

I saw Tyrell's eyes jump to the rearview mirror.

"She's not Western, she's Southern," I stammered, somewhat shaken. "She's from Kentucky. I mean she was *born* in Kentucky, then moved to Atlanta, then . . ."

"I didn't think she was an Easterner. I thought I heard *some* kind of accent. I thought it might have been a Western accent. But then I'm not very good with American accents."

"Where did you hear Becky . . . that's her name, Becky . . . Becky Ballard . . . where exactly did you hear Becky speak?"

"I was walking along Madison Avenue. I think the two of you were fussing. You were so busy concentrating on the umbrella pressing against your stomach, you didn't notice me pass by. But I most definitely noticed you."

"How 'bout that?" I remarked brilliantly, adding, "You know those redheads."

"No, I'm afraid I don't."

"They're, uh, stubborn by nature. Have tempers. You know, green eyes and freckles . . ."

"Your redhead is very pretty," said Elke. The statement was devoid of any jealousy or envy.

"She's not mine. I mean we just date. She's from Kentucky."

"You mentioned that already," said Elke.

A thin silence, like the fog outside, filled my town car. The quiet made me uneasy.

"Tell me about your family," I said, forcing myself to talk again, "like how many brothers and sisters you have, where you were born, what your parents do, you know, those kind of things."

"My life," she answered, "has been relatively boring—until recently."

(That's it? My life has been relatively boring until recently?) I asked her why she was taking Hebrew lessons.

She said she had recently converted to the Jewish faith.

"Why did you do that?"

"Convert to Judaism? I'm going to marry a man of the Jewish faith."

I anticipated Tyrell's eyes glancing up at his rearview mirror and, sure enough, there they were.

I lowered my voice and said, "I didn't know you were going to be married. Where's your husband? I mean husband-to-be. Is he living—I mean, I know he's alive, well I *assume* he's alive—what I meant was, does he live here in New York? And weren't you . . . I mean weren't *we* thinking of, talking about sleeping together the other night?"

"Which question would you like me to answer first?"

As it turned out, she answered none. Driving through West Point's main gate always seems to divert my attention. The military academy's entrance gives me goose bumps. It has ever since I was a kid. The military police, all that saluting and good manners, the yes-sirs, no-sirs, stuff like that. Then the drive up the winding streets of the campus past the Hotel Thayer. Seeing the playing fields and the scoreboard announcing next season's home football schedule. Above the fields are the old colonial brick homes built during the Civil War for West Point's commanding officers and teaching staff. On up to the parking lot next to the football stadium.

The morning was still damp and cold. The smell of freshly cut grass and wet evergreen trees was everywhere. I led Elke by her elbow through one of the stadium's tunnels and onto the playing field. We walked to the center of the fifty-yard line. I turned in a slow circle looking at the stadium's rows and rows of empty seats. I told Elke, "When I was a kid my father and I would drive here from Philadelphia several times a year to watch Army home football games. And of course the Army–Navy game is always played in Philadelphia. My father and I went to almost every one while he was alive. In high school I used to dream of marching onto Philly's Municipal Stadium someday, leading the corps of cadets. I fantasized hearing my name being announced over the public address system: 'The West Point Military Corps of Cadets is being led onto the field by Cadet Commander Chuck Barris from Philadelphia, Pennsylvania,' or whatever it is they say. And then all my high school buddies would stand up all over the stadium and cheer for me. Hometown boy makes good."

"Did you ever do that?"

"No, it never happened."

"Why not?"

"I didn't have the grades to get in."

I took Elke's hand and walked her out of the stadium. Holding her hand like that caused a faint stab of guilt to pass through me.

I thought of Becky.

Elke and I walked down a path to a marble bench. The bench, dedicated to the Vietnam class of 1966, was surrounded by large fir trees. The trees would have provided shade from the sun, if we had any sun. The same gray, damp mist we drove through from the city was still with us. It hugged the campus and hid the distant mountains. I brushed off the bench with my baseball hat and we sat down.

"Tell me about your mother," said Elke Metz.

"She's dead."

"Were you close?"

"Why do you ask?"

"Mothers are important," she answered.

"Were we close? No."

"No?"

"She stole things. Every time my mother would visit me, she would take things from my house."

"What kind of things?" asked Elke.

"Anything she could hide in the pockets of her dress or coat. Small clocks, sterling silver letter openers, watches, small sculptures."

"Was your mother poor?"

"She was rich! She was simply a kleptomaniac. Before she would leave, I would make my mother put her arms over her head and I would pat her down. Invariably, I would find all sorts of goodies."

"I don't believe it."

"Believe it," I said. "Actually, she was worse than a petty thief. Much worse. My mother couldn't love anyone, not even her husband or her children. The only one she *could* love was herself."

I told Elke about the last months of my mother's life. How I would go to Philadelphia to visit her once or twice a week. They were never pleasant trips. They were more like confrontations, right up to the bitter end. I explained how my mother was lucid but bedridden. How I sat in a small armchair at the foot of her queen-size bed. How she would be dressed in a nightgown and robe, laying on the bed over the covers with her head against the headboard, propped up on a pile of pillows. On the small night table beside the bed was her collection of prescription pills, nose sprays, and jars of hard candies. To her left, in the half of her bed where no man had slept in decades, were piles of newspapers, magazines, and books. My mother was a voracious reader.

It was during the last months of her life that I began to interrogate her. I was hoping through conversation to decide for myself what kind of mother she had been. I was convinced that she was a rotten parent, but maybe I was wrong. The way I looked at it, Ma got points for being there when little Phoebe and I were sick, at least most of the time. That appeared to be about it. As far as spreading love among her children, or keeping our family together as a unit, or giving us encouragement and advice, or letting Phoebe and I know she was thinking about us by giving us presents—not expensive ones, just thoughts—on our birthdays or on our weddings, or during holidays, or just being affectionate and loving in general, for that my mother didn't deserve a fucking thing.

At least that's what I thought.

The last six months of my mother's life didn't cause her the least bit of discomfort. She was dying from a painless disease. This allowed her to be as pompous and self-centered as ever. She held court in her bedroom when the spirit moved her. She continued to be the hostess with the mostess with friends and ancient lovers, just as she had been in her living room. When her crowd wasn't there, I was trying once and for all to clear up some matters of importance to me.

"Did we ever take a holiday together, Ma? I mean the whole family? You and Dad, when he was alive, and me and Phoebe?"

As soon as my questions started, my mother would pick up a book or a newspaper. She would speak from behind her reading material, using whatever she held as protection. Was it mean to grill a dying old woman? Probably, but that didn't stop me.

"Well, did we?" I asked again. "Did we ever take a vacation, together, as a family?"

"Every summer. We always took a family vacation in the summer."

"Every summer?" I said with surprise. "Where did we go every summer?"

"We went to different places," she said, turning a page, pretending to be reading.

"Where? Name one place."

"Stop with these questions."

"Name one place."

"Atlantic City."

"When?"

"Every summer."

"Oh, please, Ma. I remember *one* summer in Atlantic City, not *every* summer."

"Well, we did. We spent every summer in Atlantic City."

"Okay, okay. Every summer. Let me ask you this. Did the family ever sit down and have dinner *together*? The four of us? All of us around the dinner table at the same time? Did we ever do that?"

"Of course we did that."

"Who cooked?"

"Our cook cooked."

"I don't remember a cook. What was the cook's name?"

"We had a cook."

"Did you ever make me breakfast, Ma?"

"Of course I did."

"I don't remember you ever making me a good substantial breakfast. I always ate alone. I do remember when I was ten or so, you showing me how to cook a one-egg omelette and then I never saw you again in the morning."

"That's absurd.

"You also showed me how to make a small dinner steak, a minute steak I think you called it, and after that when it came to food I was completely on my own."

"Enough!"

And so it went, trip after trip to Philly.

"Ma, can I ask you something?"

"What?" she'd say, reaching for a newspaper or magazine.

"Did you ever give me a birthday party? Or give Phoebe a birthday party? I mean when we were little kids. Did you?"

"Of course you and your sister had birthday parties."

"I don't remember any."

"For God's sake, you had a birthday party at your grandfather's house when you were three. Don't you remember?"

"I don't remember, Ma. I was three."

"I have a box of pictures to prove it. Pictures of that party."

"Where?"

"I told you. It was a huge party at your grandfather's house."

"No. Where is the box of pictures?"

"Your cousin Carl Goldenberg was there, and Stevie Winkleman."

"Where's the box of pictures, Ma?"

"Who knows?"

"Did you ever give me *another* birthday party? Or give Phoebe a party?"

"Please. You're being annoying."

"Ma, did you ever buy either Phoebe or me a present? Ever? A birthday present? Or a graduation present? Or a wedding present? Or a Christmas present?"

"We don't celebrate Christmas."

"Okay, how about a wedding present? Did you ever buy either of your kids a wedding present?"

"I told you and Phoebe a million times, all your presents are in my will. Everything's in my will."

"Did you ever give me one birthday present?"

"It's in my will. All your birthday presents are in my will."

"Did you ever give Phoebe one?"

"*And* Phoebe's. Hers are in the will, too. I've told you that a million times."

"How about Phoebe's kids. Did you ever buy them *anything*?"

"My grandchildren will be taken care of in my will, just as you and Phoebe will be. Now be quiet," said my mother, reaching for some hard candy.

"Were you happy with my father?"

"When we started out."

"Then what happened?"

"He lost what little ambition he had. After we were married

he never did anything to better himself. He married me for my money. Your father was devastated when my father went bankrupt in the crash."

"You were, too, weren't you?"

"Of course."

"Would you have married Dad if you were poor?"

"Absolutely not."

"But now you're rich again from all your other dead husbands."

"Yes, I am."

"So what are you going to do with all your millions when you die?"

"For God's sake, will you please stop with the questions?"

My sister and I were in my mother's room the day she died. She passed away at six o'clock at night, straight up. My sister stood on one side of the bed and I stood on the other. I closed Ma's eyes, and then Phoebe and I went to a Chinese restaurant and split an order of chicken chop suey.

Weeks later Phoebe called and said, "Let's make a deal. Let's split whatever Ma leaves us in her will. That way if she leaves everything to one or the other, which in her spiteful way she can very well do, we will have out-foxed her. What do you say?"

I said it was fine with me.

Ma left everything—her millions of dollars, her buckets of jewelry, her tons of sterling silver trays, silverware, and pitchers, her incredible art collection—to neither of us.

Or her grandchildren.

Or her great-grandchildren.

She left everything to Israel.

Elke Metz talked all the way home from West Point. The quiet little church mouse in Hebrew School became a constant jackhammer of conversation. She went on and on about politics, religion, anti-Semitism—topics that generally

scare the hell out of me—and quoted from various philoso-
phers, mostly her favorite, the jerk Kahlil Gibran, along with
several other somatically boring purveyors of humdrum
thought." 'Let It be clearly understood that the Russian is a
delightful person until he tucks in his shirt.' You'll never
guess who said that?"

"I don't know. Who?"

"Kipling," she said.

"No kidding," I said.

"How about this one? 'Here did lie we because we did not
choose. To live and shame the land from which we sprung.
Life, to be sure, is nothing much to lose; but young men think
it is and we were young.' Who said that?"

"I haven't a clue." She was beginning to *really* drive me nuts.

"Housman," she said.

"Housman," I said, forlorn.

As the ride home neared it's end, so did all the beauty,
charm, and appeal I thought Elke Metz possessed. I was over-
joyed to drop the woman at her door and thrilled that she was
getting married. The sooner the better.

What a drip that girl turned out to be.

CHAPTER *FIFTY-ONE*

On the third day of June, 1999, I turned seventy years old. In a mere ten years I would be eighty!

The aging problem loomed as a potential downer of sizeable proportions, if I let it. Therefore, a good deal of my time that summer was spent *not* letting it.

A week later I woke and found myself laying in bed under the covers, the back of my head deep into three soft pillows, my eyes fully crusted with goop, and smiling! Also I had even awakened with the first word out of my mouth *not* being "fuck." That was because of a recent turn of events, the repercussions of which were rolling around inside my head like die in a shaker.

One of the causes of my pleasant frame of mind was the realization that marrying Becky Ballard wouldn't be the worst thing in the world. True, Becky still represented marriage and all of its evil ramifications, but the Southern beauty was becoming sweeter and sweeter by the minute. Maybe that was because I was becoming nicer and nicer to Becky. For one thing I didn't give a rat's ass about Elke Metz. Not anymore. Not after our extraordinarily depressing trip to West Point. What a bummer *that* was! Our excursion ended any thoughts of mine regarding having an affair with the bleak woman, assuming the potential existed. Consequently, there weren't any distractions from that front. And since the pressure of our getting married was on a temporary hiatus, at least for the duration of my ruse, I stopped worrying about that. And since I most emphatically agreed to marry Becky in August, she was more at ease, too. The result meant a lot less pressure between us, and more fun.

Anyway, the other happy event was the sudden appearance in my head of a good idea for a new television program. It was the first TV creation I had thought of since my disastrous visit to Rickey Manhattan at Fox TV in Los Angeles. I called the show *The Hunt*. Here's how it worked:

In four different places around the country were hidden four blank checks. Each check, worth a half a million dollars, was taped to something: a lamp pole, under a restaurant table, under a movie theater seat, in someone's mailbox. Four contestants on the stage of a television studio in New York and/or Los Angeles stood in front of a huge map of the United States. A question was tossed out to the contestants. A contestant won by being the first to hit a buzzer and answer the question correctly. If he or she answered incorrectly, the question went to the next in line. Every time a contestant gave the right answer, the map behind him or her would change from the full United States to half the United States. Then to three states. Then to one state. To a city. To a section of that city. To a street. And finally to an address. A winning contestant would have to give seven correct answers to reach an address.

At that point all those watching the television show in the area of the address would know approximately where the $500,000 was hidden. They would obviously all rush from their houses and apartments to the location and tear the place apart searching for the check. The destruction and mayhem, perhaps the occasional loss of life, would only add to the show's mean-spirited word-of-mouth. The first person to find the check would immediately be approached by one of the show's staff. The staffer would tell the finder how much money he or she had won. The following week the person who found the check in the street would meet the person who answered the seven correct questions on stage. They would be united on coast-to-coast television, hug, and then each one would happily hold up a real check worth two hundred and fifty thousand dollars!

After we had our first winner, the show would continue. Another location. More questions. The next contestant to correctly answer seven questions would divide a check for $250,000 with the person who found it. If time didn't run out, one of the two remaining contestants who answered seven questions first and the check finder would divide $100,000 between them. Of course every time a crowd gathered at an address, a film crew would appear. The crew would record the excitement of the search and discovery for posterity. The film would be shown at the end of the following week's program.

Then, just like that, the Minor twins called.

Millie and Maggie Minor.

The Minor twins were Orthodox Jews. That made them very Jewish. (Three verys, in Rabbi Angel's book.) They were also very young and very famous. Their fame was relegated to the television industry, where the girls were referred to as the "The Minor Geniuses." The twins toiled at the CBS Television Network. Their forte was finding incredibly creative people with incredible ideas. The Minor Twins' timing was legendary. Their phone call to me a day after I thought of *The Hunt* attested to that. The Minor twins talked to me on two extensions.

"We *love* you, okay?" said one Minor.

"We *adore* you," said the other Minor.

"We've been following your work since we were kids, okay?" said the first one. I think.

"You can run but you can't hide, okay?" said the other.

"We know you have something up your sleeve, Chuckie Baby," said one of them.

"What is it?" asked the other one.

"Oh, please tell us, okay?"

"You *do* have something up your sleeve, don't you?"

By now I didn't have a clue which one was speaking.

"Do I have any new ideas?" I asked rhetorically. "Of course I do."

It was a Pavlovian reaction suffered by all game-show creators and producers. That knee-jerk thing about always saying, "Of course I do," when asked if you had any new game-show ideas by network or syndicated biggies. It was a habit that stayed with you for life. Like malaria. Even if you didn't have an idea—and most of the time, you didn't—you always said you did. Then you ran into a closet, closed the door, put your hands over your ears and your head between your knees and thought of one. Oddly enough, in this case I *did* have a new show idea ready and waiting. And a great one at that. Talk about the Minors' timing.

"Actually I *do* have a new game show idea," I said, "and a great one at that!"

"You do!" screeched the Minors in unison.

"When can we meet?" chirped one Minor twin.

"Tomorrow," I said.

The next day the Minors came to visit me. I could hardly tell them apart. Both were short, had swarthy smooth skin, very curly hair, immense breasts, succulent lips, small waists, large noses, and even larger asses. If you're Jewish you had to love the mold. I definitely did. I also couldn't help but think of the many variations on a theme a night with the Minors might bring. My only complaint was their age. I appeared to be at least forty years older than the Minors. No, more like a half a century.

Fucking depressing.

Anyway, Millie and Maggie loved *The Hunt*. I mean *loved* it. In their enthusiasm, both of them kissed me on my cheeks several times. Millie's hand accidentally brushed against my balls. I wasn't sure it was an accident. I wasn't even sure it was Millie. The girls told me they were running back to CBS to rave about my idea.

The Minor twins called two days later and breathlessly asked if I could come to CBS as quickly as possible.

"*You* must sell the show to Grue, okay?" said the first Minor.

"No later than the day after tomorrow," said the second Minor.

"Time's running out and we Minors can only go so far, okay?" said the first one, I think. Or maybe it was the second one.

"Grue Henschmit's Top Gun in the CBS hierarchy," said a Minor. "He's the final word, okay?"

"He'll love it, okay?" said a Minor. "Trust me on this."

"Okay," I said. "Where do I go?"

"Come to Grue's office," said a Minor.

"When?"

"Tomorrow, okay?"

"Okay!" I said. "What's the address? East side or west side of town?"

"We're in California," said the Minors in unison.

CHAPTER *FIFTY-TWO*

That night I caught the eight P.M. United Airlines flight from New York to Los Angeles. I arrived at eleven o'clock at night California time, close to two in the morning my time. I stayed up even later working on my notes. My appointment with Grue Henschmit was scheduled for ten sharp. I entered the CBS Studios Television Programming Department reception room yawning violently as the clock struck the appointed hour. My mental responsiveness and awareness had lost all track of time, my body clock was in total disarray. I felt like a zombie and imagined I looked like one too. I stared at the opposite wall for almost an hour and a half! Just before eleven-thirty a woman came to fetch me. Both her attitude and face were flagrantly repulsive. She called me to come to her by wiggling her forefinger. I hate wiggling forefingers worse than rat poison.

"You are?" she asked.

"Guess."

"Chuck Barris," snipped the loathsome woman, not pleased. "I don't like games."

"Why did you ask if you knew the answer?"

"Follow me," she said frowning.

I thought to myself: If this hag is a portend of the future, the

303

morning is going to be a disaster. Little did I know how right I
was. Ms. Personality and I walked the long mile in silence. She
led me to an office where Grue Henschmit and fourteen of his
underlings waited to greet me. I had heard that Grue Henschmit
loved to surround himself with an army of acolytes. I had also
heard that it wasn't an unusual obsession among TV Suits. Stepping forward with his hand outstretched, Grue Henschmit
appeared to be gay and polite. Mostly gay. Good looking. Blonde
hair. A yellow cotton sport shirt open at the neck. Tan slacks.
Maroon suspenders. White sneakers. No socks. Hairless ankles.

Nice looking.

But then looks can be deceiving.

"Grue Henschmit," he said.

"Chuck Barris." I said and shook his hand.

"I love it," said Grue Henschmit.

"Love what?"

"This!" he shouted, waving my three-page typewritten program description of *The Hunt* around in the air. I had given
the Minor Twins the presentation when they visited me in
New York.

"Thank you," I said as humbly as I could.

"I love it, love it, love it. I loved it from the moment I first
read it. It's a winner." His voice sounded like Aunt Jemima
syrup coming out of the bottle.

"Thank you," I murmured more humbly than before, if that
was possible.

"I love this program idea in oh so many ways, from oh so
many levels," said The Grue.

"I'm oh so pleased."

"A super original television idea."

I hadn't felt that good in years. I looked around the room
for the Minor Twins. I wanted to share my joy with them. They
weren't anywhere to be seen. I wondered why not.

"But . . ." said Henschmit, "we don't think you're the one to produce the show."

"*What?!*" I yelled, whipping my eyes around to Grue's handsome sunburned face, realizing immediately why the Minors weren't in the room.

"I said we don't think you're the one to produce the show."

I for good news.

We for bad news.

I love it.

We don't think you're the one to produce the show.

"Why not?" I asked, barely able to hide the fury in my voice, noticing smirks here and there among the assembled.

"Don't get me wrong," preached Henschmit, "I love you. I think you're great. But we are all of the opinion that you've been out of the loop too long. We think you're just not up to speed."

I *love you*. We *think you're just not up to speed.*

I was ashamed to ask what I wanted to ask next, especially playing away from home in front of a packed house of hostile spectators. But I asked anyway. "So," I said, almost in a whisper, "who's better than me?"

"Dick Clark?" suggested a tall, thin, pipe-smoking twit.

"That old geezer!" laughed Mr. Henschmit. "He'll be gone and buried before we go into production. Give me some living candidates."

"Paul Rubens!" screamed another lunatic.

"Good one," said Mr. Henschmit, "but *not* good enough."

"Bonjourno Productions. They've got shows like this down to a science," mentioned a tall flat-chested girl.

"It's Bon Jovi Productions," corrected the learned Henschmit. "Not right."

"Ken Prager Productions!" shouted another girl, waving her arm in a bit of a frenzy, standing in the hallway.

"If you're going to say Ken Prager," said Grue the Great, "I'd rather go with Debbie Rudin."

Everybody laughed.

I had no idea why.

"Section Eight Productions," said the pipe smoker, trying again to score. "They've got a bunch of television shows on the air."

"Isn't that Steven Soder-what's-his-name and George Clooney? They know movies. They don't know the first thing about television. Besides, they're both too hyper," said The Great One.

"Cap Capezzio," suggested a wall-eyed girl with big tits.

"Of course!" shouted Mr. Henschmit. "Good call, Candice."

Grue the Great saluted the wall-eyed girl with the big tits.

She smiled her thanks, showing lots of gum. Another Meg Ryan.

"Who is Cap Capezzio?" I asked.

"Who is Cap Capezzio?" said Mr. Henschmit. "Who is Cap Capezzio? Ha, ha, ha. He asks who Cap Capezzio is?" Grue Henschmit spoke these three questions with a look of such incredulous astonishment on his face it caused a sudden hush in the room. "See?" he said, addressing me as though he was an ice cream sundae and I was dog shit. "See what I mean about being out of the loop?"

I walked across the room, grabbed a handful of Henschmit's cute little yellow sports shirt and yanked the malicious creep to my face. I pressed my forehead into his, making sure I spit saliva as I spoke. "Tell me right now, you Mexican Hairless, who Cap Capezzio is or I'll break your fucking forehead."

CHAPTER FIFTY-THREE

"Today you are a man," intoned Rabbi Axel Angel.

"No shit, Santa Clause," I muttered under my breath, turned from the podium and returned to my seat on the stage.

"What?" asked the rabbi, confused, walking behind me.

"Nothing." Lately just the sight of Rabbi Angel gave me an upset stomach. Even on this happy occasion a mere Angel glance my way irritated me no end.

It was a Thursday afternoon, August 19, 1999. I had just been bar mitzvahed. Hebrew school was such a disaster I was only able to memorize one line of Hebrew, then fake it. As the preening loonbird rabbi moved the sterling silver pointer along the Torah, I pretended I was actually reading the stuff as I went. In my religion, one Hebrew sentence committed to memory can qualify being called a bar mitzvah boy if you can also afford two seats close to the *bemah*. And now that the ceremony was over, my self-imposed sentence also ended.

I leaned sideways and whispered into Rabbi Angel's immaculate ear, "Thank you for straightening that out."

"Straightening what out?"

"That today I am a man . . ."

"No problem."

". . . and not a pineapple."

"Not a *what*?"

My seat was an ornate, high-backed, quasi-throne on the left side of the synagogue's stage, or *bemah*, I should say. Next to me was another similar throne, the one the idiot rabbi was sitting upon. On the rabbi's left was the just bat mitzvahed Elke Metz. (At the eleventh hour we decided on a double-header.) Across from us on another throne rested the temple's somnolent cantor, Herbert Block. Block had a fabulous voice. On the other hand his halitosis was outrageous. When Cantor Block hit a high sustained note, his breath might easily singe the hair of someone's head standing within range. Next to the dozing cantor was the synagogue's pretty junior rabbi, Nanci Tawil, who, as Rabbi Weirdo said months ago, *did* look amazingly like Sandra Bullock.

Rabbi Angel turned, smiled, and said, "I'm in a good mood."

"Wonderful," I replied. "Daddy's proud of you." During the closing weeks of my bar mitzvah training, I began treating Rabbi Angel as if he were a six-year-old mutant. He found this delightful.

I looked at the large audience in the "cathedral." Funny thing was, the sanctuary actually *did* resemble a cathedral. The building's interior rose up above our heads forever. There was a large aisle on the right and left of the auditorium and rows and rows of seats. The seats went back almost as far as the eye could see. The sides of the sanctuary had beautiful stained glass windows three stories high. The temple was filled to capacity. If I had to guess, I would have said a thousand people were seated in the rotunda. Where did they all come from? I'm sure neither Elke Metz nor I had that many friends combined. I suppose they were recruited by Rabbi Weirdo. He was good at stuff like that.

Most everyone wore forced smiles and joyless black suits and dresses. There was, however, one exception to that somber sea of grinning hypocrites, and that was Becky Ballard. She sat on an aisle seat dressed in a conservative gray cocktail suit over a white silk blouse with pearl buttons and black satin high-heeled shoes. Pre-wedding was written all over her face. Her smile was immense and real. She looked amazingly good, obviously happy, possibly proud, and definitely in love. Becky's long, steep climb to the altar was drawing to a close. Her painful dealings with the recalcitrant maniac she just happened to fall in love with had almost reached a happy ending. I was happy for both of us. I, too, finally realized how much I loved Becky Ballard. More than all the stars in the sky, that's how much.

The post–bar mitzvah reception was held across the street in the lobby of the Willard and Gloria Huyck Memorial Theater. The huge lobby and auditorium were a gift from the wealthy Huyck dynasty of Great Neck, Long Island. The lobby had several large showcases displaying ancient Judaic treasures. The auditorium was mandated by the Huyck family to be used solely for bar and bat mitzvah receptions, and Jewish films. I walked into the lobby with Becky Ballard on my arm, a deeply satisfied man.

Becky said, "When are you goin' to announce our wedding date, honey?"

"Next."

"Next? What's *that* mean, next?"

"Next. During the party at the Four Seasons Hotel."

Becky smiled. "Great! I'm excited."

"Me too." And I was. And I looked it.

An hour later, at six P.M., Becky and I were in my town car parked across the street from the Four Seasons Hotel on Seventh Avenue. Limousines were discharging hundreds of bar mitzvah guests at the hotel's main entrance. We watched from the back seat of the town car, mesmerized as the sea of tuxedos and fancy ball gowns filed into the hotel. Such finery drew paparazzi from miles around. They lined both sides of the entrance, snapping away as the crowd passed by. They didn't have a clue where all the well-dressed people were coming from or where they were going to, but that didn't seem to matter. A photo was a photo.

"Who invited all these people?" I asked no one in particular.

"Who do you think?" answered Tyrell. "That muthafuckin rabbi, that's who."

"That motherfucker is a man of the cloth, Tyrell!" cautioned Becky. "The sky could fall on your head, Ty, for talkin' like that. Know what I'm sayin'?"

"Yeah, you're right, Becs," he said. "I 'pologize. Anythin' I can do to keep the sky from fallin' on my head?"

"Yes. Spit on the fingers of your right hand three times and say 'poo poo poo'."

While Tyrell was busy spitting, Becky Ballard and I let ourselves out of the car.

Inside the hotel's main ballroom I asked Becky if she wanted a glass of wine and maybe a *hamantasch*."

"What pray tell's a *hamantasch*?"

I scooted off to get one without answering. I couldn't believe the great mood I was in. That's because I was about to announce my wedding to the love of my life, Becky Ballard of Bowling Green, Kentucky, by way of Atlanta, Georgia. On the way to the *hamantasch* counter I stopped by Rabbi Angel's side.

"What, Barris?" asked the visibly irritated clergyman. I think I bothered him as much as he bothered me. "What do you *want*? Can't you see I have eggs to lay and fish to fry? Thanks to me this place is crawling with fat cats."

"No rabbi, thanks to me."

"Okay. Okay. Now is not the time to quibble. Thanks to you, if you say so. It was really me, but if you want it to be you, it's you. Okay? It's you. But they came! That's the important thing. They *all* came! Thanks to me. What is it?"

"When do you think would be a good time to make an announcement?"

"What do you want to announce?"

"A wedding."

"*Whose* wedding?"

"*My* wedding!"

"Now's *not* the time."

"Now's not the time?"

"Lets get this bar mitzvah crowd worked over and out of the way before we talk about someone's goddamn wedding announcement."

"It's not *someone's* goddamn wedding announcement, Axel, it's *my* goddamn wedding announcement."

"You listen to me," raved the rabbi, poking my chest with a manicured finger, "I cannot be bothered with marital trivia right now. I'm a busy man. I must strike while the iron is hot and you are *hampering* me."

"Rabbi, allow me to introduce myself," interrupted a tall well-dressed gentleman leaning on a long cane with a sterling silver handle. "My name is Barclay Robb."

CHAPTER FIFTY-FOUR

T he sight of Barclay Robb scared me to death. Body sweats, dry mouth, the whole works.

(Why him now? Why this particular evening?)

"Who did you say you are?" asked the irritated rabbi.

"Barclay Robb. I'm a fat cat. And you must be the eminent and learned Rabbi Angel."

"Yes. Yes. That's me. Rabbi Angel. Axel Angel," stammered the confused and flattered cleric, shaking Robb's hand. "Did you say fat cat?"

"Congratulations," said the odious Mr. Robb to me. "Today you are a man." And then to the rabbi, "That *is* the appropriate thing to say on an occasion such as this, is it not, Rabbi Angel?"

"Most certainly. Most certainly. Were you teasing me, Mr. Robb, or did you *really* mean you were a fat cat. In the monetary sense, I mean?"

Ignoring the rabbi, Robb turned once again to me and asked, "Are you ready, Chuck?" his cold eyes locked onto me.

"Am I ready? What do you mean am I ready?"

"And what company did you say you were from?" asked the rabbi coyly, damn near fluttering his eyelashes, speaking to Robb's back.

"I didn't say, Rabbi," answered Robb, still looking at me.

"Oh?" replied the rabbi meekly.

"I can't tell you my company's name, Rabbi," said Robb turning toward Axel Angel, "only that we are very powerful and very, very, very wealthy."

"Three verys," giggled Rabbi Angel, "I *like* that."

"I knew you would." Robb smiled and once again turned his large back to the flustered rabbi. "I have brought you a bar mitzvah gift, Chuck." Robb handed me a rectangular box wrapped in Cartier paper.

"This is bullshit, Robb." I looked away for Becky, leaving the gift in his hand.

"A pen and pencil set?" asked the rabbi, not fond of being ignored, continuing to speak to Barclay Robb's back.

"Correct," said Robb, still facing me. "Isn't a pen and pencil set the prerequisite bar mitzvah present, Rabbi Angel?"

"That or cash. You've been doing your homework, Mr. Robb."

"Always, Rabbi Angel."

"I'm going now, but I shall return," said the smitten rabbi to Robb's back.

"Why are you here, Robb?" I asked.

"You know why," hissed Robb.

"So where to this time?"

"Jerusalem."

"JERUSALEM!" People near us turned around.

"For christ's sake, Sixkiller, keep your voice down."

I glared at him. "When do I leave?"

"Tonight."

"You've got to be kidding."

"I never kid, Mr. Sixkiller. I'm not very good at it."

"I can't go tonight."

"Oh?"

"I'm getting married. In a week! I was just about to make

that announcement. That's where I was going. I was on my way to my podium to . . ."

"Don't."

"Don't? Don't? Are you insane, Robb? Where do you get off thinking you can tell me when I can or can't get married? I'm getting married in a week and there's not a goddamn thing—"

"You," said Barclay Robb, bending down so that his nose was inches from mine, his eyes inflamed slits, "are going to Jerusalem on the ten-thirty TWA flight leaving Kennedy this evening. Is that understood?"

"I don't believe this."

Robb straightened up. "Believe it."

"If I'm going to catch a ten-thirty plane I would have to leave from here."

"That's right," said Robb. "You have less than an hour. The Duck is waiting for you. He's across the street now, opposite the hotel's entrance. He has your plane ticket. He's been given instructions not to leave your side until you are onboard and the airliner's doors are sealed shut."

"I can't."

"Sorry?"

"I can't go." I began to plead. "Just this one time, Barclay, you've got to give me a postponement. Just two weeks. No more than that. I beg of you, Barclay. This one delay. If I go tonight I'll lose my sweet, sweet Becky. I'll lose her. I know I will. She won't believe anything I say and she'll . . . she'll go home. And she won't be here when I get back."

"*If* you get back," said a smiling Barclay Robb. "And the answer to your question is an unequivocal no. You cannot postpone this trip a moment longer. The target's in place and that's that. But let me ask you, Sixkiller, why would you want to announce your marriage to a pretty young girl like Becky if there's a chance you might not come back?"

"It's not right, Barclay. It's just not right."

"It isn't right? Let me tell you something. I never concern myself with whether something is right or wrong. I do not give a damn about either. Particularly with regard to you. As I said, the target is in place now. We do not know how long the target will stay in place. If you are not on that flight tonight, you will *never* get married. Ever! Do you understand what I am saying?"

"Then *you* tell Becky," I said, sweeping the death threat aside, flailing about for some sort of acceptable entreaty. I noticed Elke Metz standing nearby, blatantly eavesdropping. She was with a thin, serious man wearing rimless eyeglasses. Must have been her intended.

"Pardon me?" said Robb.

I lowered my voice to a whisper. "*You* tell my fiancé, Barclay. I'm not going to tell her. If I tell her, she'll kill me dead. Right here in the ballroom. And I won't blame her. And won't that be a shame, Mr. Robb? Depriving The Company of that pleasure."

"You're becoming a tad hysterical, Chuck. Your fiancé isn't going to *kill* you, and I'm not telling her a goddamn thing. She's your problem." He playfully nudged my stomach with the tip of his cane, the one with the long thin silver sword inside. "Do you get my point?" he added, smiling. When the prick smiled, he reminded me of a water moccasin.

"How come they're sending you to give me my messages, Barclay. Were you demoted?" I looked around to see if Elke was still close by. She wasn't.

"No," said Robb, "I wasn't demoted. You were promoted. You're off to the Middle East on a very important assignment. On the second day after your arrival in Jerusalem, Sunday the 22nd, you will go to the Wailing Wall. You will be there at precisely ten in the morning, Jerusalem time. You will walk to the exact center of the Wall. You will have a *Jerusalem Post* under your left arm. You will stand close to the Wall, but you will face away from it, your back to the Wall. Wait there until you are contacted. Your contact's code name will be Cohen The Hawk."

"Cohen The Hawk?"

"Yes."

"Silly fucking CIA games," I muttered to myself.

Robb glowered. "Is that what you think of your work now? As silly fucking games? The Central Intelligence Agency plays silly fucking games?"

"Forget it," I said.

"Listen, you stupid little shit, these are anything *but* silly little games." Robb exhaled. "We'll speak again about this— just you and me—when you return."

"If I return."

"If you really want to get married," sniffed Robb, "you'll return. In any case, Cohen The Hawk will say to you, 'Happy pesach.' "

"Happy what?"

"Happy pay-sock. Understand? You will say, 'Happy pesach to you, too.' Cohen The Hawk will give you your instructions. I have nothing more to say to you, you simple little twat."

"Thanks for everything," I mumbled, feeling Robb's anger.

"Do well, Sixkiller," said Barclay Robb, unexpectedly lightening up a bit, "and you will be rewarded by having your letter of resignation accepted. Your connection to the CIA, thin though it may be, be severed, which is what you wish for, and we will be rid of you once and for all, which is what I wish for. One more ungrateful loose cannon gone from the ranks. And who knows, maybe you'll even be given a medal."

"A medal? Great. Who the hell can I show a CIA medal to?"

"Certainly none of *my* friends," sniffed Robb. "Let me put it this way. Do well, Sixkiller, for *your* sake."

I watched Barclay Robb walk away.

"Who was that?" asked Becky Ballard, standing behind me.

CHAPTER *FIFTY-FIVE*

I whirled around.

"Goddamn it, Becky, how long have you been standing there?"

"I just arrived. Why are you talking to me that way? What's *your* problem?"

"No problem." I had to collect myself. "I'm sorry for cursing like that. Just jumpy."

"Here. Take this. It's a Valium. Actually it is half-a-five milligram. It's nothing, but it'll calm you down so you can make our wedding announcement."

"Becky, we've got to talk."

"About what?" Her face turned white.

"We've got to move it forward."

"Move *what* forward?" She knew what.

"Am I interrupting something?" asked Arnold Hoffman, talking with a mouth full of food, tossing the glop around in the hole in his face he called his mouth like dirty clothes in a clothes dryer. Arnold always did that, talked with an open mouth full of food. It was repulsive.

"Close your goddamn mouth when you chew," I snarled.

"Good party—up to now," said Hoffman and walked away.

"Move *what* forward?" Becky asked again. "You aren't going

to tell me you want to postpone our marriage are you? I know you aren't going to tell me that. You aren't, are you?"

Rabbi Shmul Sussman sauntered up to us. He placed his hand on the back of my neck and pushed my head down to his chest. His other arm snaked around my waist. He was giving me a hug! My nose was smushed into his dirty short-sleeved sweater with the little boats sailing here and there. He smelled like rancid cheese.

Shmul let me go and said, "I'm going to miss you." His voice was cracking. He looked at the floor and jiggled some keys in a pants pocket. I was worried that he might start to cry.

"I told you he's sweet," said Becky out of the corner of her mouth, her face etched in suppressed panic.

"I'm going to miss you, too," I babbled, touched by my Hebrew teacher's surprising show of affection. "Shmul, this is my girlfriend, Becky Ballard."

"Who?" asked Shmul, his face all squinched up in confusion, jerking off some change in one of his pants pockets.

"Becky Ballard! My fiancé."

"Hello Shmul," said Becky barely able to talk, "Chuck has told me so much about you. He thinks you're one of the nicest men he's ever met. You've been a great inspiration to him."

I listened to Becky in shocked admiration.

"Thank you, Mrs. Barris."

"Not yet Shmul. Becky's my fiancé." Yet another example of Shmul's impeccable timing.

"I'm really going to miss you, Chuck," said my ex-Hebrew teacher. "I want to give you something." The rabbi searched his pockets for what turned out to be his wallet. He withdrew a dollar.

I asked Shmul what the dollar was for, amazed I was able to hold a rational conversation with anyone.

"When you go to Jerusalem," he said, "give it to a beggar.

They say if you go to the Holy Land to do a good deed no harm will come to you. Giving a dollar to a beggar is considered a good deed."

"What's this about Jerusalem?" asked an even more alarmed Becky Ballard.

"Where's the derivation about giving a dollar to a beggar in Jerusalem come from?" I asked, using a stupid question to delay talking to Becky.

"I don't know," replied the rabbi.

(Did he ever know anything?)

"What in God's name is this about Jerusalem?" asked Becky again.

"Becky, I was just going to tell you . . ."

"I apologize," Rabbi Sussman muttered to me. "Maybe I shouldn't have said anything. I heard you you shout Jerusalem a few minutes ago to that man you were speaking with. I thought you might be going to Jerusalem."

"What?" moaned Becky Ballard.

"Shmul's right, Becky. Something's come up and I have to make a hurried trip to . . ."

"Something's come up! *Something's come up!* What could possibly have come up?"

Rabbi Sussman waved to no one on the other side of the room and fled.

"Easy, Becky. The trip will only take a few weeks at the most and . . ."

"A few weeks!"

Guests close by were beginning to turn and look at us.

I felt trapped and pitiful. And embarrassed. Horribly embarrassed. I didn't know what to say. In a spasm of uncontrollable fear, I reverted automatically to the ruse. "It's important," I mumbled, "for . . . uh . . . for my conversion."

"For your *what?*" said Becky, glowering furiously.

"For my Hebraic conversion."

"*Why* is it so important? What the hell is a Hebraic . . ."

"It will round me out, Becky, make me a better person. Make me a better *husband*."

"Oh, God," she moaned, "please don't. Don't start *that* bullshit. I won't be able to go through it again. Not again. I won't be able to cope. Please. No. You can't. Don't start with your Hebraic conversion shit. I can't take it anymore. I can't!"

"Easy Becky, please."

"Okay. Okay. I'll dump all our marriage plans. We'll get married in Jerusalem. I'll go with you and we'll get married there. It'll cost us a few bucks in deposits, but what the hell. At least we'll be together and there won't be anymore postponements."

"You can't go with me."

She blinked her eyes, amazed, hardly able to whisper, "I can't go with you?"

"No."

"Why not?"

"Because you can't."

"BULLSHIT!"

I grabbed hold of Becky's arm, pulled her toward the nearest exit and hustled her out of the ballroom. We were in a long hallway. I walked Becky far enough away from the party so that if we started shouting at each other no one would hear us. When we stopped walking, I turned Becky around so she faced me. I looked her in the eyes but I didn't know what to say.

Becky said it for me. "Let's talk. Let's not fight." She put her hands on my shoulders. "Let's prove to each other that we can work a problem out *together*. Like two civilized people, okay?"

"Okay."

"So tell me what this latest . . . this latest . . . *postponement* is all about."

"I can't."

I saw her eyes widen. "That's really talking it over," she said, taking deep breaths. "What do you mean, *you can't?*"

"I can only say it's a religious thing and . . . and . . ."

"You can't explain why you're going and you can't explain why you can't take me, right?"

"Yes. No." I was confused. The ruse had become a nasty habit, a scary horror story. The CIA prohibited me from telling Becky the truth. I wouldn't have told her anyway, for her own protection. So what palatable choices did I have?

"I don't understand," she moaned. "I just don't understand."

"I need this trip to Jerusalem, Becky," I said struggling, "I really do. It's a great chance to make me religiously whole, so to speak. What more holy place is there then Jerusalem? It's literally the period at the end of the Talmudic sentence. It's the . . ."

"The what? The period at then end of the *what?*"

I felt like I was rambling incoherently, crumbling, a drowning man going down for the third and final time. "I'll finally have my faith, Becky. I'll finally have my identity, the two things I've been working so hard to get these past months. I'll finally—*finally*—nail them both down for good and always."

"I thought you got all that nailed down when you were bar mitzvahed."

"I did, but now I'll *really* nail it."

"Oh, Jesus," moaned Becky Ballard looking at the ceiling.

"I guarantee you, Becky dear, you'll be thrilled and happy about everything when I come back. And I'll marry you as soon as I do, as soon as you want. If they have a chapel at the airport we'll get married there the day I arrive home. I promise. I'll call you when I'm leaving Europe and we'll get married at Kennedy Airport the minute I land. I promise. This time I'm not kidding, or lying, or anything. I really mean it. I love you, Becky. I really, really do. Jerusalem is just too good an opportunity for me. . . ." (I could feel my energy petering out.) ". . . to waste, and . . ."

"Okay," she said, a mite more cheerful, "tomorrow when you leave let's go to the airport and hour earlier and get married in the chapel like you said, only let's do it *before* you go."

"I can't marry you tomorrow."

"You can't?" says Becky in a small voice. "Why not?"

"I'm leaving tonight."

"Tonight?"

"In about an hour. I'll just barely have time to make the plane as it is."

"Why do you have to leave in an hour?"

"Because I do," I said weakly.

Becky dropped her hands from my shoulders. Big tears started rolling down her cheeks. "Do you know what you just did?" she asked. "Do you have any idea what you just did? You just drove a spike through my heart."

"Oh, come on, Becky . . ."

"I gave you my heart to hold and protect and cherish and nurture and love and support and you tore it apart and drove a *spike* through it for good measure. Then you handed it back to me just now as though nothing happened, that's what you did."

"Aw, Becky . . ." I didn't remember ever feeling so bad.

"You can't do this to me," Becky whispered, crying. "It's not right, honey. You've made me into a crazy person. Now you want to leave me again. I'll never recover. I love you too much. I'll never get sane again."

"I don't *want* to leave you," I whispered. "I *have* to."

She didn't hear me. "I love you more than anything in the world. I know you don't believe me, but I do."

"I believe you, Becky, and I love you, too. I really do."

Becky started sobbing. "I never acted like this before in my life. I never ever cried so much. I never shouted and screamed. I would lay down and die before I caused a scene. Now all I ever do is cry and scream and cause scenes. You've made me into a monster and now you're going to leave me and I'll never see you again. And that's what I'll be for the rest of my life. A monster."

"I haven't made you into a monster. You're not a . . ."

"I've loved you from the day we met," she said through her tears. "I know I'll love you until the day I die. I've told you that. Over and over again. But you've never believed me."

"I said I believe you now, and I do."

"You're going to give me a nervous breakdown."

"You're not going to have a nervous breakdown."

"You can't do this to me. It's not right."

"Aw, come on, Becky." I grabbed her and held her in my arms as tightly as I could. Becky Ballard stood there pressed against me, her arms at her sides, her tears warm and wet on my face. "We're a perfect fit, Becky," I said. "We always were."

"You're right, sweet pea, we always were," whispered Becky. She put her arms around me and gave me a big hug.

Things were going to be alright after all.

"Chuck?" said Becky Ballard.

"What, honey?"

"When you come back, I won't be here."

PART VI

*"No sense in worrying.
Nothing's going to go right anyway."*

—JERRY SCHATZBERG

CHAPTER FIFTY-SIX

Jerusalem, August 19, 1999.

"In 1948 the Jews lost access to the Wailing Wall when the whole of the Old City was taken by the Jordanians. Nineteen years later Israeli troops stormed into the plaza during the Six Day War and fought their way directly to the Wall. Their first action after securing the Wailing Wall was to bulldoze the Arab neighborhood to create the plaza that exists today."

I looked up from my guidebook and saw the plaza and then the Wailing Wall itself. Made of ancient stones, the Wall stood half a dozen stories high. Here and there several great tufts of green grass grew between the cracks in the wall. The tufts looked like giant bunches of pubic hair. The portion of the plaza directly in front of the wall was divided by a partition that separated men from women. The mens' side was jammed with worshipers. The womens' side less so.

A pleasant but strong breeze blew across the plaza. As I headed toward the entrance to the men's side I noticed a box of cardboard *yarmulkes*. Apparently, I was required to have my head covered. I put on my New York Yankees baseball hat and walked to the Wall. On the way, I saw large tables and bridge chairs scattered about. The tables were covered with prayer books. Groups of men leaned on or sat around the tables, baiting each other in heated discussions. Others prayed. Some were dressed in immaculate long frock coats, black knickers, high black stockings, and very shiny shoes. Others—most in fact—wore dirty shirts buttoned at the neck, rumpled suits, and hats too big for their heads. I watched and listened to worshipers shouting prayers, quietly mumbling them, wailing them, and singing them. The rolling cacophony of human voices was a sound I would never forget.

I stood at the center of the Wailing Wall with the *Jerusalem Post* under my left arm, my back to the stones. Except for me, everyone stood facing the Wall. I watched the worshipers pray. Some bowed up and down. Others walked back and forth. Most simply loitered, reading aloud from prayer books and Bibles. I felt uncomfortable standing there with my back to the Wailing Wall. A group of menacing Orthodox Jews began scowling at me. I tried my best to act nonchalant. I took a deep breath and let it out. Though prayers are not my forte, I quietly prayed that my CIA contact would quickly appear.

"Hello," said a man, suddenly standing beside me.

I jumped, blurted out, "Hello."

The man asked what my name was. He spoke in a clipped tone.

"Sunny Sixkiller. And yours?"

"I am Cohen. Cohen The Hawk. Happy pesach."

"Happy pesach to you." (Silly goddamn CIA games.)

"I am with the Mossad," said The Hawk, seeming to read my mind, "*not* the CIA. The two intelligence agencies have an arrangement."

I could see why he was called The Hawk. He had a beak that would make an American Eagle proud. The Hawk looked like my Uncle Bill Barris. Same smallish height, same plain flat face, same big nose, in his sixties, gray hair, a gray stubble of a beard. The Hawk wore a wide baggy blue serge suit that covered a wide baggy body. A *yarmulke* was pinned to his head and a white prayer shawl with blue trim was draped around his shoulders. He also carried a *Jerusalem Post* under his left arm, two prayer books under his right arm, and an old leather doctor's bag in his right hand.

"Okay, what's my big important mission?" I asked, annoyed, getting quickly to the point, my voice dripping with sarcasm.

Cohen put the doctor's bag down between his shoes. "Open this," he said, giving me one of his prayer books, "and *daven*."

"Do what?"

"*Daven*."

"What's *daven*?"

"Face the Wall and rock back and forth on your heels like the man is doing on your right."

The man on my right stood inches from the Wailing Wall rocking back and forth. He was muttering prayers, I think. When the man rocked forward, his forehead almost banged into the Wall.

I opened the prayer book the Hawk had given me and began to *daven*.

"On Monday," said The Hawk, standing beside me facing the wall, pretending to be reading from his prayer book, *davening* too, "the twenty-third of August . . ."

". . . that's tomorrow . . ."

". . . you are to go to Prague."

"Prague!" I said, looking at my Bible. "Why wasn't I sent *directly* to Prague from New York, for Christ's sake?"

"Yes. Well Mr. Sixkiller, this is a good question." Cohen paused as if deciding on an answer, then said, "You are to go to Prague tomorrow morning. Your flight is Czech Air number 287, leaving Tel Aviv at 5:55 A.M. . . ."

"Five in the morning! That means I have to get up around three and then drive all the way back to . . ."

"You should arrive in Ruyzne Airport, Prague at 9:05 A.M. Here is your Tel Aviv/Prague airline ticket and some Czech money." The Hawk handed me the *Jerusalem Post* he had been keeping under his left arm. I could feel an envelop inside. "In Prague," he said, "you will proceed to the Hotel Nosticova. The taxi fare from the airport to the hotel should be under 300 korunas. The Nosticova is in the Mala Strana, sometimes called Lesser Town, near the Charles Bridge. Any taxi driver will know where the hotel is. You have the Karlstein Suite reserved for you. It is on the first floor. A bellhop will show you to your room. When you arrive there, he will give you a box of dress shirts that you will have sent on ahead of you to be laundered. Inside the box you will find your shirts that and your gun, silencer, and ammunition. After you are situated in your suite, you will spend the rest of Monday sightseeing. While sight-seeing, you will make sure you are not being followed."

"Should I expect to be?"

"On Tuesday morning, the twenty-fourth," continued the Hawk, not answering my question, "you will proceed to the Pension Pav. You will arrive at exactly twelve noon. Again, any taxi driver will know where the Pension Pav is. For your infor-mation, the Pension Pav is at Number 13 Kremencova Street in what is, known as the historic section of the city. This information is all on your itinerary, inside the magazine. When you arrive at the Pension, you will ask to speak to Anton Faust. Anton Faust, aka Karel Rziepel. Faust's body is supposed to be covered with tattoos, which is neither here nor there."

"He won't be able to be buried in a Jewish cemetery," I injected, trying my best to lighten things up.

"True," said a blank-faced Hawk. "In any case, you will telephone Faust from the lobby of the Pension Pav. You will not refer to him by name. You will simply say, 'The sky is blue.' If it is Faust, he will say to you, 'The ground is brown.' "

"Reminds me of a joke."

"It reminds you of what?" asked the Hawk, annoyed.

"What you just said reminds me of a joke. This spy is sent to Moscow by the CIA. He's told to go to a hotel, look up another spy named Goldberg and tell Goldberg the sky is blue. If it's Goldberg, he'll say, 'The ground is brown.' Then the two are to meet and exchange documents. So the CIA spy goes to Moscow, finds the hotel, asks the receptionist for Goldberg's room and telephones him from the lobby. A man answers and the CIA guy says, 'The sky is blue.' The man on the house phone says, 'This is Goldberg the furrier. You want Goldberg the spy. He's on the fourth floor.' "

"After making contact," said a blank-faced Hawk, "you will go to Anton Faust's room. His room is on the fourth floor facing the street. Once in his room, Faust will give you a leather attaché case. You will hand Faust this bag."

The Mossad agent bent down, retrieved the leather bag, and gave it to me. The bag was soft and creased, with a worn wooden handle to hold on to.

"What's in the bag?"

"Money."

"How *much* money?"

"One million, four hundred and sixty thousand dollars."

"Christ, Hawk, I'm not going to carry over a million and a half dollars around Prague with me! You crazy?"

"They're not American dollars. They are Czech Republic dollars. One Czech dollar—or a koruna—is worth twenty-nine-point-four U.S. cents. One million, four hundred and sixty korunas is approximately fifty thousand U.S. dollars."

"Oh . . . really? . . . Well . . ." I trailed off.

"You give Faust the money," said The Hawk. "Faust will give you a packet of papers. When the papers are in your hands, you will kill Faust."

"Kill him?"

"Yes. And when he is dead, take back the doctor's bag with the money."

"Kill him," I repeated. I was still on that. Lately that particular order—the one to kill someone—gave me the willies. More and more so as I grew older. But I seemed to get over it.

"Yes, kill him," said The Hawk. "Not too long ago, Faust switched to the wrong side of the playing field. Be careful. Anton Faust is a very dangerous man. Oh . . . and one other important matter. In among your airline tickets and money, inside the magazine, is a small white envelope with cyanide pills. Two of them."

"Cyanide pills!"

"If you are ever in any danger of being caught before or after you complete your mission, take these pills."

"Whoa there, Mr. Hawk. I've been in this business a long time and I've *never* been given cyanide pills. If you think—"

"A dead CIA agent cannot be horribly tortured," said The Hawk, "as the secret police are famous for in the Czech Republic."

"I am not a CIA agent, Cohen. I'm a hired gun."

"It's all the same thing to the Czech police. Also, Sixkiller, a dead agent cannot reveal any classified CIA information."

"I don't know any classified CIA information."

"You don't know that."

"Yes, I do. You know something, Hawk. This mission sucks the big banana. A dangerous assassin to take out, cyanide pills, the Czech Secret Police, and the KGB tipped off that I'm coming to town. Jesus H. Christ . . ."

"Shut up, Sixkiller, this is a holy site. Maybe the holiest Jewish shrine on this earth. Watch your goddamn fucking mouth."

"Sorry."

"I would prefer that you plant a bomb in the apartment of Anton Faust while you're at it and blow the apartment and the assassin to smithereens. As an example to other traitors. But I understand that you are not proficient in explosives."

"That's right. I just shoot people."

"Too bad. Anyway, after doing away with Faust, you will wrap your gun, silencer, and harness in a towel and place the towel in the leather bag. You will go down to the street level and enter the Cinska Restaurant next door. Can you remember all this?"

"Yes, for Christ's sake, I . . ."

"Good. Okay. You will ask the bartender his name. He will tell you his name is Franz. He has been described to me as an extremely large man, totally bald with a huge handlebar mustache who speaks with a loud, booming voice. You will give Franz the bartender both the doctor's bag with the money and your gun in it and the packet of military papers Faust gave you. After transferring the bag and packet to Franz, you will leave the restaurant and get lost in the city until it's time to go to the airport. Obviously, you will make absolutely certain you are not being followed. If you are clear, you will return to Ruyzne Airport at six P.M. and take Airline flight number 652 to London, leaving Prague at 6:55 P.M. You will arrive in London approximately two hours later. Your Prague/London air ticket is also in there, in the *Jerusalem Post*. When you arrive in London you will proceed directly to the Lanesborough Hotel, where you will be debriefed."

"By whom?"

"I don't know. You will be contacted."

"Why do I have to go to London? Why can't I meet a debriefer in Prague? Then I can go directly from there to New York."

"It is important, Mr. Sixkiller, that you get out of the Czech Republic as fast as you can. I'm sure you will agree it is in your best interest that you do."

"If you say so." I made a disgusted face for The Hawk's benefit.

"In any case," said Cohen, "it is my understanding that after the mission, providing it is successful and the debriefing goes smoothly, you will be free to return home whenever you want."

"Thanks a lot."

"It is also my understanding that upon successfully completing this mission, you will also be free to resign from your intelligence organization. Now . . . are there any questions?"

"I'll ask this once again. Why wasn't I sent directly from New York to Prague? Why did I have to go to Jerusalem first?"

"As I said before, Mr. Sixkiller, a good question."

"So what the hell's the answer?"

"To hopefully lose the trail of another assassin."

"Who's this other assassin want to kill? Faust, too?"

"No. You."

CHAPTER FIFTY-SEVEN

P rague, Czech Republic.

I didn't like the taxi driver on sight. His large, round, fat red face and thick neck, his small peaked gray wool cap, everything about him angered me on sight. I figured him to be an anti-Semitic Czech thug. I asked how much it would cost to take me to the Hotel Nosticova. He shrugged his thick shoulders. He didn't know. He didn't speak English, either. And he didn't give a fuck, which is what the shrug meant. The gesture pushed me over the edge. Nervous tension and all that crap. I leaned forward so that I spoke right into the cabbie's hairy right ear and said, "The fare better not be over three hundred fucking korunas, you fat turd, or I'll take a back door with me when I leave this shit taxi of yours." I am always amazed at the amount of anger and fearless nerve a psychotic like myself can accrue. In any case, I think the fat fuck understood English. At least some of what I said. His neck turned bright purple and he glared at me through his rearview mirror.

A Czech Duck.

The weather in Prague was hot and the stupid cab didn't have air conditioning. Even with all the windows open, it seemed to be roughly a 140 degrees Fahrenheit in the back seat. The heat made me extremely uncomfortable. I pulled my tie down and unbuttoned my shirt collar. My suit coat was already on the seat beside me.

Putting my discomfort aside, the bright sunshine turned Prague into a glorious sight to see. The buildings' burnt orange roofs, pale yellow walls, ornate black art nouveau trim that framed apartment windows seemed to me like a living water-color painting. Below the apartment windows the serene Vltava River flowed quietly through the city whose skyline was filled with spires and the tops of centuries-old cathedrals and castles.

I stopped the taxi somewhere near the city center and decided to walk the rest of the way. When I asked the thug how much the fare was, he said two hundred and ninety korunas. He was under my three-hundred-koruna limit. Just. Both of us were glad to see the last of each other.

With my guidebook in hand, I started walking. Dark tunnels opened onto immaculate squares filled with sunshine and strolling Czechs. A jazz band was accompanying a girl singing American songs somewhere nearby, *"It is wonderful. It is paradise. That you belongs to me."* Electric trolley cars rattled by outdoor cafés. I walked along Karlova Street, crossed the Vltava River on the Charles Bridge.

A few minutes later I saw the Hotel Nosticova. The hotel was at the corner of two cobblestone streets, Nosticova and Praha. It was a white building with black trim painted between the roof and the building proper. Flower boxes of red and blue flowers were under all the windows on the second floor.

A suit of armor stood by the reservation desk. I wondered if anyone was inside the armor. A bellhop in an ill-fitting uniform led me to my room. He carried a cardboard box under his arm. Once we were inside the suite, he said in English, "The TV is attached to a satellite. The rooms are with valuable antiques. E-mail and facsimile facilities are here as is also a baby-sitter available. Private parking and theater and film tickets downstairs. And I have your laundered shirts." He handed me the box.

I thanked the porter for the information and gave him a generous tip. He smiled.

After he was gone, I opened the box and found my gun and silencer. My handlers had also conveniently included a shoulder harness. I loaded the gun, attached the silencer, put the gear into the harness and my arms through the straps. I adjusted the thing to fit comfortably and left the hotel. I saw the bellboy on the way out, but we didn't acknowledge each other.

It was about four in the afternoon. I was going to go sight-seeing and try to determine if I was being followed. It took me less then six minutes to realize that I was.

CHAPTER FIFTY-EIGHT

The three of us were walking along the large Boulevard Karmelitska Ujezd—me and the two bloodhounds behind me. One bloodhound was taller than the other, but they wore identical large black Stetson hats and black suits. They had been trailing me since I left the hotel. They always walked in tandem on the opposite side of the street. Every time I turned they quickly stopped and looked into the nearest store window. Clever little fellows. The two were now pretending to be doing some serious evaluating in a store window a half a block away. The store sold ladies' shoes. Just what those two bohunks needed.

I crossed the street, stopped in front of them and said, "Do either one of you speak English?"

"Yes," answered the tall one on the right, startled, his eyes the size of half dollars.

"You guys following me?"

"Yes," said the shorter one on the left.

"You're not very good at it."

"We know," said the one on the right.

"Neither am I," I said and shrugged. "Any idea what we should do next?"

"We are on your side," said the one on the right.

"*My* side?"

"Yes. We were sent to keep an eye on you, to protect you," said the one on the left.

"Who sent you?"

"Cohen The Hawk," said the same one.

"What's my code name?"

"Sunny Sixkiller," answered the one on the right.

"Fuck!"

"What?" one asked.

"Go away," I said. "I don't need your goddamned help. You're only in the way. I appreciate the gesture, but just go away."

"We are here to protect you," whined one guy.

"I don't want your fucking protection. You're in my way."

I left the sulking bodyguards on Boulevard Karmelitska Ujezd and returned to my hotel.

The next day I awoke to a gray, depressing morning. I puttered about the room wasting time and then wrote a letter to Becky. The letter was pitiful. I tore it up, tried a few more, quit, and read a book. I left the hotel close to twelve noon, hailed a cab, and went to the Pension Pav. I entered the hotel's lobby and talked to the receptionist, a dried-up old lady with a pinched and pointed face. She wore wire-rimmed eyeglasses, had a wart with several long white hairs growing out of it under her chin and thinned-out prickly gray hair. She reminded me of Becky's dog Bernice. I asked for Anton Faust. The receptionist told me he was in Room Four-One-Zero, that she would connect me and pointed sourly to the house phones at a desk across the way.

I walked to the desk and picked up the ringing telephone.

A male voice answered.

I said, "The sky is blue."

"The ground is brown," said the voice. I thought again of my joke. I'm Goldberg the tailor. The spy's on the fourth floor.

As I got off the elevator I checked the hallways. They were empty. I knocked on the door of Room Four-One-Zero. A heavy set man in rumpled clothes answered. He had dark circles under his eyes and a thick, short black beard.

"Who are you?" he asked.

"Sunny Sixkiller. Who are you?"

"I am Anton Faust."

I shot him in the chest.

He fell to the floor, landing half in the hallway, half in his room.

I pulled his body into the hotel room by his wrists. I shut the door and shot him again, this time in his ear.

I had decided to kill Faust when he opened the door. It was the easiest and safest way to do the job. My precipitous action solved one problem but created another: If I couldn't find the information Faust was supposed to hand me I would have a disaster on my hands, and most certainly another failed mission. So with a wildly beating heart I searched Faust's room for the package of stolen secrets. Almost immediately I found them hidden under his mattress. (Thank you, Jesus, for Faust's lack of imagination.) I went to the bathroom to get a towel. I wrapped my gun, silencer and harness in the towel and placed the bundle in the leather bag. I let myself out of the hotel room, closed the door, and took the stairs to the lobby. The entire operation had taken eight minutes and thirty two seconds.

Almost too easy.

I walked out of the hotel and stepped into the Cinska Restaurant next door. The restaurant's bar and dining room were dark and depressing. So was the furniture and the dreadful paintings of saints and nuns that hung from various walls. The place was packed with a lunchtime crowd of dispirited patrons. The food appeared to be as dreary as the clientele. The only beacon of joy was the bartender. His bald head glistened. His mustache curled at both ends like a Cossack's. He was a large man with a voice that boomed when he spoke. The bartender stood drying a beer glass with a small white towel. He wore a blue work shirt and jeans. The shirt and jeans were covered by a white apron that slipped over his head and was tied behind his back. I went to the bar.

"Franz?"

"Yes!?"

"I'm Sunny Sixkiller."

Franz immediately lowered his voice twenty octaves. "Hello, Sixkiller."

"I have this doctor's bag for you and a packet of papers." I handed Franz the bag and papers.

"I will take good care of these, Sixkiller," whispered Franz, adding; "Did it go well?"

"Yes, it went well."

"Good. God be with you Sixkiller."

Out on the pavement again someone behind me yelled my name. "Chuck! Chuck! Wait up!"

I turned.

It was Elke Metz!

"Elke! What are you doing in Prague?"

She said nothing, just pulled a revolver and silencer from her hand bag.

"Hey Elke!" I hollered, "what the hell—"

Then she shot me.

CHAPTER *FIFTY-NINE*

The force of the shot spun me around and threw me into a storefront. I slid down the store's wall until I was sitting on the pavement. I felt a searing pain on my right side.

As a crowd formed I watched Elke Metz run to the curb, where she stepped into a waiting taxi that drove quickly away. I sat against the brick wall fascinated by the blood spreading across my white dress shirt. I looked at the crowd gathered in a semi-circle around me. Among the shocked pedestrians was the easily recognizable bald head and mustachioed Franz, the bartender from the Cinska Restaurant. His face was ashen. I also noticed the two bodyguards Cohen the Hawk had sent to protect me. And then I recalled that the taller one had bumped into Elke as she fired her pistol. If I lived, he was the one who had saved my life.

The police and an ambulance arrived in tandem. Two paramedics put me on a stretcher, pushed me into the ambulance, and raced to the emergency ward of the Hospital Fakultni Poliklinika on 32 Karlovo Nam Street. I was clearheaded but felt extremely hyper. I guess getting shot will do that to you. This was all new to me. I had never been shot before.

When we arrived at the hospital, I was wheeled through a long white and green hall into the Emergency Ward. I was stripped to the waist by nurses, doctors, and interns hovering around me. I asked an English-speaking nurse if the wound was serious.

"Not at all. Just a crease along your right side."

"I wonder," I said, "if I could have two milligrams of Valium to ease the pain?"

"I will give you something better," she promised.

I told the nurse I was only allowed to take Valium. "Doctor's orders. I'm allergic to most everything else."

I thought it best not to ingest unfamiliar drugs, since I had no idea what kind of reaction I might suffer. I didn't want to start babbling about things I shouldn't be babbling about. I needed a clear head and if I had to endure pain, then so be it. I was far from out of trouble and light years away from the safety of London.

"It was a superficial wound," said a young baldheaded English speaking doctor. He was wearing granny glasses resting on a long, thin nose that hooked over a bushy mustache. "Your assailant was a poor shot."

I wanted to say she was pushed, but I didn't.

"I am told it was a woman that shot you. Her bullet grazed your side. Hell hath no fury like a woman scorned, eh?" The doctor beamed, proud of his English quote.

"Yes," I said, aching and bummed and thinking the doctor was an asshole.

"How is my English?" he asked.

"Good. Can I go?"

He told me I wasn't allowed to leave the hospital until I spoke to the police. It was routine procedure for all gunshot wounds. "Someone from the police department should be here soon."

An hour an twenty minutes later a short, plump, disheveled man walked up to me. Sweating profusely, he held a cap in one hand and a handkerchief in the other. "I am Detective Prager. Dov Prager. I am with the Prague Police Department. Come over here with me and sit. Are these two chairs okay? At least this emergency room is air conditioned. This is okay, is it not?"

"Yes, this is fine."

"It is hot, no? Look how I sweat. Being fat as I am makes one sweat. This handkerchief is very wet. I should send it to the wash already. Okay, so . . ."

The detective opened my passport, which he pulled out of his suit coat pocket. I wondered how he got it. Then I remembered I gave it to someone when I was admitted.

". . . your name is Chuck Barris, is it not?"

"Yes."

"I see you are an American?"

"Yes."

"Does your wound hurt?"

"No. Well yes, a little."

"Yes, is it? Do you want me to try and get you something to ease your pain?"

"Thank you, but no. I'm fine."

"Okay. Let me ask you something. Do you know the person who shot you?"

"Her name is Elke Metz."

"A wife? A girlfriend?"

"Neither."

"Neither? Then what kind of relationship does this . . ." he checked his notes ". . . this Elke Metz have with you?"

"A friend . . . I thought."

"But obviously she is not. Do you have any idea why she is not the friend you thought she was?"

"No."

"Is this . . . her name I can't remember . . . it is why I write everything down in this notebook . . . this Elke Metz woman, is she a Czech?"

"I don't know. I met her at a bar at my hotel last night," I lied. "She spoke English. With an accent. We had . . ." I felt a bit of panic settling in. I told myself to be calm. ". . . we had sex. I was supposed to see her . . ." I took a deep breath. I was getting the shakes. ". . . I was supposed to see her . . . this morning . . . but I didn't. I stood her up. Do you understand the expression 'stood her up?' It means not being someplace when you are expected."

"Yes, I understand. Thank you," said a visibly tired Detective Prager.

"Maybe she was angry about me not meeting her."

"Maybe," said the detective. "Phew, I am hot. A crazy woman, this . . . this . . ." He checked his notebook again. ". . . this Elke Metz woman, wouldn't you say?"

"A crazy woman?"

"To shoot you for not coming to meet her? *Shoot you!* You do not think this is maybe excessive?"

"Maybe," I whispered.

"And Mr. Barris, no one heard a sound. I stopped off at the Cinska Restaurant before I came here. I asked some of the patrons who were there when you were shot if they heard anything. Noise, like a pistol shot. No one heard noise like a pistol shot. Which makes me think this angry woman shoots you with a revolver equipped with a silencer. Do you recall seeing a silencer on her revolver?"

"No, I don't remember seeing a silencer," I lied. Why was I lying about a silencer?

"Strange. . . ."

"What's strange?" I asked softly.

"Strange this woman, this Elke Metz uses a silencer."

"I told you, I don't remember seeing—"

"Of course you remember," snapped the detective, "and of course she used a silencer. Now you tell me, would an angry woman use a silencer to shoot a lover? I think not. I think just a plain gun would do. On the other hand, would an assassin from a competing spy network use a silencer? I think so. And *why* would an assassin from a competing spy network try to kill you, do you think? To stop you from carrying out a mission, maybe? Or failing that, to kill you for revenge? Or out of anger at having *failed* to stop you? In any case, there are reasons. Most of them quite serious."

I didn't know what to say.

Detective Prager was almost bald. The few hairs he had hung damp and uncombed over his ears. The detective perspired freely. Parts of his shirt clung to his chest and sides as if he showered then dressed. He was constantly mopping his brow with his handkerchief. Finally he said, "I saw the body of Anton Faust."

I flinched. Prager noticed.

"Perhaps this Metz woman was too late to prevent you from killing Faust so in anger she sought to kill you? And would have, if she hadn't been pushed. Mr. Barris, by any chance are you carrying any cyanide pills?"

"Cyanide pills!" The question practically paralyzed me. I hoped I didn't showed it. *"Absolutely* not!"

"I am thinking of searching you. Would you object?"

"I . . . uh . . ."

"Mr. Barris, I know you are working with the Central Intelligence Agency."

"I told you, Prager, I am absolutely not working for any intelligence service." I was becoming frightened.

"Are you Jewish?"

The hair on my head tingled. "What's my being Jewish have to do with anything?"

"It is not good," said the detective, "to be a captured Jewish CIA agent in the Czech Republic."

"I am *not* a CIA agent. And I'm *not* . . ."

"Will you come with me to the mens' room please?"

"Why?"

"So that I can search you. I know you have rid yourself of your gun. I want to see if you are carrying cyanide pills. I also want to see if you are circumcised."

I became woozy. What I really became was scared. Scared shitless. It seems I've been scared shitless all my life. It's what should be on my gravestone.

CHUCK BARRIS 1929/?

HE WAS ALWAYS SCARED SHITLESS

R.I.P.

The detective took hold of my elbow forcefully, helped me to my feet and, never letting go of my arm, led me to a mens' room. My arm would be black and blue tomorrow.

If I was alive tomorrow.

Inside the bathroom, Prager checked the stalls to make sure they were empty. I leaned against a sink, feeling unexpectedly dizzy. Prager returned and stood in front of me.

"Mr. Barris, I am a detective with the Prague Police Department. I am also Jewish. There are not very many Jewish detectives in our Police Department. Less than the fingers on your right hand. My parents were born here. Hitler forced them to leave. They moved to Brooklyn where I was born. My parents missed their native country and returned to Prague after the war. I was twelve when we came back to Czechoslovakia. That's what this country was called when we returned. I have always missed America and I do not like the Czech Republic under its present rulers. Why do I tell you all this? Because, Sixkiller, I want you to realize—"

"How did you know my . . . how do you know about Sixkiller?"

"I, too, am an undercover agent for the Israeli Mossad. I was about to tell you when you interrupted. How lucky you are. In the first place," Prager pulled on his thumb, "this Elke Metz isn't Elke Metz at all. She's Elke Slasky. That's her real name. And she is a Russian agent. In the second place, you are lucky that," Prager pulled on his forefinger, "this Elke Metz is not a good quick shot. In the third place," Prager pulled on his middle finger, "you are lucky she got pushed by one of our agents. In the fourth place," he pulled on his ring finger, "you are lucky she panicked and ran away before she made sure you were dead. In the fifth place," the detective pulled on his little finger, "you are lucky I knew you were on this mission and was available to be on call. Are you with me so far, Sixkiller?"

"Yes, I am."

"We in the Mossad knew this Slasky woman had been trailing you for a long time. Did you know this, that she has been trailing you for a long time?"

"No."

"If *we* knew, then surely the CIA knew. It is strange they didn't warn you?"

"Yes, it is."

"She was trailing you in New York. I also wonder why she did not kill you there."

"I have no idea. Maybe someday I'll find out."

"She is still out there somewhere," said Detective Prager.

"I know."

"So watch yourself. Oh, and one last thing."

"What's that?"

"Leave this country as soon as possible, Sixkiller. As soon as possible."

"I'm leaving tonight for London."

"Good. Well, Sixkiller, go with God."

"Thank you. Same to you, Dov. And Dov, can I ask you something?"

"What?"

"Why did you scare the living shit out of me out there in the Emergency Ward? What was all that stuff about searching me and checking to see if I had cyanide pills or if I was circumcised? What the fuck was all *that* about?"

"I had to get you alone before I could tell you these things and who knows who could be listening?"

I nodded. He was right. He did what he had to do.

"Oh, and Sixkiller."

"Yes?"

"Good job on Faust."

PART VII

"Please don't tell me it all adds up in the end.
I'm sick of that one."
—JOHN ASHBERY

CHAPTER SIXTY

I flew from London to New York on August 31, 1999.

Tyrell picked me up at Kennedy International Airport. We hugged.

"You put on some weight, Tyrell."

"I was worried about you. I overcompensated with some Krispy Kremes, know what I'm sayin'?"

As soon as I was in the car I called Becky's office in Atlanta on my car phone. Her secretary told me that Becky was on vacation. The secretary didn't know when she would be back.

"Where'd she go?"

"To Europe."

"Did she go by herself?" I asked.

"No," said the secretary icily, "she did not go by herself." And that's all the woman intended to say.

I was crushed.

I telephoned Becky's sisters in Bowling Green, Kentucky. Both were married now: Faith still to the proctologist Neil Copelander and Hope to a veterinarian, Dr. Bunky Garvin. When I telephoned Faith, she flat-out refused to talk to me. She said I had treated her sister "despicably," adding that she never wanted to speak to me again and hung up.

Her sister Hope was nicer.

"She went to Paris, Chuck," she said. "I think she was goin' to Rome, too. She was a mess. For all I know, she still is. I really like you, Chuck. I thought the two of you sure were a great couple. But you treated her poorly, you really did. Can't rightly blame her for goin' and gettin' herself some R&R. Not after what you put her through. She surely needs it. It's a shame, you two breakin' up like that."

"She go alone, Hope?"

"Nope, went with someone."

"She did?"

"Yep."

"Do you know who she went with?"

"Yep, I do."

"You want to tell me who it is?"

"Nope, I don't."

Hope was being nice to me. She's a nice person by nature.

The news of Becky's trip and the fact she didn't go alone just about did me in. It took me a week to ten days before I could get myself out of my green armchair to do anything. And what I was able to do wasn't much. I puttered around my apartment, putting it back in order. I started a regime of eating properly and exercising faithfully. I boxed old clothes and gave them to Goodwill. Eventually I went back to the gym and began playing racquetball again. But not as well as I used to play. Unfortunately, racquetball wasn't my only problem. Other problems were banging around inside my head. So one night I went to my dining table with a pad and pencil and made a list of what was bothering me:

1. I don't know who Becky's with in Europe.
2. I don't know what to do with myself.
3. My slice of Arnold Hoffman's goddamn Pie of Life is getting thinner and thinner.
4. Becky Ballard is nowhere in sight.

5. I'm slowing up on the racketball court.

6. My right shoulder hurts.

7. Becky's not looking for me.

Four months later, New Year's Eve arrived.

I sat in my green armchair, sipping wonton soup and tearing up a half order of pork fried ribs from the China Fun restaurant down the street. At midnight, I watched Dick Clark bring in the millennium on TV. I was faintly glad to see the old codger. I guess that was because there were moments during the past few months when I wasn't sure I ever would again.

Clark bellowed, "Hap-py New Year!" and then he kissed his wife Kari. It was the first time Clark ever did that, kiss his wife at midnight on coast-to-coast television. It was slightly cute but mostly nauseating. And she upstaged him to boot! She placed her face in front of his so the camera saw mostly her, rather than him, which I know he didn't like at all. He winced, then shot daggers at his wife on coast-to-coast TV.

"Let's take a look at the millions of happy revelers in Times Square celebrating the year 2000!" Clark ordered.

"Fuck you," I growled.

I was miserable.

I missed Becky Ballard something awful.

I started the new year doing exactly the same thing I did the year before—reading books and moping. I had grown older, grumpier, snappish, repulsive, and I was falling apart at the seams. Every day brought a new ache—only these aches never went away. They just stayed and ached. But then, as my doctor recently said, "Chuck, let me tell you something. At your age, the day you wake up and nothing aches, you're dead."

As usual, out of nowhere something new was bothering me. Really bothering me. It was my right shoulder. When I finished a game of racquetball, it ached a lot. Since Elke Metz bounced me off that wall in Prague, I was sure I had injured my right rotator cuff. I went for a CAT scan at New York-Presbyterian Hospital. The scan revealed a touch of bursitis in my right shoulder, not my rotator cuff, that was probably the cause of my pain. What the radiologist *did* find, quite by accident, was something else.

Lung cancer.

CHAPTER SIXTY-ONE

Today they got me out of bed, placed me in a wheelchair and rolled me to "Hell's parking lot," the place where we sick and dying patients go to be X-rayed or CAT-scanned and stare at nothing while we wait. They line us up all in a row against a wall. We sit there ignored, looking helpless, half dead, pitiful. It's why I nicknamed the wall "Hell's parking lot." Most of the patients spend their time sneezing and coughing, then staring fascinated at the globs of sputum in their Kleenexes. Is the stuff good white shit or bad green shit? Sometimes the really old ones piss in their wheelchairs. They're either incontinent or have lost the will to live. We call them the "don't-give-a-shits." The patients with flu or pneumonia never cover their mouths when they hack and wheeze. They'd much rather blow their goddamn germs all over the place, hoping we catch whatever they have, too. I should care but I don't. Does it matter what I finally die of? So I sit in my wheelchair staring at nothing like everyone else.

The operation took place during the second week in September. Half of my right lung was removed. The fortuitous CAT scan found the small tumor early enough so that I didn't need radiology or chemotherapy. I came through the operation with flying colors. After four days I left the hospital, losing a mere half a pound. I went home exalted. I told my driver Tyrell Massella it really wasn't as bad as all that.

But I had to return to the hospital the next day, suffering from a staph infection I had apparently contracted in the operating room. The infection centered around the long incision across my back. There was also blood in the remaining half of my right lung. It was that staph infection and the blood in the lung, not the cancer, that almost killed me.

On Friday the 13th of October, I came close to dying.

The problem was the blood-sucking machine. It wasn't doing it's job.

A tube that went from the machine into the remaining half of my lung tried to pull out a puddle of blood that had formed there. But the blood wasn't coming out because it had coagulated into a hard mass. They pumped some sort of fluid into that lung that hoping to break up the coagulated blood. The doctor explained that there were two types of de-coagulation fluid he could use. One was risky and *might* do the job quickly, and one wasn't risky at all, but might not work.

"How risky is the risky one?" I asked.

"We don't know," answered the doctor. "The side effects can run from a bad headache . . . to death, I'm afraid. But if we don't bust up the hardened blood in your lung, a dangerous infection can set in and you might die anyway."

I told them to use the risky one.

The sun was shining brightly on the Hudson River the afternoon they shot the dicey fluid into the remains of my right lung. The doctor inserted a long needle into my side from the large syringe he held. While he did that, I watched a boat sail slowly north. I thought to myself: At least the last thing I'll see on earth will be this sweet sight.

That night I suffered the sweats and chills of a malaria victim.

"Bad grass never dies." That concerned intern's dumb expression got me through the night. And he was right, I didn't die.

The risky fluid broke up the coagulated blood.

The next day Bridget Phelan walked into my hospital room. She was small and skinny as a stick, with wispy hair and a pixie face. Her eyes twinkled and she's was always smiling, unless she was pissed. Even though we had never met it was great to see her walk through my room door and say, "I'm your nurse, whether you like it or not. I've got to weigh you. You've got to start to walk, even if it's just a few steps."

"Weigh me? Walk? You crazy? I hurt too much to walk, let alone get weighed."

"You have to," she said. "You're retaining your liquids from not moving. Look at your ankles."

I looked at my ankles. They were immense. So were my legs.

Little Bridget rolled a large scale into my room, pulled me out of bed and walked me to the scale. I weighed 185 pounds, more than thirty pounds overweight! Then Bridget dragged me to the bathroom and made me look at my face. It was grotesquely fat. That was the day I started walking. At first the two of us went slowly down the long hospital hall, little Bridget carrying the blood-sucking machine and me pushing the intravenous stand I had named Herbie. As the days and weeks went by, we walked further and further.

I was hospitalized throughout the most beautiful October in the history of New York City. There wasn't one rainy day during that entire month. Not even a cloudy one. Just sunshine and flowers, bright green grass and lots and lots of leaves turning brilliant orange and red. I spent almost eight weeks in the hospital, most of that time watching cars travel up and down the West Side Drive. They went to the city in the morning and returned at night. In the afternoons, I napped on my crossed arms on the window sill, lulled to sleep by the breeze and the hypnotic movement of barges, tugs, and pleasure boats sailing back and forth on the Hudson River. On the weekends the automobiles would head north to mountain homes and festivals, the yachts and sailboats to restaurants along the river's banks. I watched the leaves turn and die, then fall. That October I felt very much like the dried-up, dying leaves. And if I survived, so what? I had neither a wife, nor a creative idea, nor the motivation to find either of them. I saw a bleak future devoid of fun, with just the crossing-off of days as my only amusement for however long or short the rest of my time on earth might be.

I thought about Becky Ballard all the time. I would put myself to sleep at night and wake up in the morning thinking about her. I wondered how she was. I missed her as a mourner misses a dead loved one. But soon I grasped an understanding that thinking about Becky was absurd and that I should put her out of my head as soon as possible. I was a sickly man. I had one lung and no future. I was thirty years Becky's senior. Why would I even bother to consider burdening her with the likes of me? Though I wanted to telephone her a million times, I never did.

My sister and brother-in-law visited me in the hospital almost every day. Tyrell came frequently with huge selections of home cooking I never ate. I knew the food was delicious but had simply lost my appetite. I gave the food away as soon as Tyrell was gone. I retired my secretary, Mrs. Poltz, telling my loyal companion the truth; there was nothing for her to do anymore.

Eventually I didn't need the blood-sucking machine. A few days after they removed it, Bridget said it was time I went home, and it was. The hospital released me and Tyrell drove the two of us down Lexington Avenue toward my apartment. About ten blocks from home, Bridget made me get out of the car and walk the rest of the way. Bridget and I said our good-byes that afternoon.

I came back to my apartment with a permanent intravenous needle imbedded in the top of my left hand. I ingested bags of antibiotics hooked to Herbie. The antibiotics flowed down a tube through the needle in my hand twenty-four hours a day. I had three nurses working eight-hour shifts. My deeply infected incision that ran halfway across my back had to be cleaned every three hours.

I watched holidays come and go from my apartment windows, just as I had the days and weeks in the hospital. Thanksgiving became Christmas. Christmas became New Year's. I spent all of that time in my green armchair reading. I read thirty-seven books during the month of December alone. When I wasn't reading, I watched the bags of antibiotics drip into my body. The intravenous tube fascinated me. It ran under the skin from the top of my left hand up my left arm and across my chest. I had no idea how it got there or where it ended. They must have put it into me in the operating room.

On December 31, 2000, I watched Dick Clark on television holler, "Hap-py New Year Everybody!"

I told him to go fuck himself and went to sleep.

CHAPTER SIXTY-TWO

I t was now the middle of January, 2001.

I would be seventy-two years old in less than five months.

Over the past few weeks my old CIA buddy Coulter Bean had come to my apartment to visit. He explained the whole story about Elke Slasky, aka Elke Metz.

Elke was born in 1957 in Homvel, USSR. Homvel is near Kiev. Elke's father, Petor Slasky, was a Major in the KGB, Russia's State Security Agency, who was killed in 1959. He died defending Khrushchev's life during a secret attempted assassination on the Soviet Chairman. The failed attack took place while Khrushchev was on a state visit to Albania. Elke Slasky was two years old when her father died. After his death, she was raised by her mother and her widowed grandfather, Colonel Gregory Slasky. Colonel Slasky was one of Russia's legendary spies, whose work caused the United States and its allies a great deal of damage. In 1972, a CIA hitman operating under the code name "Sunny Sixkiller" put three bullets into Colonel Gregory Slasky's face. Slasky died half on the pavement and half in the street across from the Hotel Saint Pierre on the Left Bank of Paris. Elke Slasky was fifteen when her grandfather was murdered.

In 1973, Sarah Trepper Slasky took her daughter Elke to England. Sarah Trepper Slasky was a descedant of Leopold Trepper, the cofounder of the NKVD's Red Orchestra, a renowned spy network during World War II. While in London, Sarah Slasky worked as an English interpreter attached to the Russian Embassy. Elke enrolled in an Oxford University preparatory school, moving on to Oxford in 1975. After Elke's graduation, her mother was transferred again, this time to the United States as part of the Russian delegation to the United Nations. Shortly after their arrival in New York, the two women moved into an apartment close to the UN building on 50th Street and First Avenue. Elke Slasky entered Barnard College on the Columbia University campus, majoring in language studies. Seven years later she left the Columbia campus with a doctorate in languages. She was now thirty-one years old.

"The trail gets a little murky here," said Coulter one winter afternoon, "but accordin' to her trackers down on the Farm, they figure somewhere durin' this period of time was when she changed her name to Metz and started to plan your assassination. And contrary to all our assumptions at The Company, targeting you for extermination was not a mission, not officially, not something ordered by the NKVD. She decided to do it on her very own."

"What prompted her?"

"I'll tell you later," he said.

Most of what Coulter told me next I knew. I knew Elke Slasky joined Madison Avenue Synagogue in April of 1999, I didn't know she was forty-two years old at the time, but I did know she claimed to have converted to Judaism. I didn't know she flew from New York to Prague in August of 1999, arriving on the 30th, but I most certainly knew she shot me on the last day of that month. I had a hunch that Elke Slasky left Prague after the assassination attempt. She did. She flew to Moscow. Like I said, I knew most of that stuff.

What Coulter told me next I did *not* know. Elke Slasky was captured by the British Secret Service six months later.

CHAPTER SIXTY-THREE

Elke Slasky was taken into custody as she stepped off a British Airliner at Heathrow Airport, London. At approximately the same time, Elke's mother—Sarah Tepper Slasky—was picked up and questioned by CIA agents in New York. Sara Slasky's questioning was short. After three days the high ranking KGB spy was placed on a British European Airliner and sent to London. There, Sarah Slasky was transferred to a Russian Aeroflot jet and flown to Moscow, where she remains. A trade that included two CIA intelligence officers held by the Russians and returned to Washington was rumored to have taken place. Unfortunately, events didn't move as quickly for Sarah Slasky's daughter. Elke was sent to a safe house in Bicester, a small town between Oxford and Buckingham, and questioned for close to three months.

"Here's what the MI5 interrogators basically found out," Coulter told me one snowy day in March. We were sitting by a roaring fire in my apartment, as roaring as a fire could get in my small fireplace. It was a dark gray afternoon, the snow coming down in swirls, a splendid afternoon for talking about Elke Slasky. Coulter consulted a file of notes he had pulled from a worn leather briefcase. He placed the notes on his lap and said, "She got her idea to kill you after seein' you on a television interview here in New York. She said the more she thought about how prosperous and smug you looked, the more furious she became. She knew it was you who had killed her grandfather—everyone in her family did—and to think, she said, you were livin' the good life and had been for years,while her grandfather lay dead in his grave. Somethin' snapped, she told the Brits. Suddenly she was determined to avenge the death of her grandfather (who had been like a father to her) and the family honor by killin' you. Somethin' like that. By the way, she told the MI5 guys that it was durin' the TV interview that you mentioned doin' that ceremony you Jewish men do—"

"Getting bar mitzvahed?"

"Right. You mentioned it was unusual to do that ceremony so late in one's life. Anyway, that's where she got the idea to find the same church you were goin' to go to."

"The synagogue. I go to a synagogue, not a church."

"Excuse me. The synagogue. Anyway, after trailin' you to the synagogue, Slasky explained to the rabbi there . . ." (Coulter consulted the notes in his lap)". . . a Rabbi Angel I believe . . . that she wanted to convert from Russian Orthodox Catholicism to Judaism in order to marry her Jewish fiancé. Of course the fiancé was nonexistent. Slasky told the rabbi she wanted to perform a certain female ceremony, too—"

"Bat mitzvahed," I said. "It's what girls do."

"Right, so she signed up for Hebrew lessons. Doin' that allowed her to get as close to you as anyone possibly could. Butt-to-butt, so to speak."

"So to speak," I said, disappointed in myself that I fell for her, if only for a few weeks.

"Now get this," said Coulter Bean. "She tells these MI5 dudes that it was about this time the KGB gave her permission and put resources at her disposal to continue her plan to assassinate you, *but* about the same time, her plan goes awry because she falls in love with you. How 'bout them apples, Chuckie Baby?"

"Stop calling me Chuckie Baby," I muttered.

"So she changes her mind about assassinatin' you. You know what they say, don't you? They say fallin' in and out of love is a major reason a lot of intelligence plans get all messed up. But then you know that, don't you?"

"No, I don't know that."

"Well, it is. Love can fuck up an agent royally. Anyway this Slasky woman tells her Brit handlers that *you* apparently lost interest in *her* which *really* pissed her off. So now her assassination plans are back on, this time with a vengeance. You know what they say, Chuckie Baby, 'Hell hath no fury like a woman scorned.' "

"I've heard that before."

Coulter scratched his head and said, "In some ways you gotta give her credit. I mean she worked hard in the preparation, don't you think? Remember, for a while there she was doin' it all alone. Trying to find the right moment and location to kill you. Changin' her name, the converting-to-Judaism scam. Trackin' you to that synagogue you went to. Talkin' the rabbi into lettin' her take lessons. Endin' up sittin' cheek-to-jowl with you in that classroom. Like I said, you gotta give her credit. It takes time to prepare like that, and you gotta admit she did it well."

"Not me," I said. "I'm not admitting dick when it comes to that—"

"It's all in the prep," continued Coulter, oblivious to my anger. "You taught me that, Chuckie Baby. Thank God for you her only mistake was chokin at the moment of truth."

"She didn't choke."

"What?"

"I said she didn't choke, she was pushed."

"What are you talkin' about?"

"Never mind, Coulter. Go on with what you were saying."

"I was just going to wrap it up by sayin' there were obviously others involved in the woman's plan to kill you."

"Like?"

"Like the taxi driver who was waitin' for her and whisked her away after she shot you in front of that restaurant. Then there were the Aeroflot airline people, who slipped her onto a departin' flight back to Russia without goin' through the proper exit channels. I mean this was an action planned down to the last detail."

"Except the action failed."

"Yeah. You're one lucky dude, Chuckie Baby. And you're a free man now! Your letter of resignation has finally been accepted by the D.O. . . ."

"Thank you, Jesus."

". . . and you can expect some serious severance pay."

"Swell."

"And a medal."

"You can have the medal, Coulter."

"Can I have the severance pay, too?"

"No. Can I ask you something, Coulter?"

"Sure. What?"

"If the entire intelligence community seemed to know this Russian assassin, this Elke Metz slash Slasky, was following me all over Manhattan for months and months, was actually sitting *next to me* in goddamn Hebrew school, how come nobody told *me* about it?"

"Don't really know."

"Well, that's comforting, Coulter. So tell me, where is the fair Metz slash Slasky woman now, pray tell?"

"Dead."

"*Dead?!*" I said, shocked.

"Automobile accident. In England. Not far from Oxford, her old alma mater."

"Pity," I muttered.

"Really unfortunate," said Coulter Bean.

"Yeah," I said, and hugged him good-bye. I wasn't sure I was hugging a friend or an enemy.

On January 15, 2000, I began writing a book tentatively titled, *Bad Grass Never Dies*. It would start where *Confessions of a Dangerous Mind* ended.

The same day I started that book, I got a phone call.

"Chuck, is that you?"

I felt flushed and dizzy. My heart may have stopped. "Becky?"

"Do you want to have dinner?"

"Where are you?"

369

CHAPTER SIXTY-FOUR

I covered the horrible intravenous nozzle that hung from my left hand with a long-sleeved sweater under a long-sleeved blazer under a long-sleeved topcoat and raced down to the lobby. I thought my heart had stopped again when the elevator doors opened and she was there! She really was, sitting in a lobby armchair, her arms on the chair's arms, her legs crossed, and a big smile on that gorgeous face of hers. Becky looked so pretty she almost took my breath away.

"Hey, Becky." What a lame greeting.

"Hi, darlin'."

"I love you, Becky," I suddenly found myself saying, "I really really do."

Our doorman, Nelson Quatman, beamed.

"Don't leave me again," I told her, locking her in my arms.

"Right now my chest is achin' so much I can't stand it. The longer we're apart, the more I hurt."

We ate at an Italian restaurant called the Isle of Capri. We sat in a corner booth by the window. When I looked at Becky Ballard sitting next to me, I saw the most beautiful and sweetest woman I had ever met in my entire life. I wondered sadly why I hadn't married her years and years ago. I was such an idiot.

"What's the matter?" asked Becky. "You look so sad. Are you sorry I called?

"*Are you kidding*? Exactly the opposite. I'm just sitting here thinking what a fool I was not to marry you when I was thirty-eight and you were eight. I am violently in love with you, Becky." I was so filled with emotion that my eyes watered up. "I haven't called you because I didn't want you to come back. Better you be mad, I thought, than throw your life away. You know, marry me out of sympathy or guilt, stuck with a sick old man for the rest of your days. Besides, I didn't know how long I had to live. But the doctors told me they caught the cancer so early I beat it. And I'm getting stronger every day. I can feel it. Hell, six months from now, I'll be the same tough old cranky lion you met three years ago. Maybe just a little more scarred up than before." I couldn't think of anything else to say, so I stopped talking.

"Could that possibly have been a proposal?" asked Becky.

"Yes, I believe that was."

"I thought you'd never ask, sweet pea."

Becky and I were married two months later on March 14th. The ceremony took place in my apartment in the company of twenty good friends. I didn't know Becky and I had twenty good friends. I guess we did. Anyway, marrying Becky Ballard was the best decision I ever made in my entire life. I mean that. Now every time I pass the Isle of Capri, I smile.

EPILOGUE

> *"To be useful, to earn rewards, the trick is to survive."*
> —Marshall Browne

I t's hard to believe that I was sick and alone just a little more than a year ago, with a future as bleak as the hospital room I was confined to. Or that I would find Becky again and actually marry her. Or that they would make a movie of *Confessions of a Dangerous Mind*. Or that Becky and I would be walking up the red carpet of a full-blown Hollywood premier with all the flashing cameras and screaming craze-o-fans. Or that my *Dating Game, Newlywed Game,* and *Gong Show* television programs would still be on American TV in the twenty-first century.

During the winter of 2002, I toured the country promoting my book, *Confessions*. In February, I returned to New York to make appearances in two or three bookstores in Manhattan. One evening, with the temperature hovering somewhere near zero, Becky and I approached a Barnes & Noble on Astor Place. As the two of us walked toward the entrance, I mumbled to Becky, "No one's going to come out on such a cold night just to hear me pitch a book. You watch. The manager's going to tell us because of the frigid weather nobody showed up and would I please just sign a few books before I left."

"I betcha you're wrong," said Becky. "The place will be packed."

And it was.

"There's an overflow that quite frankly is a bit dangerous," said the nervous lady bookstore manager. "Also we can't bring you in the usual way. We're going to have to go around the back and come in through the delivery door."

When I walked up to the podium, the huge crowd cheered for what seemed like forever. Standing there waving and smiling and bowing, I suddenly I recalled that dreadful night in Philadelphia when sixteen thousand hockey fans booed. My sister Phoebe and my brother-in-law Herman and all their kids and their kids' kids were there. So was my driver, Tyrell Massella, and his wife, Tulip, and Laverne Beesley from my favorite Krispy Kreme store, and my old cronies Will Balliett, Don Weise, Arnie Hoffman, Ben Lorca, and Sidney Hirschman. Even Hoffman's daughter, Luci-with-an-i was there. I'm not sure, but I may have seen Coulter Bean and The Duck. That freezing evening on Astor Place was a night I'll never forget. As my grandmother would have said, "Go know."

Becky and I bought a cozy little home near West Point that we had to renovate. One day while we were watching the construction guys at the house, I pulled Becky aside and said, "Honey, can I ask you something?"

"Sure."

"When we were apart last time, who did you go to Europe with?"

"Are you sure you want to know?"

"Yes, I'm sure."

"I went with Martha."

Martha Johnson had been Becky's girlfriend since first grade.

We had cleared the last hurdle, allowing me to enjoy what Marianne Williamson calls "the love we were born with." Soon, I became unrealistically happy in a manner I suspect few people ever enjoy.

A final footnote. When Becky and I are either driving to our new home or going back to the city, we take the West Side Drive along the Hudson River and pass the hospital. We can even see the window I used to sit behind and watch automobiles go by. Every time our car passes in front of that window—either one way or the other—I put my arm outside our Lexus, hold my hand straight up in the air and give that goddamn hospital room the finger.

Becky always says, "Honey, that's not nice."

And I always say, "I know it's not."

But I do it anyway.

ACKNOWLEDGMENTS

I would like to thank Will Balliett and Don Weise for making me a better writer and my book a better book, Jennifer Lyons for her unwavering support, Riki Wagman for her poo-poo-poos and, of course, Mary Barris for all the rest.

ABOUT THE AUTHOR

CHUCK BARRIS is the author of *You and Me, Babe* and *Confessions of a Dangerous Mind.* He and his wife live in Manhattan.